∾ Adventurous Americans ∾

Adventurous Americans

Edited by
Devere Allen

Illustrated with etchings
by Bernard Sanders

FARRAR & RINEHART
INCORPORATED
On Murray Hill   New York

∾ Contents ∾

TRUMPET TO THE PEOPLE, 3
Oswald Garrison Villard

AN EVOLUTIONIST ON THE BENCH, 18
Oliver Wendell Holmes

JUSTICE FIRST, 38
John A. Lapp

EVERY CHILD A WANTED CHILD, 52
Margaret Sanger

IF I WERE A POLITICIAN, 69
Norman Thomas

PREACHER WITHOUT AUTHORITY, 84
John Haynes Holmes

LABOR MUST LEARN, 99
A. J. Muste

PROPHET OF ISRAEL, 118
Judah L. Magnes

EDUCATION IN ACTION, 130
John Dewey

FORTY YEARS AT HULL HOUSE, 141
Jane Addams

GALAHAD OF FREEDOM, 154
Roger Baldwin

CHANGING THE MIND OF A NATION, 165
Carrie Chapman Catt

ECONOMIST OF TOMORROW, 179
Paul Douglas

"WINGS FOR GOD'S CHILLUN," 192
Burghardt du Bois

CONTENTS

THE WORLD IS TOO SMALL, 203
SHERWOOD EDDY

A DIFFERENT EMPLOYER, 217
WILLIAM P. HAPGOOD

LABOR CAN LEAD, 233
SIDNEY HILLMAN

A STATESMAN CAN BE A PROPHET, 248
FRANCIS J. McCONNELL

A PURITAN REVOLUTIONIST, 263
SCOTT NEARING

AMBASSADOR TO THE COURT OF ST. FRANCIS, 277
VIDA D. SCUDDER

GREAT-GRANDSON OF THE REVOLUTION, 290
JOHN NEVIN SAYRE

BISHOP TO THE UNIVERSE, 304
PAUL JONES

BARRICADES AND BUSINESS MANAGEMENT, 321
B. CHARNEY VLADECK

CHAMPION OF WOMEN AND CHILDREN, 333
GRACE ABBOTT

FOREWORD

Lives of authors oft remind us
We can write about The Great,
And, departing, leave behind us
Proof that we were second-rate.

In a moment of juvenility, the editor of this book once published the foregoing lines. Whether or not they possessed insight at the time, in foresight they were sadly wanting. For the method of biography subsequently changed until it became almost mandatory for a biographer to elevate himself upon the ruins of his subject.

The twenty-four sketches gathered here were written neither to canonize nor to destroy. They are brief and unpretentious. But they deal with living persons who, by forthright struggles for principle, have built up loyal followings. These men and women differ vastly in origin, training, and present-day activity; yet they have in common an impatience to improve the social order. Most of them are especially interesting because they emerged from a conservative milieu. Such labels as Pink, Red, Progressive, Liberal, or Radical have been applied to all of them, sometimes deservedly, sometimes not; sometimes with friendliness, sometimes with venomous hostility. About some, colorful legends have arisen; regarding the majority, nothing intimate has ever been made public hitherto.

The editor himself has not contributed a single sketch. He conceived the plan, outlined the subjects with the aid of friends, conducted many quests for facts and gossip, made innumerable suggestions and revisions. But in every instance the bulk of the writing has been done by a close acquaintance of the person depicted. With some of the criticisms expressed the compiler takes issue; but he has let them remain, believing that there has been an abundance of sympathetic praise, and that the persons criticized are strong enough in character, repute, and accomplishment to withstand any unfair accusations. Least of all has he desired to make these leaders of American life seem beyond human weaknesses; thus occasionally, so unblemished have been the portraits, he has instructed his collaborators to insert some of the things "they say," for if these products of chatter have no basis in truth they nevertheless belong in the public picture.

The actual writers have been willing to remain unknown, cheerfully renouncing any credit to themselves, in order that they might speak without constraint, and promote a wider understanding of people whom they deem superlatively worthy of respect. Their chief satisfaction will accrue from the production of what, it is hoped, may be found a heartening and human book. They have recorded authentic experiences which give the lie to cynicism and should serve to tone the systems of our "tired radicals."

Exactly why some natures rebel against social injustice while others tolerate it can hardly be made plain by any written words. But if these Americans are at all typical of rebels and innovators their lives should make it easier for those who vaguely fear "radicalism" to comprehend the motivation of all prophetic personalities. For these are, indubitably, modern prophets. And just as we look back today upon the cluster of alert minds that gave force a hundred years ago to the movements against slavery, the subjection of women, war, fiendish cruelty in prisons, and other social wrongs, so historians evaluating our civilization will not be able to chart the twentieth century without reference to leaders like those whose lives are here portrayed.

The subjects of the sketches have been selected so as to present a small cross-section of American revolt against orthodoxy. Clearly, it would have been impossible to include even a substantial fraction of those who might justly belong in a Who's Who of the American Left. The series was not compiled in a desire to set forth the country's two dozen greatest crusading figures, or even the best companions for a desert isle. Nor has any attempt been made, were it possible, to do comparative justice to the various "causes" which these leaders serve. Let no one feel aggrieved, then, because some favored enterprise or seer has failed of mention in these pages.

Were justice really done, however, the book would bear the names of Gladys E. Meyerand, for the major editorial work on certain chapters and assistance with the entire manuscript; of A. Albert MacLeod, for his many resourceful suggestions; of Kirby Page and Reinhold Niebuhr, for their unfailing help. Indeed, when the extent to which the editor is thus indebted is appreciated, and the work of the anonymous authors is considered, it becomes manifest that he is himself morally guilty of exploitation. This sin he condones because he is eager to make better known, in the only way compatible with frank intimacy, some of the bravest spirits of our time.

DEVERE ALLEN.

Heyst, Belgium,
September 7, 1931.

∾ Adventurous Americans ∾

Trumpet to the People

OSWALD GARRISON VILLARD

WHEN a boy, Oswald Garrison Villard used to ride his pony up Fifth Avenue behind his mother's victoria. The progressiveness of his parentage—that of the railroad-building Henry Villard and of Fanny Garrison—showed even in the manner of their residence, for the Westmoreland, where the family dwelt in the early eighties, was the first elevator apartment in New York. The "excelsior" note has been a family heritage. It lives today in the battling *Nation*, champion of the downtrodden, even though the contemporary Garrisonian journalism no longer suffers the *per aspera* trials of the months when William Lloyd Garrison slept on the floor of his garret in order to publish *The Liberator*, and the penniless immigrant youth, Heinrich Hilgard, fled from military reaction in Germany following the '48 revolution. But the *ad astra* pathway is being blazed in the new pioneering amid the wilderness of our complex twentieth century civilization. The crusading urge derives from both the Hilgard and Garrison ancestries. Oswald Villard got both barrels.

The Westmoreland Apartments in which he spent part of his childhood recently made way for a new Tammany Hall, but the suggestion that the wigwam be adorned with a tablet recording the fact that William Lloyd Garrison had died there met with no encouragement from the grandson. He deemed the juxtaposition of the civic idealism commemorated and the municipal *realpolitik* materialized in stone wholly incongruous, though he tactfully based his objection on the technical point that the new edifice was not the one in which the abolitionist had breathed his last.

The boy on horseback riding up America's most famous street was father to the man some twenty years later. Bob Duffus's "The Grandson of the Liberator," accepted as the official monograph by its reprint from *The American Mercury* for the tenth anniversary of the new *Nation* celebration two years ago leads with this savory anecdote:

"One morning late in 1898 Fifth Avenue pedestrians paused to gaze at what even then was an unusual sight on that respectable thoroughfare. A spirited steed was curvetting up the avenue with a gentleman in the late twenties clad in a brownish-yellow riding costume in the saddle. A wide hat-brim dropped over a pair of spectacles and shadowed what seemed to many observers to be a decidedly familiar moustache. The Spanish war was just over and reverence for martial achievements was high. Here and there along the line a hat was waved and cheers broke out. Policemen drew themselves up to their full height and saluted.

"The rider received these tributes with some astonishment, but continuing modestly on his way, turned down a side street and rode his mount aboard a Brooklyn ferry. A small group of passengers assembled and gazed respectfully. No one spoke. Finally a grimy stoker emerged from the hold and shouldering the other spectators aside stared hard. 'Say,' he demanded, 'are you Colonel Roosevelt, or ain't you?' "

Oswald Villard enjoys telling this story about himself, and it is a curious fact that between the militant and military Theodore and the militant pacifist Oswald there is more than physical resemblance. The same "strenuous life" is there, the same catholicity of interest, the corresponding expertness in a variety of widely diverse fields. Villard nearing sixty is a superb horseman and can swim a mile without fatigue. He can speak as well as he can write, with the same fine fire, when he is aroused. He may justly claim expertness as a political observer—his Washington correspondence for the *Evening Post* equals the best in America's journalistic tradition; he is an authority on the press—and its most caustic critic—and cites with some pride that the family's four generations in journalism are equalled only by the record of the Bowleses of the Springfield *Republican*. He is a musical connoisseur; his presidency of the Philharmonic was rooted in his love for symphonic excellence. He takes pride in his expertness in military strategy and tactics. An enormous crop of post-war memoirs of generals, great and near-great, gravitates to his desk for review, a literary inheritance, perhaps, from his father who distinguished himself as a war correspondent with the Union Army.

Nor is the Villardian ability to chronicle events purely journalistic. Oswald could with ease have followed a professional career. His first adult occupation was teaching history at Harvard—his alma mater—after graduation. He has served on the "committee to visit the Department of History," an honorary post which at least signalizes the recognition of the academic world. And his *John Brown—a Biography Fifty Years After* is the classic and, to use a modern term, the "definitive" biography of the martyr of Harper's Ferry. Which leads naturally to one of O. G. V.'s major interests—in the colored people, with whose emancipation his grandfather's name is so imperishably linked. In him, the abolitionist tradition, which has petered out in the third generation of so many other families whose sires crusaded from the thirties to the sixties, burns with undiminished flame. For three decades his voice and pen have been unceasingly directed against the injustices, cruelties, and discriminations erected by American race prejudice against Americans of African descent. He was one of the founders of the American Association for the Advancement of Colored People, established in the dark days of race rioting and lynching a quarter of a century ago. He was for many years the chief supporter and the president of an industrial school for colored youth at Manassas, Virginia.

Does the picture conjure up an impractical idealist merely tilting at windmills? It is suggestive that in a recent issue of one of our best monthlies appears an uproariously triumphant article from his pen, entitled "Our Crumbling Color Line." In it he takes delight in recording the transformation which, still unknown and unnoticed by many, is bringing to the American Negro a new emancipation, economic, political, and even social.

But it is not merely in the realization, actual or prospective, of the one-time apparently unattainable goals that Villard may be exempted from a category of "tired radicals," the connotation of whose every effort is glorious defeat. The fiscal genius which enabled the elder Villard to complete the Northern Pacific—ties, rails, stocks and bonds—and to worst the redoubtable Jay Gould in one of those titanic catch-as-catch-can struggles of the days of railroad trail-blazing and financing, has transmitted a few chromosomes to the son. Villard, the younger, on occasion admits that had the accumulation of more wealth been his goal, he might have been a figure in Wall Street, have associated his name with the upbuilding of some huge business enterprise, have successfully administered some nation-wide trust. It might conceivably have been Villard and Company of Wall Street, or Villard Frères of New York, Paris, London, and Frankfort; or, following the paternal bent toward transportation, the Villard Motor Company of Detroit, or the Villard Steamship Line. As it is, he has managed uniquely to lift a crusading weekly "out of the red," an

OSWALD GARRISON VILLARD

achievement which none of the endowed competitors in the field of liberal weekly or monthly journalism have been able to approach. Indeed, most of them have long since given up the struggle. Likewise there is his *Nautical Gazette,* a journal of marine news and comment which aims to aid the restoration of the American merchant marine to its one-time glory. If his *Yachting* has passed out of his hands it remains today the exact publication he visioned when he founded it.

To be sure, his critics—who are often his warmest admirers —deplore what seems to them a needlessly economical streak running through the escutcheon of financial wizardry. Likewise *Nation* contributors are wont to assert with some unction that *The Nation,* which waxes fervent in behalf of the "exploited" workingman, exploits its literary workers with complete inconsistency when it accepts their pen products at a cent a word. No one, however, gainsays Mr. Villard's ability to continue to secure their literary contributions. Moreover he maintains stoutly, with the logic of the ledger on his side, that it was only by holding down at every point that *The Nation* has been possible at all. While certain friends have contributed to take care of deficits in the leaner years, Villard has borne the greatest part of the load out of his own pocket. Of course he draws no salary himself, pays his own travel expenses when he is reporting for *The Nation,* and pays the weekly's entertainment bills.

For some years Villard has thought of retiring. Yet of course retirement for him would be anything but innocuous desuetude. His tongue and pen would doubtless continue active in behalf of the causes to which he has given his life. He talks at times with a certain amused sadness of an autobiographical "Confessions of an Unsuccessful Journalist." His lack of success is not apparent to anyone—unless it be himself— although his greatest defeat was the loss of *The Evening Post* which, since its founding by Alexander Hamilton, had variously continued under the editorships of William Cullen Bryant, of Carl Schurz, and of Edwin Lawrence Godkin. For more than a century it had been a beacon to American journalism. Never attaining a great circulation, it entered homes where ideas were current, and its readership constituted an intellectual aristocracy in America. Especially was the *Post* read by other American editors from coast to coast. The editorial page of the leading Boston morning daily was not "put to bed" until, at about 10:30 P. M., the five o'clock limited from New York brought in the afternoon's *Evening Post* with the day's topics lucidly exposed and vigorously discussed in its editorial columns. The same practice prevailed in Philadelphia and Baltimore "sancta."

It was precisely this respect for the editorial leadership of *The Evening Post*—even among the editors whose expressed views on many topics were wholly at variance—that made the paper so formidable. In his *Some Newspapers and Newspaper-Men,* Villard cites the remark of Governor David B. Hill of New York in the course of the Maynard campaign in which the reformers, with *The Evening Post* leading the press, waged a successful, though at first apparently hopeless, campaign to thwart the efforts of the Hill machine to place a totally unfit man in a high judicial office: "I don't care anything about the handful of Mugwumps who read it (*The Evening Post*) in New York. The trouble with the damned sheet is that every editor in New York State reads it."

Fearless, uncompromising, high-principled, the uniqueness of the *Post* lay in the complete editorial freedom given its editor by the ownership, and its disregard of financial considerations in carrying out policies which the helmsman deemed right. It was the relentless foe of corruption in high and low places, but especially did it engage the powerful in mortal combat. It early fought—at great cost to its exchequer—the battle against the pressure of department-store advertisers, a chapter not always glorious in the past life of many an American daily. Such policies should have led to permanent financial success; and indeed it is the sorrow of Villard's friends that he did not keep *The Evening Post* alive even at some sacrifice to his fortune and demonstrate the soundness of a non-commercial newspaper. The effort would have been worth making, for the *Post,* if not a great financial success as newspaper properties went in those days, was a consistent though not a large income producer in the generation of Villard ownership (1883-1918). In one of these years, it made over $100,000. The yearly net revenue until 1900 was substantial. In the second seventeen years, it averaged a small percentage of profit, and its circulation increased. Its course of intellectual honesty, rather than expediency, in opposing the United States' entry into the World War, and thereafter fighting for the maintenance of civil liberties at home that seemed consonant with the waging of a war "to make the world safe for democracy"—an objective which *The Evening Post* denounced as illusory—led directly to the paper's sale. The *Post* suffered for its at that time unpopular views just as did the owner. Mounting costs of production spelled increasing deficits, and the paper was sold. Its name, with the prefix of "New York," survives.

On the other hand it should be remembered that Villard received the paper without one dollar of working capital, carried it through two panics, and made a very strenuous effort to finance it before letting it go. At that time it was losing at the rate of $175,000 a year. Unionization immediately after the sale cost another $75,000 annually. Mr. Villard maintains that had he foreseen the great boom in newspaper earnings which came immediately after the war, he would have mortgaged himself to the hilt, but that there was no reason for anticipating such prosperity. As it was, a group of his friends sought to guarantee $100,000 a year but could not attain that goal.

Villard, freed from the larger responsibilities of daily journalism, strove in *The Nation* to set forth his convictions, and the views which, with the general regimentation of opinion incidental to the war, found no expression elsewhere. He did not escape unscathed. He and his family for a time suffered social ostracism. He tells with relish some of the incidents of these days.

"My Gawd, what a club this is!" one of his fellow-members at the University Club was heard to remark, "a club that has in its membership Oswald Garrison Villard and A———— P————."

"Just supposing I had remained 'regular' at the beginning of the war," Villard has remarked on various occasions, with keenly evident satisfaction at his irregularity, "supposing I had not opposed our participation in the war. Through my friendship with Woodrow Wilson at the time, I might have been a brigadier-general." In the intelligence department of course, for which, with his proficiency in German and French and his knowledge of military affairs Villard would have been well qualified.

Well, possibly Villard might have worn a general's stars, if he had ever had a hankering for rank and decorations. His accumulation of honorary degrees—Litt.D., Washington and Lee, LL.D., Lafayette—was cut short by his non-conformism. Still his imagination of "what might have been," occasionally runs away with him. It was not without expectation that he was slated for the Vice-Presidential nomination on the La Follette Progressive ticket in 1924. This optimism he applies not merely to himself but to men and measures generally. He is always hopeful that men, especially in public office, will turn out far better than they do. Hence his frequent disillusion which causes him to rend them with his pen and has given him a somewhat undeserved reputation for "bitterness." Actually he keeps his estimates of the private virtues and the public attainments of public men correctly distinct. Evasion and pussy-footing are non-existent in Villard's or *The Nation's* lexicon.

With all his achievement in several fields as journalist, biographer, publicist, and as a reckonable force in the formation of public opinion—for *The Nation* has really been the voice of American liberalism for nearly a decade and a half—Villard refers to himself at times as a "failure." Mood may partly account for this wholly unwarranted self-castigation. "Oswald is not happy unless he's miserable," was the penetrating comment of a friend who knew him well. His mood may vary quickly from sunny cheerfulness and confident optimism to great depression. His capacity for sympathy and understanding is great. And the suffering and sorrow that he witnesses on every hand affect him deeply. His occasional despondencies about himself are temperamental rather than buttressed in fact. For life has dealt kindly with him and he has had the extreme good fortune of being able to follow his bent, to feel the pulse of great events, and to play some part in their shaping.

He attributes what may be set down as a lack of greater success to an inferiority complex which was fastened upon him by being at the outset of his journalistic career on *The Evening Post* surrounded by older men of repute and prestige—E. L. Godkin, Horace White, Rollo Ogden, and his uncle, Wendell Phillips Garrison. Some of his associates whose journalistic judgment and aptitudes he now considers inferior to his own, never, he asserts, permitted him to know that they considered his editorial writing—at times when he was stirred and aroused

—the best on the paper. In consequence he long distrusted his own judgment.

Villard likewise believes that his being born to affluence and social position was a great handicap in his effort to achieve success as a radical journalist. It would have been far easier, he thinks, had he, like his grandfather, been born poor and been obliged to sleep on the floor of the composing room. Wall Street friendships, those derived from his father's financial connections, were not easy to reconcile with editing a gad-fly weekly. This is Villard's own explanation. Others, while conceding that inherited wealth carries with it certain disadvantages, will not consider it the obstacle he himself does. Moreover, his heritage of wealth was accompanied and fortified by other more important legacies—culture, ideas and ideals, a noble tradition of service, and physical health.

Wealth, however, did impose a limitation on Villard of which he is probably unaware—namely an inability to realize that he cannot fairly apply his own standards of conduct to men dependent on their efforts for their livelihood. The castigation, "He has sold himself" springs easily to Villard's lips about some of his fellow-journalists. He fails to understand that what Stuart Chase calls "the luxury of integrity" has been his by inheritance, and that most other men engaged in journalism are confronted with the dilemma of forfeiting in a measure their freedom of expression and action or letting their families starve. Villard has never had to face such an alternative.

That he is capable of superb writing is recognized by all Villard's associates who assert that in any *Nation* issue to which he has contributed, the best—and likewise the worst—pieces and paragraphs are likely to be the products of his pen. At any rate no one else attains quite the lyric and dramatic quality of his literary craftsmanship when he is profoundly moved.

His invocation to George W. Norris when that noble old
Roman, weary and discouraged, was planning to retire from
the United States Senate, is an excellent sample:

"For twenty years you have sat in the seats of the powerful
in Washington and served your country faithfully and well.
During all that time, unlike many of your legislative associates,
your soul has been your own, your vote the vote of conscience.
Wherever you have gone men have respected you, political
opponents have envied and feared you. They saw you enter
the Senate a reformer, a progressive; some of them laughed
cynically and, pointing to many an example in the Senate
Chamber, declared: 'The system will overcome him.' The
system found itself baffled by a brave and honest man. The
years passed; you were progressive still. The Great War came,
beclouding men's minds, instilling passion into their hearts,
making them give out only words of hate and unreason. You
remained clear in vision, temperate in speech, loyal to the core.
You voted against the war which was a crime against America
and its every ideal, and in so doing you kept the American
faith. You have kept it ever since. Always you have been the
captain of your soul."

It will be noted that it is almost invariably on a subject related to pacifism, to detestation of war, to passive resistance, to
moral values, that Villard rises to his greatest heights. Thus
in his moving and eloquent editorial, "The Soul of McSwiney,"
written after the martyr to Irish liberty had died as the result
of a 72-day hunger strike. Thus in his analysis of Woodrow
Wilson written immediately after the President's death:

"And so, once upon a time, there came out of the vineyard
to speak brave words one as with a silver tongue. Young and
old, rich and poor, stopped their work, gathering in the market-
place, saying: 'Behold, there is one who tells the truth. But
do you not see that he is not of the Philistines? Let us listen

and be guided of him.' Whenever he spoke men echoed his words, so that more and more came to listen and to revere. When all the tribes of Israel went to war it came to pass that his words winged their way wherever men battled and women suffered; as men lay dying of their wounds they cried out to him to prevail in order that none others might perish like unto themselves. Widows with starving babes at their breasts called down blessings upon his name. Serfs and bond-slaves lifted up their voices before his image, saying: 'Lo, He has come again.' And when the day dawned when men fought no more, and he went abroad, humble folk kneeled down before him, crying: 'Thou art the man!'

"Yet one day, falling upon evil companions, his strength and wisdom went out from him and his voice was no longer as the trumpets before Jericho. Conceiving greatly he yielded greatly, doing wrong in the hope that some little good might come. Beholding, the people cried: 'He is no longer the Messiah that he was. Do you not perceive how now he strikes hands with those who have misled us?' Soon were heard lamentations throughout the land. Men beat upon their breasts, declaring that woe was theirs, that darkness was now indeed upon all His people, and that there was no light upon the waters. Returning thence to his own tribe, men cast him aside, saying: 'Thou hast no longer the voice of thy other days; we are betrayed and by thee shall we be led no more.' "

* * * * * * *

"Now for truth's sake, it must be written down that when Mr. Wilson passed, the curtain fell upon the greatest tragedy in our history. William Dean Howells once declared that there were but two great tragic and dramatic figures in our past, John Brown and Abraham Lincoln. Surely we may add Woodrow Wilson as well. For what could be greater tragedy than to have ruled eight years and to have left so few enduring

marks upon our institutions; to have preached visions and
ideals to one's countrymen for eight years, only to yield office
to the most material, the most corrupt, the most sightless Administration ever to hold its sway in America. If Mr. Wilson
could but have learned from John Bright that 'War is the grave
of all good, whether in administration or legislation, and it
throws power into the hands of the most worthless of the
class of statesmen!' he could not have betrayed America and
her democracy as he did by going to war. There is no treason
in our history of similar magnitude, and the evil thereof will
endure for generations to come. Probably only an Aeschylus
could do Woodrow Wilson justice today. Certainly no element of the sombrest Greek tragedy was lacking in Washington when Woodrow Wilson left office.

"Upon these things will the historians of the future pass, each
according to his bias and to his interpretation of state papers
now sealed, documents now hidden, events yet to take place.
Philosophers will always wrangle as to whether that man's of-
fence is worse who deliberately destroys the rights and liberties of a people or the crime of him who exalts the spirits of men
by a glorious vision of a new and inspired day, only to let the
uplifted sink back, utterly disheartened and disillusioned, into
the darkest slough of despond. As to the merits and demerits
of Woodrow Wilson, books will be written to the end of time.
Those who worship him will continue to keep eyes and ears
closed to facts they do not wish to hear; those whose very
souls he outraged and betrayed will judge as through a glass
darkly. But one fact no one can deny: Aspiring to the stars
he crashed to earth, leaving behind him no emancipation of
humanity, no assuaging of its wounds, only a world racked,
embittered, more full of hatreds, more ready to tear itself to
pieces today than when he essayed the heavens. The moral of
his fall is as immutable as the hills, as shining as the planets.

If humanity will perceive and acknowledge it that will be
Woodrow Wilson's priceless legacy to the world he tried to
serve so greatly."

It may fairly be said that no man in America has served
the peace movement more faithfully, more clear-sightedly than
Oswald Garrison Villard.

For thirteen years *The Nation* has gone merrily on, attack-
ing militarism and imperialism, stoutly supporting the traditional American liberties, and being lustily iconoclastic—an
irrepressible gadfly to smug complacency and to the deity of
"things as they are." One of its issues was temporarily barred
from the mails after the Armistice by Solicitor Lamar, for no
less heinous an offense than a caustic criticism of the labor
leader Sam Gompers. Three years ago it celebrated its tenth
anniversary—that is, the decennial of its metamorphosis from
a staid and academic mentor, dry and authoritative, to a "liberal weekly"—with banquets of *Nation* readers in a score of
cities from coast to coast.

Villard, of course, has ever found it difficult to share the view
of his associates that *The Nation* is—and should be—an institution, conducted like a soviet by its staff, and not his personal
property. He has repeatedly endorsed their idea in principle,
but in practice editors come and go, somewhat disillusioned
by too prolonged service, and needing a spell of distance to
restore their earlier enchantment.

While the contributions of his fellow editors have played a
considerable part in making *The Nation* what it is, nevertheless
it stands today as a Villard monument, wholly consonant with
the journalistic traditions of four generations. Its virtues (already amply suggested) and its vices (sentimentalism, moraliz-
ing and occasionally biased presentations) are alike Villard's.
For twelve years it has been dedicated to the perpetuation of
principles which are representative of the worthiest striving in

the American experiment. It has left an imperishable mark
on contemporary American thought. With all its internation-
alism, it has kept alive a peculiarly American spirit and tradition of independence and decency in an epoch of great confusion. The credit is chiefly Villard's.

Fifteen years ago, Gustav Pollak wrote *The Nation's* story
in a brilliant collection of editorial extracts from the writings
of American immortals that had appeared in its columns—
Lowell, Howells, James, Charles Eliot Norton and the rest. He
called the volume "A Half Century of Idealism." That characterization is not less merited with the added years as *The
Nation* nears its three score and ten.

An Evolutionist on the Bench

OLIVER WENDELL HOLMES

WE WHO think of Mr. Justice Holmes as the great dissenter should remember that his first public act was to join with the majority. The Harvard class of '61 was graduating when the bombshell of secession exploded, and most of the seniors volunteered. Wendell, as his classmates called him, obtained a lieutenancy in the Massachusetts Twentieth Infantry, fought at Ball's Buff, was wounded, went back and was wounded twice again.

Still another explosion shook that generation. Darwin jolted those young minds. Old, rockbound concepts lost hold. The scientific attitude of examining the accepted gave rise to the realization that life is a process of adjustment, and to young Holmes, who had a taste for philosophy, it was evident that social organisms, too, must constantly adapt themselves to changing conditions. Just as Freudian psychology has given new values to us in the twentieth century, evolution brought doubts and liberation to the nineteenth.

William James was studying medicine in Cambridge at the time Holmes was buckling down to law. James would wrangle with him on optimism and pessimism and then go home to think up an answer to put in the mail. James considered him "the only fellow here I care anything about . . . a first-rate article, and one which improves by wear. He is perhaps too exclusively intellectual, but sees things so easily and clearly and talks so admirably that it's a treat to be with him."

The tall and lank fellow of Charles Street, Boston, who had a gentle, philosophic humorist for a father and the serene and aphoristic Emerson for a house visitor, was developing a character of his own. James could not have too much of him. Writing to him from Berlin, the budding pragmatist said, "Good golly! how I would prefer to have about twenty-four hours' talk with you up in that whitely lit-up room—without the sun rising or the firmament revolving so as to put the gas out, without sleep, clothing, or shelter except your whiskey bottle, of which, or the like of which, I have not partaken since I have been in these longitudes! I should like to have you opposite me in any mood, whether the facetiously exclusive, the metaphorically discursive, the personally confidential, or the jadedly *cursive* and argumentative."

The young sceptic Holmes was no mere heckler. He had the thirst of a scholar. His persistent energy drove him to stacks and stacks of volumes, searching in the past for the roots of present usage—discovering the mutability of truth. Though gifted with a facility for assimilating and assembling knowledge, he was a hard worker. "I should think Wendell worked too hard," James observes, at the same time finding him "in very jolly spirits." Again, James records, "W. is to take no vacation."

Whether nature or nurture deserves the honors for fashioning this interesting person is a matter for argument between eugenists and behaviorists. Born into uppercrust Boston society in 1841, he had a New England lineage long enough for any complacent scion to brag about. Father was a physician who never practised anything but literature. Grandfather Abiel Holmes had been for forty years minister of the First Congregational Church in Cambridge and a historian of parts. Summers were spent at Beverly Farms on the seacoast in the privacy which is the privilege of the well-to-do. Built against precipitous rock, the house was covered with luxuriant vines and the rocks with jasmine. Of course the Autocrat of the Breakfast Table was not free from admiring callers; many a stranger pulled his bell, and young Oliver got an eyeful of autograph hunters. But there must have been plenty of stimulating talk on that veranda where literary nabobs rocked to the rhythm of the Autocrat's sceptre.

Intellectual playfulness was a Holmes family trait. The doctor's brother John, a lawyer, pleased the boy who was otherwise overburdened with serious thoughts about life's problems. Uncle John had a flair for nonsense and was given to impromptu monologues spinning out into irresponsible sequences. His letters were full of foolery. He even twisted the tail of the law. One of his expressions, as the venerable justice remembers it, was "the ambulatory will, with all its little codicils running around after it." Every solemn youngster needs an Uncle John.

Levity must have been congenital, although the Justice maintains that the virus was acquired late in life among other vices, including print-collecting. Father ascribed his own mental inheritance to the Wendells. Sarah Wendell, wife of the Rev. Abiel Holmes, was of New York Dutch stock that settled in Boston and married descendants of Governor Bradstreet and Governor Dudley. The doctor married Amelia Lee Jackson, whose father was Chief Justice of the Massachusetts Supreme Judicial Court until 1824. Recently, when Justice Holmes was being conducted through Harvard Law School to see his own portrait unveiled, he stopped in front of a painting of this forebear and remarked, "That old bird was my grandfather."

Let others stress the significance of this grounding in the spiritual beginnings of New England—the Justice has other ideas. He appreciates the Founders but believes that the great currents of the world's life ran in other channels; that the future lay in the hands of Bacon, Hobbes, and Descartes rather than in John Milton's. And now: "I think that the somewhat isolated thread of our intellectual and spiritual life is rejoining the main stream, and that hereafter all countries more and more will draw from common springs."

His resemblance to his father is not so distant as is supposed by an offhand comparison which poses innocuous gracefulness of expression on one side and vigorous analysis and public importance on the other. Charles W. Eliot remembered Holmes, Sr., as an *enfant terrible* in the medical world, accusing physicians of carrying puerperal fever from one confined woman to another, and as a pioneering professor of anatomy and physiology at Harvard Medical School, fond of provoking the conservatives of the faculty. This was in the days before the advent of bacteriology, which vindicated his insistence that maternity mortality would be reduced if doctors washed their hands.

Dr. Holmes spoke of his double professorship not as a chair but as a settee. His task was to instruct students who were obliged to listen to thirty lectures a week. Entrusted with these fatigued hopefuls, he brought vivacity and earned popularity. He lectured without notes, enlivened the boys with his gift of clear and charming speech, and illustrated his talks with engravings from his own library. President Eliot credited him with foresight in the science of medical instruction. The professor put histology on the map and required every student to learn to use the microscope.

His conversation was said to be better than his writing. He was a past master of the lucid, useful thought, and delighted in rapid sparring with foemen worthy of his wit. His was the kind of mind that is best stimulated by a challenging tongue. (Perhaps this explains why his son is better at dissenting opinions than at decisions of the court.) The good professor had a distrust of many of the beliefs accepted in his set and a sunny willingness to let the truth, the whole truth, be known. Reaching his eighty-first year—"a kind of off year," he said—he admitted lacking his old enthusiasm for writing and often looked into Boswell to see what Johnson was doing at the same age one hundred years before. His handwriting was like Jefferson's—the same slope and absence of ornament. It is remarkable how closely his son's hand resembles it.

"I always thought that I was the ugliest of men, especially in my youth," Justice Holmes is quoted by the artist, Walter Tittle. "In my early conceptions of masculine comeliness curly hair was an indispensable requisite." (He was gangling, with expressive dark brown eyes and glossy brown hair that lay quite flat away from its part high on the left.) "My father gave me a conviction of physical inferiority by pointing out the weakness of mankind, using himself and his son as illustrations. I was positive that I was a very inferior person. He kicked me into the law and thereby did a fairly good job in determining my life for me. In spite of his theory of human frailty, father wrote a book at eighty, and at eighty-four I am still going strong."

Age has been an amusing, not a reverential, matter to him. Often he refers to an imminent end of his span, but he has always managed to live on. Every year, when a new secretary comes down to him from Harvard, he reminds the young man that he cannot guarantee a full year's job. Ten years ago he spoke of himself as "an old warrior who cannot expect to bear arms much longer." In 1902, when he was appointed to the Supreme Court, objection was raised on the ground of his age, sixty-one, but he was expected to continue of use for another fifteen years. At seventy he signed letters, "Your aged friend." On his ninetieth birthday the man who never uses a typewriter or a radio sat before a microphone in his Wash-

OLIVER WENDELL HOLMES

ington home and told listeners-in that "the end draws near."

The red brick house he occupies in I Street (he writes it Eye Street) is the same to which he came with Mrs. Holmes on his appointment. There she remained his gracious companion for twenty-seven years longer, abstaining from Washington society, deriving pleasure from the visits of a new crop of brilliant youngsters and from their own banter. The Justice frequently read aloud an entire book to her. Summers they repaired to the old homestead at Beverly Farms for their long June-to-October vacation from Court. They moved back to the capital just before the opening of the new term and settled down to another round of cases and opinions, as well as foreign and domestic literature.

The house is a library, and a separate niche is given over to the works of his father, Oliver Wendell the first. Books line almost every wall from floor to ceiling. Where any wall-space is left, you will find a print. Holmes covets prints. Rembrandts and Whistlers are his joy. Goya reproductions give him as much pleasure as originals, since he collects for the fun of it, not for the sake of being "a trustee for posterity." Talk to him about engravings and he will probably want to exchange duplicates or buy one you need in return for your second copy which he must have. He may exhibit his collection and say with cocksureness, "Holbein is *it!*"

Mrs. Holmes is gone now. One supposed her passing would undo him, but he took his grief like a Stoic and applied himself to the balance-wheel of his judicial work. (A few months after her death he wrote his dissenting opinion in the Rosika Schwimmer case, a vigorous and sparkling essay on liberty which may become immortal.) Mrs. Holmes had been the merry and popular Fanny Dixwell, daughter of the man who conducted the private Latin school Holmes attended. They were married in '72 when he was editing the *American Law*

Review. If anyone knew the human foibles of a great man it was this wife. One day when a painter called to finish a portrait of Holmes and word was sent down that the subject was regretfully too busy, Mrs. Holmes laughed and told the artist, "You'll probably find him hiding behind a new French novel and smoking a cigarette."

The boy of twenty who joined up with the Union Army before graduation, burrowed into law on his return, and people realized that he was a more strenuous worker than his genial father. It looked as if he were going to make his mark some day. After growing a drooping mustache and loitering in Europe—it must have been a pretty wide-awake loitering—he was admitted to the bar in '67 and into partnership with his only brother, Edward Jackson Holmes.

He taught constitutional law at Harvard one year and lectured on jurisprudence the next, meanwhile editing the *Review* and revealing his talent for the compact sentence. Leaving the editorial desk for the courtroom, he practised as a member of the firm of Shattuck, Holmes and Munroe until his literary achievements brought him fame and a new station in life.

Holmes's interest in the law as a science and his researches into the common law were manifested during his editorship. He had already put in a painstaking job editing the twelfth edition of Kent's *Commentaries* when the Lowell Institute, before which his father had given a series of lectures on the poets, asked him to lecture on the common law. Those who heard him said that his manner of delivery was a marvelous intellectual performance. He spoke without referring to a manuscript as though narrating an absorbing story offhand. Steeped in his theme, he did not need to memorize; he appeared to be going through a process of reasoning at the moment. In preparing these lectures for book publication he put in enough work rearranging, rewriting, and enlarging to render most of the book practically new.

Its publication in '81 made him internationally famous. (*The Common Law* remains a classic.) Harvard gave him a professorship in '82, but he held it only a few months. At the end of the year he was appointed to the Supreme Judicial Court, following in the tracks of "that old bird."

It is not true, however, that he followed anybody's trail. In those days, despite the reproaches of public opinion, he spoke up for war as an institution. This recalls Emerson's remark—"sometimes gunpowder smells good." In Memorial Day addresses, on other patriotic occasions, and in conversations at the club his speech was replete with metaphors of the battlefield. His Civil War experience imbedded in him a faith in the rôle of the soldier, the soldier's sense of duty, heroism, glory. Life, to him, was action and passion. If a man did not share the action and passion of his time he ran the risk of being judged as one who had not lived. If the nation was to be involved in war, the highest attributes of man were called forth.

"There are many," he said, "who think that love of country is an old wife's tale, to be replaced by interest in a labor union, or under the name of cosmopolitanism, by a rootless self-seeking search for a place where the utmost enjoyment may be had at the least cost." He would rather share "the incommunicable experience of war" and feel "the passion of life to its top." He said he did not know the meaning of the universe but there was one thing no man "who lives in the same world with the rest of us can doubt, and that is that the faith is true and adorable which leads a soldier to throw away his life in obedience to a blindly accepted duty." Ideals in the past, he said, have been drawn from war. "For all our prophecies, I doubt if we are ready to give up our inheritance."

These things he uttered a few years before the Spanish American War. Liberal opinion was worried about him, especially since he seemed to be a champion of the common man in his opinions in labor cases. But to Holmes life meant battle. We bear a bundle of burdens, and the societies aiming to mitigate the struggle ("from societies for the prevention of cruelty to animals up to Socialism") are simply shifting the incidence of those burdens. His upholding of legislation benefiting workmen had merely legal foundation. If the people wanted improvements and were willing to pay for them and the Constitution permitted them, he might have his doubts about the benefits but he was not going to be an obstructor.

Hence in the controversies that shot out of the new industrialism Holmes sustained the right of unions to picket, strike, and boycott. His mental integrity saved him from the influence of the vested interests of Massachusetts, while the majority of the court were disposed to keep a conventional regard for precedent. But Holmes, dissenting, would point out that a patrol of workers in front of a place of business did not necessarily carry with it a threat of bodily harm, and that a union had a right to dissuade other men by peaceable means. Combined workmen had the same liberty as combined capital to support their interests by the bestowal or refusal of advantages in their control. Speaking for himself, he felt it was pure fantasy to suppose that labor gained much by "the strike, a lawful instrument in the universal struggle of life," except "at the expense of the less organized and less powerful portion of the laboring mass." However, he upheld labor's rights, and that is what counted.

Small wonder that President Roosevelt, who was something of a reformer, appointed this man to the first vacancy in the United States Supreme Court.

The seed of the long Holmes tradition on that bench is

contained in a paragraph which he wrote while on the *Review*. It combined the elements of his social philosophizing—his belief in the will and power of the majority, his acceptance of change with the shifting of burdens, his emphasis on the current realignment and the justice of society's self-defense against minorities. The occasion was an English decision involving a gas stokers' strike in London. The thirty-two-year-old editor took issue with Herbert Spencer's position on class legislation and he wrote in part:

> It has always seemed to us a singular anomaly that believers in the theory of evolution and in the natural development of institutions by successive adaptions to the environment, should be found laying down a theory of government intended to establish its limits once for all by a logical deduction from axioms.

Holmes's objection was that the different parts of a community did not have an identity of interest and that Mr. Spencer was wrong in assuming that a change in the law was inexpedient if society as a whole failed to ease its burden as a result.

> . . . The struggle for life, undoubtedly, is constantly putting the interests of men at variance with those of the lower animals. And the struggle does not stop in the ascending scale with the monkeys, but is equally the law of human existence. Outside of legislation this is undeniable. It is mitigated by sympathy, prudence, and all the social and moral qualities. But in the last resort a man rightly prefers his own interest to that of his neighbors. And this is true in legislation as in any other form of corporate action. All that can be expected from modern improvements is that legislation should easily and quickly, yet not too quickly modify itself in accordance with the will of the *de facto* su-

preme power in the community, and that the spread of an educated sympathy should reduce the sacrifice of minorities to a minimum. But whatever body may possess the supreme power for the moment is certain to have interests inconsistent with others which have competed unsuccessfully. The more powerful interests must be more or less reflected in legislation; which, like every other device of man or beast, must tend in the long run to aid the survival of the fittest.

Moreover, to object to legislation because it favors one class at the expense of another was, he declared, a weak point; most legislation does that, even when it is in behalf of greatest number as against a minority consisting of the most intelligent. The welfare of the living majority was paramount simply because the majority had the power in their hands.

. . . The fact is that legislation in this country, as well as elsewhere, is empirical. It is necessarily made a means by which a body, having the power, puts burdens which are disagreeable to them on the shoulders of somebody else. Communism would no more get rid of the difficulty than any other system, unless it limited or put a stop to the propagation of the species. And it may be doubted whether that solution would not be as disagreeable as any other.

Holmes came out of war with faith in the righteousness of martial combat. He rose from his studies with the conviction that individual rights may be sacrificed without a scruple whenever the predominant power is thought to demand this last measure of self-preservation. That is why it is easy to understand how as a judge he gives some people the impression he is a liberal and gives some liberals the certainty that he is not. Though he accepts the deliberations of legislatures on such matters as minimum wages, maximum hours, child labor,

woman labor and trade unions, and the safeguarding of civil
liberties, there comes a time, he feels, when freedom of speech
is curbed by the same reasoning which permits a state to protect itself from the multiplication of imbeciles by requiring
sterilization. "I used to say, when I was young, that truth
was the majority vote of that nation that could lick all others."

The nature of truth thus early conceived identified itself with
what most people were willing to believe. Subjectively, truth
was "the system of my intellectual limitations. . . . I do not
venture to assume that my inabilities in the way of thought
are inabilities of the universe," and it became truth for others
only in so far as it coincided with their limitations. Writing
to James in 1901, the year before the chief justice of Massachusetts became an associate justice in Washington, he said,
"I have been in the habit of saying that all I mean by truth is
what I can't help thinking. . . . My *can't helps* are not necessarily cosmic. . . . I can't help preferring champagne to ditch
water, but I doubt if the universe does. . . . The great act of
faith is when a man decides that he is not God. . . . It seems
to me that my only promising activity is to make *my* universe
coherent and livable, not to babble about *the* universe."

Going back to the formation of these subjective truths
Holmes asserted: "One cannot be wrenched from the rocky
crevices into which one has grown for many years without
feeling that one is attacked in one's life. What we most love
and revere generally is determined by early associations. I
love granite rocks and barberry bushes, no doubt because with
them were my earliest joys that reach back through the past
eternity of my life." Seeing thus how his preferences developed, he could realize that "others, poor souls, may be equally
dogmatic about something else. And this again means scepti-
cism." Not that he would not fight for his own—"we all,
whether we know it or not, are fighting to make the kind of

a world that we should like"—but he realized that others would fight with equal sincerity.

Deep-seated preferences cannot be argued about—you cannot argue a man into liking a glass of beer—and therefore, when differences are sufficiently far-reaching, we try to kill the other man rather than let him have his way. But that is perfectly consistent with admitting that, so far as appears, his grounds are just as good as yours.

We can see how this philosophy was brought to bear on a case arising from the World War:

Persecution for the expression of opinions seems to me perfectly logical. If you have no doubt of your premises or your power and want a certain result with all your heart you naturally express your wishes in law and sweep away all opposition. To allow opposition by speech seems to indicate that you think speech impotent, as when a man says that he has squared the circle, or that you do not care wholeheartedly for the result, or that you doubt either your power or your premises.

On the other hand, he makes it clear that "if in the long run the beliefs expressed in proletarian dictatorship are destined to be accepted by the dominant forces of the community, the only meaning of free speech is that they should be given their chance and have their way."

However unhappy we may be about some of the eggs in his basket, Holmes has the ideal judicial temper. He has no final truth in his vestpocket, no patent panacea good for today's maladjustments and tomorrow's; his truths you do not have to swallow—you must gulp them down only when they happen to be the law. Thus the nonagenarian judge differs from your callow world-firing evangelist in not trying to make over mankind in his own image. If the lack of an ultimate objective leaves the socially-minded stranded, for Holmes at least there is a Constitution to define the rules of the game. The vague drift of life in general, of American government in particular, he is willing to countenance so long as there is no unreasonable interference. Holmes the evolutionist admits change where the die-hards don't; admits that minorities may agitate for it within their (qualified) rights and that legislatures may have the utmost freedom to experiment. As an expounder of the Constitution he is not concerned with approving measures, much less with intruding his private beliefs; he must determine whether legislative or individual courses of action are not forbidden by the holy scroll.

More than once he has asserted that the Constitution should not be made the partisan of an economic theory; that judges should not read their prejudices into that instrument. (He has none of the false modesty which checks a man from repeating himself.) He scathes "encysted ideas" which prevent further investigation. He takes judicial cognizance of "these days," "modern times," the need to respond to "the changing opinions of these times." The soundness of a statute is not the court's business—"the law knows nothing but legal rights." And the substance of the law at any given time "pretty nearly corresponds, so far as it goes, with what is then understood to be convenient."

When differing with his brethren on the bench he is not loving capitalism less or states' rights more; he insists that they must not judge by their own conceptions of public policy or morals. They should permit, in his deathless phrase, "free trade in ideas." The best test of truth is "the power of the thought to get itself accepted in the competition of the market." This is the theory of the Constitution, he says. "It is an experiment, as all life is an experiment. Every year if not every day we have to wager our salvation upon some prophecy based upon imperfect knowledge." Just as reformers who spout universal dogmas are not to his liking, he cannot entertain the conclusions of his associates when they cling to *status quo*. This is why he has so much fondness for the company of Justice Brandeis.

"Judicial dissent," Holmes has said, "often is blamed as if it meant simply that one side or the other were not doing their sums right, and, if they would take more trouble, agreement inevitably would come." Holmes shows that it is not faulty arithmetic on the part of those who disagree with him but "too literal a meaning" of the Constitution. Sometimes this narrow view reveals a reactionary or conceals him. When the Constitution does not plainly, to Holmes, forbid, he does not see why it should not permit. His addiction to the word "penumbra" indicates that he is not taken in by what he stigmatizes as "delusive exactness." The weight is on the side of reasonableness.

According to the dissenter's way of looking at a decision, the Court is not listening to the will of the community:

> This case is decided upon an economic theory which a large part of the country does not entertain. If it were a question whether I agreed with that theory, I should desire to study it further and long before making up my mind. But I do not conceive that to be my duty, because I strongly believe that my agreement or disagreement has nothing to do with the right of a majority to embody their opinion in laws.

A constitution is made for people of fundamentally differing views, he said. A statute's constitutionality is not to be determined by finding the opinion it embodies either "natural and familiar or novel and even shocking." The occasion for that statement was the refusal of the Supreme Court to permit the State of New York to limit the working hours of bakers. The court held that the right to buy or sell labor was a liberty guaranteed by the Fourteenth Amendment. Again, when Congress enacted a law prohibiting the discharge of railroad workers for the reason that they were members of a union, Holmes dissented from a decision which found the law unconstitutional.

I quite agree that the question what and how much good labor unions do is one on which intelligent people may differ,—I think that laboring men sometimes attribute to them advantages, as many attribute to combinations of capital disadvantages, that are really due to economic conditions of a far wider and deeper kind—but I could not pronounce it unwarranted if Congress should decide that to foster a strong union was for the best interest, not only of the men, but of the railroads and the country at large.

The widest possible latitude should be given to legislatures because, theoretically at any rate, they are supposed to represent dominant opinion. So we find this jurist saying, when the court struck down an Arizona law prohibiting injunctions in labor disputes, "There is nothing I more deprecate than the use of the Fourteenth Amendment beyond the absolute compulsion of its words to prevent the making of experiments that an important part of the community desires, in the insulated chambers afforded by the several states, even though the experiments may seem futile or even noxious to me and to those whose judgment I most respect."

A minimum-wage law for women in Washington, D. C., was invalidated. Holmes declared that the criterion of constitutionality was not whether the judges believe the law to be for the public good but what a reasonable person reasonably might believe. New York limited theatre ticket brokers' re-sale

profits to fifty cents a ticket, and the Supreme Court held that
this piece of legislation contravened the Constitution by invading private property; that no duty to nurse the drama devolved
upon any American government. Holmes once more dissented:

> We have not that respect for art that is one of the glories
> of France. But to many people the superfluous is the neces-
> sary, and it seems to me that government does not go beyond
> its sphere in attempting to make life livable for them. I am
> far from saying that I think this particular law a wise and
> rational provision. That is not my affair. If the people of
> the State of New York speaking by the authorized voice say
> that they want it, I see nothing in the Constitution of the
> United States to prevent their having their will.

Likewise, when the case before the court involves a pioneer
for a better world, the peaceful advocate should not be denied.
Rosika Schwimmer, for instance, is opposed to the war system
which is part of the Constitution. She wants the Constitution
improved in this respect, at least, and is pledged to refuse war
service. Because of her capacity for baneful influence she was
denied citizenship. Holmes said he did not share her optimism
that war will disappear, "nor do I think that a philosophic view
of the world would regard war as absurd." But he added:

> If there is any principle of the Constitution that more im-
> peratively calls for attachment than any other it is the princi-
> ple of free thought—not free thought for those who disagree
> with us but freedom for the thought that we hate. I think
> that we should adhere to that principle with regard to admis-
> sion into, as well as to life within, this country.

His written opinions do not tell the whole story. Besides
the thousands of occasions since 1882 that Holmes has put his

deliberations into words, there have been the tens of thousands of times when he silently concurred in decisions or dissents rendered by other members of the bench. We have recently seen him joining a majority in invalidating the Minnesota newspaper "gag" law and the California red flag law (in part) and sustaining the Indiana chain-store tax. We have likewise seen him side with a minority in refusing to interpret the Naturalization Act so as to debar from citizenship Professor Douglas Clyde Macintosh and Marie Averil Bland on account of anti-war convictions. These concurrences of Holmes hardly came as a surprise. They are mentioned simply in allusion to that tall cairn of intellectual loyalties which does not crop up in his written works.

What a pity it would be if Holmes had stuck by his early declaration, "I think it useless and undesirable, as a rule, to express dissent." We are grateful that he broke the rule often, for the body of his dissenting opinions aside from being studded with literary gems gives us the heritage of a continuous record of revolt. It is insufficient to turn a neat phrase in one such conflict with his colleagues and let that aphorism do duty for subsequent disagreements. Instead of casting an opposing vote with silent discontent he has stated his grounds and become the articulate promise of a new order.

If at times his conclusions diverge from the shibboleths of progressives, they must not think that they alone possess the true article. No one was more startled than President Roosevelt when Holmes failed to support his trust-busting campaign and voted to uphold the Northern Securities railroad merger. In another anti-trust case Holmes again sided with the combination, seeing nothing in its conduct which would not be practised, "if we can imagine it, by an all-wise socialistic government."

The war, crisis of crises, brought disappointment and loss

of hope. What price tolerance when at the supreme moment a Holmes condemns a Debs? In the venomous days of prosecution under the Espionage Act many among us felt that the test of liberalism had come. And as liberalism closed the door in defense of the established system, evolution by revolution gained adherents. The folly of force against force is not within the province of the present writer. We can see how Holmes naturally came by sustaining the bayonet behind the conscript and approving conviction of resisters. He himself does not disbelieve in war—although that is not supposed to bear any weight—but the government he has sworn to uphold, the Constitution he has sworn to defend, countenance war; they provide for war and the machinery of it. Congress, supposedly responsive to the people, declares war in conformity with the power bestowed by the Constitution, and it votes for enabling acts and for punishment of enemies foreign and domestic. We have the picture again of a majority making truth.

Where the dragnet of the Attorney General swept in offenders of the Espionage Act criticising some aspect of the war or using the occasion to preach radicalism, the criterion of "clear and present danger" was ignored by the court, and once more Holmes (and Brandeis) dissented:

> It is only the present danger of immediate evil or an intent to bring it about that warrants Congress in setting a limit to the expression of opinion where private rights are not concerned. Congress certainly cannot forbid all effort to change the mind of the country.

After all, we are dealing with the law. While we have laws, constitutions and governments we shall have authority. Within the realm of authority our best fortune is to possess, as a last word, a mind compounded of fairness, wisdom, and grace. If he believes in the greatest good of the greatest number, whereas we may be thinking of the greatest good of future generations, to quibble with him is to claim that we have the patented nostrum. The short way is to dissent. Holmes has said that "an evolutionist will hesitate to affirm universal validity for his social ideals, or for the principles which he thinks should be embodied in legislation. He is content if he can prove them best for here and now. He may be ready to admit that he knows nothing about an absolute best in the cosmos, and even that he knows nothing about a permanent best for men."

But he looks for lone thinkers like Darwin and Pasteur who will discover the principles basic to new adjustments. He cheers on these adventurers in solitude who "must face the loneliness of original work." And yet men of destiny are not far removed from the plane of the workaday world. "The man of the future," said Mr. Justice Holmes, automobile companion of Mr. Justice Brandeis, "is the man of statistics and the master of economics." There is no need to talk of Olympian grandeur in connection with Holmes. He is full of humor, sometimes saucy, sometimes colloquial. "Young feller," he says, and when he fashions a bright epigram in writing a letter he beckons his secretary and makes him listen. Olympian? He is human to the point of having a wart on his cheek!

Justice First

JOHN A. LAPP

HE SEEMS a strange and lonely figure, this interpreter crying aloud for fellowship between two great groups where mutual suspicion is usual and frank hostility not seldom met. He is a teacher of sociology in a Jesuit university and a foremost figure in promoting legislation usually termed "radical." Because at the present day there is an idea, blown strongly from Russian storm clouds, that to be radical one must fight God, John A. Lapp seems to stand like a herald of peace, summoning armies hidden from each other to meet as friends.

It is difficult to write a just estimate of his work and quite impossible to write it without giving offense on one side or the other. There are two frames of mind involved which frankly do not understand each other: the modern crusading liberal and the immemorial liberating crusader. The difference is perhaps made clear by a quotation from one who has long been a personal and intimate friend of Lapp:

"We were talking about a Roman Catholic bishop who is famed for his strong stand in behalf of economic justice," said this friend, a Protestant minister. "I was glorying in having such a champion of social justice in that church. And I happened to add a sarcastic remark—perhaps it might even fairly be called a sneer—because this same bishop has just returned from Rome with a package of the bones of some saint. And John Lapp, while he said nothing, was profoundly hurt. I

JOHN A. LAPP

apologized for hurting him, but I still can't get the idea."

Novenas asking the Little Flower to intercede with God to provide work for the unemployed—the blessing of throats on St. Blase's day—medals of St. Christopher on automobiles to avert accidents—invocations to St. Anthony to find lost articles —the type of mind of which these are expressions is simply not intelligible to the average modern Protestant, and even less so to the modern liberal and agnostic.

Perhaps the most extreme example of this frame of mind was the announcement by the Cardinal of Ostia that the Italian earthquake was God's punishment on a race which permits women to wear such abbreviated bathing suits and such short, provocative dresses. Influential Italian daily newspapers ventured a protest, saying that if this were so, divine justice showed singularly poor judgment, since the people killed were mainly mountain women who seldom go swimming. To this the Vatican official newspaper rejoined that the editors of these daily papers were not theologians, and hence not competent to pass judgment.

Between this primitive view of life and that of the scientifically trained collegians who form the great bulk of the social workers in this country, there is a wide gulf. And one who stands at the point of impact between two such spiritual battle-lines is bound to be somewhat uncomfortable.

I have seen John Lapp on a lecture platform leap up in a blaze of emotion to answer an atheist who had sneered at his church, an emotion quite alien to the smiling Protestant minister who occupied the same platform and who passed off a similar sneer at his own church by the same atheist with a laugh and a wave of his hand. To Lapp, it was as though his mother had been insulted. To the Protestant minister, it was as though his club had been criticized.

Here perhaps lies the root of the difference. The modern

crusading liberal feels that he is a new man, that he is applying novel principles, of which he is not yet sure, to a novel situation that he has not quite analyzed. To him social distress is apt to appear as a problem to be solved. He is always conscious of the excitement of pioneering, of a feeling of blazing fresh trails through untrodden woods. But to a Catholic the chief thought is that he is the bearer of a sacred trust, a soldier on an immemorial firing-line, attempting to carry out a world-old strategy under conditions perplexing to him but completely understood at headquarters. To him the war is an old custom; he serves in an army with a tradition of heroism. He is a crusader in the sacred old meaning in that he is fighting for the cross. To the Catholic it is quite as natural to appeal to Saint Therese or Saint Anne for advice and help regarding unemployment as it is to the modern liberal to consult with the Secretary of Commerce or the chairman of the Federal Reserve. These saints are in a position where they know more and can bring more influence to bear than can he. And, above all, to the Catholic economist social distress is not simply a mathematical problem to be worked out but a family difficulty to be solved, with the chief aim in view of preserving the moral integrity of the persons distressed—the victory of the soul being the great goal, and not the mere comforting of the body.

Here is the basic element of all Lapp's thinking, as set down in his most characteristic work, *Justice First*.

"The starting point is that man is a spiritual being; that he is not mere muscle or power. Man is morally endowed with essential rights not merely of life, liberty, and the pursuit of happiness, but of protection of his integrity—physical, economic, civic and spiritual—against adverse forces that surround him. The central purpose of all efforts to control economic life by social action is the protection and promotion of the

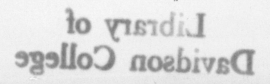

rights of human beings—the attainment of justice for mankind."

Why is it that the Roman Catholic Church is so frequently considered a reactionary on all social and economic matters? Let us analyze if possible the attitude of the church toward any radical movement.

In any question affecting large numbers of people the attitude, actual or potential, of that church looms like the orbit of Neptune. It is not always pressure directly exerted. More often it is a state of mind, generated by teachings and customs, a system of values which are entirely incomprehensible to the person to whom its spiritual exercises are unknown.

Within the past twenty-five years, something like twenty million immigrants have been poured into the current of American national life. Myriads of them found in this country only one thing that bore the slightest resemblance to anything they had left in their homeland and that was the church. Language was different, laws were different, customs, transportation, habits of buying and selling, hours and days of working, labor laws, rental customs—everything was madly, bewilderingly different. Only the Latin of the mass sounded like home, and the glittering constellations of the altar candles shone like familiar stars. To the church then, these transplanted immigrants clung.

But in hundreds of thousands of cases, children of these immigrants felt a rift widen between their new life and the old habits. So the Roman Catholic Church in the United States finds itself battling vigorously to retain its hold upon the younger generation. It makes rigid lines and erects strong barriers to keep its younger folk from joining in any organization with other young folk on equal terms. It has its own system of schools from kindergarten to university. Its gymnasiums, sodalities, Knights of Columbus, Daughters of Isabella—

all impress its members with the idea that they are different from the surrounding Protestant world.

It is certainly not to be wondered at if the surrounding world reciprocates the feeling, with the result that the gap widens to a gulf. But there are forces seeking constantly to bridge the gulf, promoting human understanding, seeking to "co-ordinate"—in the terms made familiar by the war experts—enterprises of common moment. Among these forces John A. Lapp is one of the most conspicuous and certainly one of the most significant.

Lapp is believed by most of his associates to be a convert to the Roman Catholic church from Protestantism. This, however, is not true. His father was a Lutheran, but his mother was a Catholic. He was reared in a part of the country where there was no church nearby, only a mission station. All his education and professional activities were in secular fields until, well along in his career, he found that the principles and ideas he had worked out in his own practice sprang naturally from, and were quite in conformity with, the tenets of his religion. This discovery is his spiritual romance.

The amount of work he has done is enormous. In one year, 1926-27, as President of the National Council of Social Work, he delivered 150 addresses in 32 states. Sales of his books have mounted to a half-million copies. He has left a deep impress upon the methods of procedure of every state legislature, as well as on the methods of practically all relief systems in the country. "I do not know anybody who is on more committees," he says with a smile. Among them are: National Council for the Prevention of War; Civil Liberties Union; Executive Committee of the League for Independent Political Action; American Association for Labor Legislation; National Conference of Social Work, as well as fifteen or sixteen more. But John A. Lapp is not merely a yes-man, joining committees to keep things moving. He is a pioneer by profession, starting things, then moving on.

Educated at Alfred University, he later did graduate work at the University of Wisconsin and was awarded a fellowship in economics at Cornell. It was during this period, 1906-1907, that the field of legislative reference was just beginning to develop. Under the impetus of the La Follette movement in Wisconsin, scientific methods were being utilized in the interests of state government. Professor Charles A. McCarthy started the idea of scientific legislation through a system of compilation of all laws on given subjects. Lapp was his first pupil, and as such was put in charge of the Indiana Bureau when it was established.

In Indiana he pioneered all the time, building from the ground up. He was the legislative guide of three governors—Marshall, Ralston, and Goodrich. He framed most of the legislation for their administrations during five successive legislatures. He developed the idea of co-ordinating the University of Indiana with this legislative work, and through the university he trained a number of young men as scientific lawmakers, men who later went to the legislature.

The first problem left on the doorstep of the new bureau was that of vocational education. A preliminary bill met with little success. Further study led to the drawing of a bill which passed the next legislature in its first session—unchanged. This attracted national attention and President Wilson appointed a vocational commission, of which Lapp was a member. He drafted the national measure which had the extraordinary fate of being passed by Congress without change—an all-time record. Most commissions just flounder along. Under the name of the Smith-Hughes law, this measure is still in effect, and through its provisions the Federal Government spends $12,000,000 a year, in cooperation with the states, to equip young people, through vocational education, for their work in life.

Having accomplished this, Lapp went on to the next phase—vocational rehabilitation for men injured and disabled in industrial accidents. This brought him into the field of child labor laws, compensation work, and social insurance.

In 1917 the Ohio Health and Old Age Insurance Commission invited him to assist with their work. He served there for a year and a half, presenting the report in 1919. Not much has come of it except agitation, largely because of the vigorous opposition of life insurance companies, against which Lapp has a deep and merited grudge. Health insurance might be a reality, he says, except for the uncompromising battle they put up against it. The Committee on the Cost of Medical Care, headed by Ray Lyman Wilbur, he condemns just as heartily, on the ground that it tends to avert health insurance.

About this time Father O'Grady of Washington became interested in the problem of old age pensions. Together with Lapp he devoted eight months to this inquiry, doing most of the field work. Just as it was completed O'Grady was made secretary of the National Catholic War Council, and invited Lapp to come to Washington. This organization afterward became the National Catholic Welfare Conference.

"Up to that time," said Lapp, "I had never had any work in connection with any religious organization. My experience had been purely political and scientific. But I found—I must confess to my amazement and pleased surprise—that the formulas I had worked out as the result of these surveys fitted perfectly into the framework provided by the Catholic doctrines. Especially was this true of Pope Leo XIII's Encyclical on labor. I never read this until 1916 and it gave me tremendous satisfaction to see how timely it still was."

At the time that his connection with the Catholic council

began he was offered the editorship of a magazine called *The Nation's Health*. He remained at that post for four years. At the same time, as a director of the Social Action Department of the National Catholic Welfare Conference, he set up in Washington a program for civic education—a system of study of civics in schools, both parochial and public, and work among the foreign-born. The publications of this movement gave the story of the American government, civil life and social problems. They embodied the elementary things men need to know about our country and its ways. They were translated into fourteen different languages, published serially in foreign newspapers and later issued by them in pamphlet form. Altogether they must have run to 5,000,000 copies. Meanwhile Lapp talked all over the United States on the need of education in citizenship.

Shortly after his consecration as archbishop of New York, the present Cardinal Hayes placed Lapp in charge of a survey of the charitable work in the archdiocese. He wanted to know what was going on and why. Two or three of his young priests were sent to study in a school of social sciences, and kept in touch with Lapp's survey so as to be able to use it intelligently when completed. As many as fifty people were working under Lapp's direction. They covered New York's charitable activities, taking seven months to do it. On the basis of their report, a new system of charities was set up. The archbishop asked for half a million dollars to cover his budget and the church responded—in the spring of 1920—with a solid million, which has now been doubled, in the archdiocese, all of it spent scientifically, in accordance with the survey.

All this time Lapp was coming to understand more and more how "the other half" lives, and it was a discouraging knowledge. For seven years he was joint director of the Social Action Department of the National Catholic Welfare Conference.

Then, suddenly in 1927, Bishop Muldoon of Rockford died. A new bishop took Muldoon's place as head of the Social Action Department. This bishop, Lillis, of Kansas City, knew nothing about Lapp's work. Lapp received a letter one morning from Bishop Lillis saying that it had been decided to reorganize his department, that it was to be moved to Washington, and that another director would be put in charge immediately.

Why such brusqueness? Lapp will not have it that there was any connection between this sudden action and his frank championship of the cause of Sacco and Vanzetti, whose condemnation and execution he openly denounced as an outrage. He insists that it was entirely a matter of budgetary reform. Well—it may be so. Whatever the cause was, within a few weeks Lapp was in charge of the department of social sciences at Marquette University in Milwaukee.

During the four years he has been there, the registration in his department has grown from practically nothing to 525. From five courses, poorly attended, the department has increased so that it now includes nineteen courses, nearly all overcrowded.

Marquette is a Jesuit university in the sense that the order owns it. But half of the board of managers are non-Catholic, more than half of the faculty and very much more than half of the student body come from outside the Church of Rome.

"Do the Jesuit fathers interfere with your teaching?" I asked.

"Don't you know them better than that?" he replied, smiling. "Nobody has ever interfered in the running of my department. Being put in charge of it, I am left to run it."

He is not muzzled by ecclesiastical superiors in his frank opposition and strong assaults on vested wrong. No man has battled the power trust more trenchantly or taken a more vigorous stand in exposing its attempt to subsidize the colleges.

Frequently he goes visiting as a lecturer. Addressing a synod of the Episcopal Church, he assailed "flippant Menckenites" and other advocates of the ancient jungle theory of the survival of the fittest. "Survival should not be governed only by biological laws," he said. "The struggle must be moralized by charity and justice. Competition of individuals will go on. Society would be drab and desolate without the rivalry of in. dividuals for place, property, and power." This was in answer to a blast by the "American Citizenship Foundation" of Chicago, which seemed to hold it a patriotic maxim that the weak should perish.

When Lapp was elected president of the National Conference of Social Work, he was sitting at the very top of the balcony in the Masonic Auditorium in Cleveland. There had been misgivings in some minds about electing him on account of his membership in the church whose hierarchy, led by Cardinal O'Connell of Boston, had recently made a bitter attack against the national child labor amendment and prohibition.

Miss Gertrude Vail, the retiring president, spied him in his obscure seat and called him to the platform. His first words cleared away any doubts about his independence of spirit.

"I shall not put my individual conscience into cold storage but shall insist upon speaking my beliefs," he declared. "And this is what I believe. I believe in social action. I denounce the attempt to decry legislative action, when the only remedy that can be given evils is legislative action. . . . I believe in civil liberty not only for the strong but also for the weak who most need protection. Not every action can be justified by the pretext of individual liberty. I do not believe that a man has a right to drink or get drunk. I do not put the right to get drunk among the fundamental liberties guaranteed to our people by the Constitution. I am a prohibitionist. I believe in the complete enforcement of the Volstead Act. I stand for justice first of all, especially justice for children; I believe that the Twentieth Amendment to the Constitution, providing for the prohibition of child labor, ought to be ratified as quickly as possible."

When he sat down, all fears in the minds of the members regarding his independence had been removed. If his opening statement was electrical, his closing address, printed in pamphlet form as *Justice First* was epoch-making. It has become a classic—the clearest statement ever made on the relation between justice and charity. Brief as it is, every word, every phrase, is carefully calculated and built into a structure of impassioned protest against the misconception and abuse of the two qualities—justice and charity—which are at the very heart of God.

"Charity discovers needs. It rouses men to moral duties. It points the way to justice. Justice is the goal, and, as it is attained, the obligations of charity are taken over by the institutions of justice. That which we care for out of charity today is prevented or provided for through systems of justice tomorrow. Charity, intelligently given, looks to the elimination of the need for its ministrations."

John Lapp battles heroically and with all the force of a wide experience marshaled by keen intelligence against the doctrine of "survival of the fittest" and "let things alone." The survivors are not necessarily the fit. They are the lucky, he maintains. Are the victims of a tornado unfit? he scornfully demands.

"Investigation proves," he says, in *Justice First,* "that people are poor in the main through social injustice or unavoidable causes. A mere fraction only are responsible for their own downfall. War, floods, tornadoes, sickness, unemployment, under-employment, accident, mental deficiency, death or desertion, inadequate wages, business failure, and dependent old age are the causes of 90 per cent or more of all the poverty in the United States. Is it within the power of the individual to control these disasters?"

Peace movements both here and abroad claim much of what Dr. Lapp laughingly calls his "spare time." He was a delegate to the International Catholic Conference on Peace in 1925 at Oxford, and has been an officer of the American Association for Peace Education, and the National Council for Prevention of War.

He went abroad in 1928 and again in 1929 as a delegate to the preliminary conference on International Peace through Religion, which is preparing for a World Conference in Washington in 1932. He has also taken an active part in the meetings of the World Alliance for International Peace through the Churches. But this pacifist activity is a lesser issue. "In my own thinking," he says, "all is subordinate to the idea of justice. There is a deep and growing animosity in my mind toward the kind of talk that is put up in community drives for charities. The talk is all in terms of charity, never of justice. I feel a strong revulsion toward the 'charity games' of football they are promoting this fall. Why? Because a lot of wealthy people think they are doing all that can be expected of them when they go to see a football game. It puts the emphasis in the wrong place. Jesus said, 'Seek ye first the Kingdom of God, and his Justice—and all these things shall be added unto you.' "

Leo XIII's utterance which he quotes most frequently is the following: "Justice demands that the interests of the poorer class should be carefully watched over by the administration. Whatever shall prove to be conducive to the well-being of those who work should receive favorable consideration. Let it not be feared that solicitude of this kind will be harmful to any interest. On the contrary, it will be to the advantage of all, for it cannot but be good for the commonwealth to shield from misery those on whom it so largely depends."

But on one point Lapp runs counter to the pontiff's utterance—that in which Pope Leo holds that "human nature cannot be changed." Lapp's constant thesis is that the conditions under which human beings live and labor can be changed and are being changed, that alteration of environment for the better creates an instant response for the better in human beings.

"Juvenile delinquency can be cut seventy-five per cent with the right kind of recreational facilities and leadership," he maintains. "Why do we have so many youthful criminals? Why do we find them originating in certain sections of our cities? The answer is that we have left youth in our congested centers to the evils of their surroundings and the influence of bad companionship.

"Recreation teaches honesty. True sport is an honest affair. If the public should ever insist on public honesty to the same degree that it now insists on honesty in sports, we would have a pure and undefiled government.

"To help people help themselves is what the world has got to do. Show men and women how to lift themselves out of poverty and give them social protection." To do this Lapp advocates progressive social education and legislation.

Perhaps it is for this reason that in thinking of John A. Lapp one sees a picture, not of the man, but of his work. One remembers not the sound of his voice but the things he says. He does not impress one as a general, but rather a messenger, bearing and translating instructions from a headquarters not everyone sees. His importance to the future is the interpretation he makes between two great masses of thought, two atmospheres which are often hostile but which must, for the sake of saving the world, come to an understanding and join in a friendly crusade. After meeting him, one carries away not so much a sense of a dominating personality as of a dominating purpose. He is a general who effaces himself in his strategy, bent not on winning his laurels but on bringing about a victory for his cause. He carries on the tradition of Stephen, the first organizer of poor relief, and of Francis, content to be merely the "poor little brother," and of the hospitallers of the Temple, with their motto *Non nobis, Domine.*

We shall be feeling the influence of his mild, persistent efficiency for many years to come when his name is perhaps forgotten. And like Francis, he is well content to have it so.

John A. Lapp is a "radical" in the original meaning of the term, which signifies one who goes to the root of things. Having got to the root, he finds that root is God.

Every Child a Wanted Child

MARGARET SANGER

THE killing of an obscure Archduke fired the World War; the killing of an obscure woman by the laws preventing knowledge of birth control fired the accumulating pain and revolt in the heart of a simple, unassuming trained nurse named Margaret Sanger to a battle the echoes of which have reverberated in every civilized country in the world.

Those were the days of home nursing; poor people didn't go to the hospitals readily. She was called one violently hot July to the tiny flat of a couple desperately trying to rear three children. Another young mother—she had seen so many —lay apparently dying of septicemia caused by a self-induced abortion with a knitting needle. The children were terrified, the boy father distracted. How could they ever get along without this mother? To Margaret Sanger difficulties were like hurdles to a thoroughbred; work was exaltation; failure something never thought of as a possibility. But this case taxed every resource of knowledge and skill and a delicate physique. She had left her own husband, her own children to undertake it; the only help she had was from kindly neighbor women. Everything had to be carried down three flights for disposal, and ice, milk, and food brought pantingly three flights up.

At the end of several weeks the patient was out of danger and Mrs. Sanger, almost ill herself with exhaustion, was about to leave. The doctor came in and dismissed his patient with the warning that another such escapade and she would be finished.

"But Doctor," in a frightened voice, "what can I do? How can I help it?"

"Well, I'll tell you the only sure thing," laughed the doctor good-naturedly, "tell Jake to sleep on the roof!"

He left and the young woman turned a despairing face to Margaret Sanger. How many poor mothers had looked at her like that! But the only information she could give her were methods depending entirely on the husband—and the girl burst into tears. Deeply troubled Mrs. Sanger promised to try to find something better for her. But she could not; so she kept away, constantly haunted by that pleading face. And then three months later—only three months—the same call came again from the same woman. In an agony of shame and a fury of rebellion at the utter futile waste, the hoplessness of palliative measures, she went once more to make that hard fight and—if the mother could be saved—to make it again and again. But she was too late.

She went home and took off her uniform for the last time. She would never nurse again.

Margaret Higgins Sanger was the sixth of the eleven Higgins children. She knew the meaning of large families from intimate experience. She tells how impossible it was to study at home because there were always babies to be put to bed, knees to be washed, food to be prepared, clothes to be mended and remodeled for the smaller ones. She was very young when she commenced making decisions for herself. Her mother had been born a Roman Catholic and Margaret started out in the parochial school. But after one week she decided walking six miles a day to the public school and back would be preferable, and as she was a born leader even then, the other children soon followed her example. It was Mr. Higgins who had the voice of authority in that household, and he always encouraged independent thinking in his children. He had an impressive personality and his wife adored him; he was a Free Thinker himself—a member of the Knights of Labor—and he made his living by carving gravestones for Catholic cemeteries! He rejoiced in the most stimulating friendships; such radicals came to visit him in Corning, New York, as Henry George, the agnostic Robert Ingersoll, and the astonishing Father Mc-Glynn. Often they would make the small house ring and keep the children tossing until dawn with "the feast of reason and the flow of soul." Their neighbors thought they were heathen.

Thus plain living and high thinking nurtured this twentieth century Joan of Arc, who was born with a touch of the leprechaun, of mystic Irish superstition which was to make symbols of dreams to her through all the teeming years. Naturally tender and warm-hearted, she has never lost a certain child-like charm and naïveté in spite of an invincible determination too often unjustly called by her enemies, stubbornness, waywardness or even bullheadedness! Yet she was up against the most bitter realities from her earliest years; and nursing was no new job when she undertook her training. Her father had been practically the only doctor the family ever had. He brought the babies himself, and he treated every ailment from an abscess caused by mumps to pneumonia itself with his favorite infallible remedy—"good whiskey."

But Margaret's childhood was too full of responsibility, and she was too sensitive to have been happy in Corning. Finally, one day when a stupid teacher made fun of her, she gathered up her books and came home declaring she would never return. Nothing, not even her father, could make her. No one could ever make her change her mind, once it was made up, not even judges, lawyers, or jails. So she was sent to the Methodist Col-

MARGARET SANGER

lege, Claverack, at Hudson, New York, which has another famous graduate—Stephen Crane. Here she was really happy in an atmosphere that favored the expression of opinion. It supported William Jennings Bryan and Free Silver—and even Woman Suffrage, that still more radical cause whose sponsors were considered "masculine" by the other girls.

She finished at sixteen. It seemed too soon to go to college and, besides, she was needed at home for Mrs. Higgins was ill. During that year at her mother's bedside Margaret became deeply interested in medicine; and after her mother died, there being no more money for college, she entered a hospital in Westchester County and graduated after three years of grinding, gruelling study and work.

It is probably this training that has made Margaret Sanger's attitude toward birth control professional. A trained nurse is taught first and last to believe in the physician; where others adopting the cause have favored free knowledge for all from any source, she, since her first visits to the Holland clinics, has been convinced that contraception is an individual medical matter and that individual clinical diagnosis and technique are essential. Her first clinic was served by nurses only because she could get no doctor to officiate. For years the doctors would not listen; it is a great triumph that at last, in the winter of 1931, the American Academy of Medicine has endorsed birth control, recommending that contraceptive methods be taught in the medical schools throughout the country.

Romance came riding by one day in the person of William Sanger, a well-established young architect who was by temperament and would have been, by preference, an artist. There were times when he could afford the hyacinths he brought home instead of bread and times when he couldn't; but it was always the hyacinths he brought. Life was tempestuous and idealistic. His wife wanted to help him and also she wanted to be independent; so they both worked six months of the year and played the other six. She wanted to keep her maiden name although she had never heard of the Lucy Stone Leaguers; but her father, not her husband, couldn't bear the idea and she gave it up. For all his broadmindedness, Mr. Higgins was entirely conventional on the subjects of marriage and motherhood. He could not endure the mention of sex. When he heard of his daughter's first magazine *The Woman Rebel,* he thought she had gone insane. He called it a "nervous breakdown" and urged her to go to a sanitarium! But when, even as he was talking to her, officers arrived at the house to arrest her, he instantly championed her regardless of his own private feelings.

Three children were born of this marriage, three carefully planned and deeply wanted children. Stuart is now a graduate of Yale, and Grant is about to graduate from Princeton. Peggy, the longed-for little girl, died when she was six years old at a time when her mother was hardest pressed on all sides. This loss was the deepest sorrow of Margaret Sanger's life.

On the morning Mrs. Sanger put away her uniform forever, she threw away all personal life for herself. Of course she was freely criticized: "How can she leave her children? They'll turn out badly, you'll see; she's neglecting her husband"—and more of that sort of thing. People seem to think that genius, the single-track mind, does not have the common human emotions. Nothing could be more mistaken. Mrs. Sanger was tortured constantly by the thought of her children, even though she always had her sisters or mother-in-law looking after them. To leave her little girl was a special daily heartache—"Mother, you don't have to go to the printers *this* morning, do you?"

But Margaret Sanger is that rare being, a really self-less person. She was even more tortured by the thought of other children—that vast army of the unwanted, the inadequately fed, the scantily clothed who were kicked early into the streets to beg or into the mills to work. "Oh God, that bread should be so dear and flesh and blood so cheap."

She was driven by that vision as only genius or insanity is driven. That necessity took her—she did not deliberately take it. She had to obey as she had to eat or sleep, no matter what her naturally strong maternal instincts dictated in her personal life.

First she talked to the doctors: how could they forbid babies on pain of death and yet offer no aid in preventing them? Some were sympathetic, others were hard, all were afraid. It was against the law; it was a dangerous business; they did not know what to tell them; there was nothing one hundred per cent safe.

Then she went to the medical libraries, even to the Congressional library, but she found hardly a reference to methods of contraception. She turned to the various so-called radical, liberty-seeking groups. Surely here there would be understanding and response. But there was none. Always she received the same answer, "Wait." "Wait until we get the vote," said the Feminists. "Wait until we get a Socialistic government," said the Socialists. Only the I. W. W. listened at all and helped with names of labor leaders and in other small ways.

She turned away from her own free country and looked toward Europe. She knew that in France family limitation had been practiced for generations, regardless of the law, regardless of all governmental prizes for large families, regardless even of the Pope himself. She decided she would go there and also to England. Her artist husband was instantly filled with enthusiasm; what artist would not be at the thought of Paris! To be sure there were the three children and where would the money come from? They blithely sold their house, and took the children, all under ten, along. What was a house compared to the fulfilling of a destiny!

France was a gold-mine of information. With the aid of interested English friends, Mrs. Sanger went everywhere, meeting many influential people but talking to women particularly —women from all walks of life from the most sophisticated *grande dame* to the humblest peasant. From them all she got their precious secrets, their methods tested for generations.

Then she wrote—this was about 1914—the first of a long line of works on her subject, a small pamphlet entitled *Family Limitation* which was published in England along with three others also by Mrs. Sanger. But this one, the most important since it was addressed to the working women who needed it so badly, has been translated into several languages. In America she tried twenty printers before one brave man would touch it, and he did the job secretly after hours. By that time the young author had come within the arm of the law, and the hundred thousand copies were bootleg material. Nevertheless—or for that reason—they penetrated everywhere, and women in the highest social circles schemed to get one of those prized pamphlets as eagerly as the poorest women; those lucky enough to secure one, copied it over and over for their friends. The practical and propaganda value of that tiny booklet cannot be overestimated.

She returned from Europe with her children, but without Mr. Sanger. Their interests had become too widely different; the perfume of hyacinths and the cabbagy odor of tenements could not mix. They separated in a friendly manner and were divorced somewhat later.

Mrs. Sanger now decided to start a magazine calling attention to the need of contraception, or "birth control," as she termed it. Those words were not accidental; they were the result of much thought and were chosen because they could be easily understood by the most simple or ignorant people. She was obliged to manage every department of the *Woman Rebel*, as her new venture was called, including the financing, even though it meant that many times she had to draw on her balance at the bank down to the last eight or ten dollars, and the rent went temporarily unpaid. Remember what she was: an unknown woman without any financial or civic or social backing; so modest and unassuming in demeanor that even today when her name rings with meaning in every country, she is never recognized in restaurants or on the street. When she is in a group or being introduced with other women, invariably and inevitably a hand is extended to the largest and most impressive woman in the crowd with a "So happy to meet you, Mrs. Sanger." She is inconspicuous; her manner is never militant, and she is intrinsically gentle, although her gentleness is sometimes deceiving because it covers a purpose of steel.

In addition to her other handicaps, she had the most precarious health. It is not generally known that from 1900 to 1921 Mrs. Sanger waged a constant war against tuberculosis—during the very years when public opinion was most against her, when she was being knocked about by policemen, and when she was working eighteen hours a day on her magazine, besides lecturing whenever she could be heard. Five different times she had to stop long enough for operations; once she was sentenced definitely to the Saranac Sanatorium, only to rise up in the night and run away to New York, determined to die on her feet, if she had to, rather than in an atmosphere of eggs and milk.

The Woman Rebel with its proud slogan "No Gods, No Masters" went to England where it received a wide circulation among the Feminists. In America, two issues of the magazine reached three thousand subscribers, who were obtained, except for a sprinkling of writers and poets, as a result of publicity and advertising in the labor journals. This list, secured after Mrs.

Sanger's flight abroad and without her knowledge, formed the nucleus of the first National Birth Control League.

The other seven issues were suppressed by the Post Office authorities under Section 211 of the Postal laws which makes the whole question of contraception not a medical one, not one of health, but one of obscenity. Following the ninth magazine, in September 1914, came her arrest. There were nine indictments—one for each issue—and sentence would mean forty-five years in jail. Yet there was not one scrap of actual information in the journal. There really never was a legal case against its editor. *The Woman Rebel* was simply like the child rebel who "mocked 'em and she shocked 'em and she said she didn't care." Mrs. Sanger was saying to the rich people, to the educated people, to the ministers and the politicians: "You are all so smug—you have this information and you won't give it to the poor people who need it most—I'll show you!" That was all.

She would like to have said it in court, but there was no one there to listen or to care. War news had crowded out any publicity the case might otherwise have attained, and there was no one to champion or protect her. She did not even have a lawyer, insisting characteristically that she would be her own lawyer. Who else knew so well the justice of her cause—unless it be the host of grateful and therefore damaging witnesses she could already have brought into court? But she wanted time so that she could present her case more effectively. Harold Content, the prosecuting attorney, was against anyone with radical ideas; he conferred with the Judge, and they gave her just one day. One day! It was unfair and Mrs. Sanger said so the next morning. She tried to make them understand that she was not a criminal sneaking under cover, but a soldier fighting to emancipate women from the most ancient form of slavery in the world. She asked for a month in which to prepare her case. Mr. Content objected in alarm. The idea—that woman to be free and at large for a month, spreading obscenity! Birth control information was obscenity—what better authority than the law itself to prove that? The judge looked puzzled and embarrassed. He gazed sternly into the quiet, honest eyes of the prisoner. There was nothing about her to suggest the fighter unless it was her auburn hair, and even that was red in a soft, not flaming way. She had not wept, she had not ranted, she had not even lost her temper. She treated her opponent not as if she hated him but as if she pitied him. Yet he said she was dangerous. He ought to know; he had made it his business to know about such people. Very well, she must stand trial the next morning; he would hear nothing further.

Margaret Sanger had come to another cross-roads in her life. There were many of them and never enough time to speculate as to which road to take. The habit of individual, unadvised, quick decisions had long been forced upon her; sometimes it led her into difficulties, but more often this habit plus her almost mystical Irish intuition saved her as it did now.

She went from the court house straight to a hotel where she engaged a room so that she could be alone to think it out. The responsibility was solely hers; she wanted no one to share in her tremendous decision. For hours she walked the floor. She knew she would be convicted if she stood trial; public opinion was against her; the judge was against her; the prosecuting attorney saw another notch in his gun. She was unable to fight financially—there was simply no chance for her. Suppose she went to jail? There would be nothing to gain because she was not well enough known. And what of her children? Was it to be jeered at them, "Your mother went to jail?" Even worse, was it to be leered at them, "and for obscenity?" That she could not bear. They had already been sacrificed enough in various ways.

She must leave. Those who did not understand would call it running away; in her own soul she knew it was not that. Loving her own integrity, it was the hardest course to choose. But once decided, she acted promptly. Putting the children in her sister's sympathetic care, she packed just one suitcase and took a train for Montreal. The next day, under an assumed name, she was on a steamer bound for the British Isles. There was to be some trouble over passports at the other end, but finally she succeeded in entering England.

England was always kind to Margaret Sanger. Such men as H. G. Wells, Havelock Ellis, and Arnold Bennett listened to her and were not ashamed to stand publicly for her cause. Feeling was aroused in the United States; after two years she returned to this country uncertain as to whether or not she would have to stand trial.

At first, the National Birth Control League would have nothing to do with the source of their movement. But when they heard of the prestige she had won abroad, they, with other timid intellectuals, came out for her. Thousands of letters went to the district attorney and the judge from people all over the country. Editorials and articles were published in her defense, and suddenly all nine indictments were quashed.

Following this publicity came opportunities to lecture in many cities as well as opportunities to get into print (carefully censored) in several well-established magazines. But Margaret Sanger was not to be spoiled by publicity. She says there are three tests of character: sudden wealth, sudden power, and sudden publicity. Few people can stand the last, and she made it a point not to read what was said about her; she was not to be influenced by praise nor discouraged by criticism.

Mrs. Sanger now found herself at the head of the Birth Control Movement. But there is no use talking—she is not fitted to work in organizations. She has a terror of them, too.

"They cut your wings," she says; "you cannot soar in an organization." Hers is not the filing-cabinet type of mind. She has no knowledge of or interest in red tape; she will not consult, she will not postpone. Not that her mind is closed to suggestions—there is no one more easily reached or more tolerant of other peoples' ideas providing they also countenance immediate action—but usually they want to wait. Mrs. Sanger does not wait. How could she wait to ask anyone what she should do? It would be like asking your cook whether you should use oleomargarine or butter. If she saw something to do, she did it regardless of the means. Over and over she would throw her board of directors into a frenzy by her unbusinesslike methods. She would go out and hire a hall, engage speakers, invite crowds without the least idea where the money was coming from to pay for it all. "Why do you worry?" she would protest in genuine amazement. "The money will come. It always has come." But sometimes it had to come from the directors' own pockets. She made enemies, of course, but she herself has never been vindictive. She is as impersonal in her relationships as a man—a rare quality in a woman. To her the principle is everything. "Personalities come and go, but the principle must never be deviated from."

In her lecture tours she had been advocating the opening of birth control clinics wherever possible. State laws were so different that in many places clinics were illegal so long as the Federal injunction against the use of the mails was observed. In New York, however, a clinic seemed clearly forbidden. That law needed testing.

Her sister, Mrs. Byrne, also a trained nurse, was another brave spirit who had succeeded to the Higgins heritage. Mr. Higgins had said, "I can't leave you riches, my children, but I leave you unchained from dogmas." So these two, after many rejections from faint-hearted landlords finally were able to rent

a store in Brownsville, Brooklyn, for their attack on Section
1142. Here in a district where most of the workers were making barely a living wage, swarmed the largest families, in spite
of the appalling number of abortions.

In ten days, four hundred and eighty-eight women had
stormed the clinic; ten crowded days of incredulous, exulting
women marvelling at these two courageous nurses who were
ready to do for them what no one else would. Then came the
police; only this time there were plenty of reporters and photog-
raphers, as well. There was no dearth of publicity now. Mrs.
Byrne was sentenced to the workhouse for thirty days. For
eleven days she went on a hunger strike and a thirst strike as
well, and after very nearly dying, she was pardoned by Governor Whitman. A month later Mrs. Sanger went to the Queens
County Penitentiary with prostitutes and procuresses for thirty
days. As a result, the dormant tuberculosis became active again.

The worst two hours were the last, when they tried by force
to effect the finger-printing she had so far successfully resisted.
Incredible as it sounds, even two burly keepers could not succeed in getting her fingers onto the pad. Political prisoners,
she felt, ought not to be subjected to such a humiliating indig-
nity.

During this time the case was before the Court of Appeals.
In 1918, Judge Crain sustained the conviction under Section
1142, but he also startled the public with the announcement
that under Section 1145 of the New York State laws, it was
permissible for licensed physicians to disseminate contraceptive
information among those suffering from disease. This was
hailed with joy as a real triumph; it meant the legal establishment of a clinic which, if it could not benefit all, could serve a
great number of the most needy.

Hitherto Mrs. Sanger's thought and effort had been directed
largely to the laboring classes, to the poor who were daily using

the only sure preventives they knew—abortion and occasionally infanticide. Now she saw that it was to the women of leisure she must turn, to women of wealth and influence if the birth control movement was to be put on a sound, practical basis. She gives much of the credit for her success in this to Juliet Barrett Rublee. Mrs. Rublee would be entertaining prominent professional or literary or social leaders when the subject of Birth Control would come up. "Isn't it disgusting," someone would murmur, "the space the papers are giving to birth control and that awful creature, Margaret Sanger?"

Mrs. Sanger's telephone would ring. "Darling," it was Mrs. Rublee's voice, "come right down here as fast as you can. Never mind what you are doing—Dr. X and Professor Y and Mrs. Z are here—hurry." And Mrs. Sanger would drop everything and rush for a taxi. Mrs. Rublee would pull off her hat "so they can see what a fine head you have" and, taking her hand, lead her in. "Here is that awful creature Margaret Sanger! Now tell me—do you really think she is so awful?"

Thus the snowball grew. In 1920 Mrs. Sanger was asked by the Kaizo group of liberals publishing Kaizo Magazine to go to Japan as one of four speakers, the others to be Bertrand Russell, H. G. Wells, and Albert Einstein. This trip was finally made in 1922, a few months after the first American Birth Control Conference at which a mass meeting in the Town Hall of New York City was prevented by the Catholic Archbishop Patrick Hayes, using the police power entirely without authority—a splendid bit of publicity for the cause.

The Japanese trip demonstrated again Mrs. Sanger's "calm force for difficulty" and also her Irish luck! For at the last moment the Japanese government refused to visé her passport. Mrs. Sanger quietly got one for China and sailed on the same steamer she had planned. On board were the Japanese delegates returning from the Peace Conference! How was it possible that this little mouse could be such a firebrand? Of course she landed! Among other apologies came one from the Rickshaw Men's Union, haltingly delivered: "You do not mind," begged the coolie humbly, "sometime Japanese Government, he little autocratic." She did not mind. Sometime American Government, he little autocratic, too.

For the past six years in the well-equipped New York City clinic, women who for health reasons should bear no more children have been receiving medical advice from trained physicians acquainted with the best that science can offer so far. It is not the best that can be hoped for—Margaret Sanger is sure of that. Much of her effort in recent years has been expended in stimulating research in all parts of the world to find what an English enthusiast has styled "the perfect pill"—a simple, fool-proof method which will protect careless or feeble-minded women in spite of themselves. So far the propaganda side has been developed far more than the scientific side. Propaganda had to come first; women had to be aroused to demand knowledge from the doctors. But now it was time to put the question back into the medical hands that had so long rejected it. She arranged the first International Population Conference at Geneva in 1927 from which sprang the Population Union composed of distinguished scientists from all over the world. And in September, 1930, a real triumph—the first International Birth Control Conference on Contraceptives—was held in Zurich, attended by a brilliant roster of physicians, chemists, and bio-chemists from all the leading countries including Japan. Surely better methods and improved technique are now only a matter of time.

Meanwhile the New York clinic was exceedingly busy, and according to the carefully kept records, extremely successful. Then in the spring of 1929, after no interference from the authorities for six years, there was a sudden raid by the police, private records were seized and the two physicians in charge were arrested. A woman with a most pathetic story had come to the clinic; her husband was a confirmed drunkard, she had three children already, ages five, three, and one. After being given sympathetic attention, she turned out to be a police-woman with a taste for notoriety! She probably expected promotion for her bravery and daring, but instead she was promptly demoted. The case was dismissed after a righteous furor of public indignation such as has never been equalled in previous birth control history.

The winter of 1931 brought two spectacular capitulations: that already mentioned of the American Academy of Medicine with the recommendation that contraception be taught in the medical schools of the country, and that of the Federal Council of the Churches of Christ in America which publicly approved contraception on the grounds of morality, health, and family happiness. A short time thereafter, one minister, John Haynes Holmes, listed Mrs. Sanger as one of the ten greatest women in the world. Even the Pope could not maintain his previous strict silence; he mentioned contraception in his Encyclical this same winter of 1931 with emphatic disapproval, although he was deeply grieved for those families which "thought" they had more children than they could support! Any number of Catholic patients clipped this out and brought it to Mrs. Sanger at the clinic, saying firmly, "I don't believe a word of it."

A few years ago Mrs. Sanger was married to Mr. J. Noah H. Slee, president of the Three-in-One Oil Company. He has helped her in every way to realize her dream and best of all for her thousands of grateful admirers, he has made her take a little care of herself.

How old is she? Well, if you really want to know, you must look in *Who's Who*. But you will have to look quickly. She says she is the only woman in it who has given her birth date, and now she's left orders to have it omitted from the next edition. But perhaps she ought to be dated, like other battles!

Mrs. Sanger has withdrawn, except for her clinics, from state work and is now working on the Federal statute. Her so-called "doctor's bill" aiming to place the whole matter of contraceptive education in the hands of competent physicians and clinics died in committee March 4, 1931. But that, too, is only a matter of time to this intrepid, tireless, indomitable and yet always gentle woman.

If I Were a Politician

NORMAN THOMAS

IT IS late afternoon of a sweltering June Sunday when the
New York City Socialist convention turns from formu-
lating a municipal platform to the nomination of a mayoralty
candidate. There is no debate now as there was over the
wording of platform planks on taxation, transport, and public
health. In perfect unison 300 delegates enthusiastically acclaim
Norman Thomas as their candidate. He strides to the front
of the crimson-bedecked hall to acknowledge a nomination he
dare not refuse. Suddenly the persistent hand-clapping swells
to a roar of wild applause; his very appearance has galvanized
a tired convention into a demonstration that lasts twenty
minutes.

Norman Thomas may have been a hero to that convention,
but the New York papers characteristically greeted the nomination of a Socialist with a few casual sticks on an inside page.
Yet three months later those papers were hailing his candidacy
as the feature of the campaign. The Scripps-Howard *Tele-
gram* found in him an ideal leader of a new labor party it
hoped would soon emerge: "He is striking the public fancy
by the mere power of his voice, his fine intelligence, and his
wide and intimate knowledge of the problems of the people
and of city government." Regretting that he called himself a
Socialist, the Democratic *World* nevertheless declared: "In
quality of mind, in integrity of character, in the uprightness
and dignity of his bearing, in the shrewdness and fairness of

69

his argument, in the magnanimity which he has displayed, he has fully justified the judgment of the Citizens Union." The latter had said, "If personal merit alone were to decide the contest Mr. Thomas would win easily."

No one prophesied the election of this tall, genially dignified and magnetic candidate of a hitherto dwindling party; yet in a dull campaign he injected a new spirit into the politics of a blasé city and, with a high-water vote of 175,000, reestablished the Socialist Party as a serious contender for municipal office.

The Norman Thomas that New York City discovered in the autumn of 1929 is the man who has become the idol and inspiration of hundreds of young collegians, and who for a decade has been a tireless champion of causes dear only to a small circle of liberals and radicals. His courage, scholarship, humor, catholicity, and perhaps above all his practical-mindedness mark him, even in the estimation of many who disagree with his Socialism, the leader of a new day in Amercian politics. Indeed, there are political "experts" who predict his election to the mayoralty of New York within a decade. An anomaly in American life, a spokesman who has never held public office nor manipulated the machinery that put other men in office, his pronouncements as the head of a weak and little-respected party have a wide, if not at times an almost magical, influence. Except for his efforts it is unlikely that there would have been forced the several investigations in New York which have revealed corruption and racketeering in the municipal government more scandalous than at any time since the plundering of Tweed and Croker.

Until his campaign in 1929, Thomas considered himself primarily an educator. He had previously run for Governor, Mayor, Alderman, and President, simply because of the dearth of available candidates in his party; even now his public-affairs

NORMAN THOMAS

activities are conducted in addition to his full-time office of executive director of the League for Industrial Democracy. The innocence with which he has regarded his political aspirations was once revealed in a chance remark. A group of editors, professors, and peace advocates had been called together at Manhattan's Town Hall for practical planning in support of the Kellogg Pact. The discussion turned toward the pending Presidential campaign, and suggestions were sought toward securing a warm endorsement of the Pact in the Democratic and Republican party platforms. The most practical suggestions came from the none-the-less perfectly sincere Socialist Presidential candidate, who stirred not a little amusement with the preface, "Now if I were a politician. . . . "

Marion, Ohio, in 1884, the year of Norman Thomas's birth, had passed through its pioneer days and was already developing the complacent normalcy that in later years was to flower into Warren Gamaliel Harding. Even the earnest and eloquent preaching of the scholarly Welling Evan Thomas failed to arouse the social consciences of the store-keepers and doctors and lawyers who filled the pews of the Presbyterian church. Indeed, Welsh crusader though he was, it is to be doubted if the Reverend Doctor Thomas realized the full implications of the faith to which he was so devoted. Religion at that time concerned itself with personal virtues and an oppressive formalism. The forces of a rising and ruthless industrialism that unleashed the furies of a World War, which in its backwash sent Marion's editor to the White House and the Reverend Dr. Thomas's son, Norman, almost to jail, had not yet made their impact on the church.

Norman's boyhood was lively and fully occupied. He delivered Mr. Harding's *Marion Star,* acquired a proficiency at boxing, and read avidly in his father's library. As the eldest he was expected to carry on in the profession that his father and both grandfathers had honored, and this tacit understanding the boy unquestionably accepted. After a brilliant high school record, he enrolled in Bucknell University, but with little zest. Princeton, glorified by the short stories of Jesse Lynch Williams, was his heart's desire.

A relative's assistance helped him reach Princeton in his sophomore year. There he partially supported himself and plunged into his studies with an enthusiasm that carried him to the top of his class. He displayed a flair for debating, and in the classes of Professor Woodrow Wilson developed a keen interest in politics, government, and economics. Perhaps it was from Wilson that he acquired his eloquent, balanced-sentence style of writing and speaking.

In 1905 young graduates out to remake the world might go into the foreign missionary field, or if less pious, into a community settlement house whose magic touch would soon banish poverty, drunkenness, uncleanliness, and ignorance. Two years young Thomas spent in a settlement in the midst of the congested Spring Street slums of New York, and then made a trip around the world in which was laid the foundation for his solid knowledge of world affairs today. Returning, he went to the Christ Church Settlement as an assistant pastor. There he met Frances Violet Stewart, who had come to organize one of the first clinics for the treatment of tuberculosis in New York, and in 1910 the two were married.

Soon he had become assistant to Dr. Henry Van Dyke at the Brick Church on Fifth Avenue, meanwhile studying at Union Theological Seminary and growing more rebellious at the restrictive orthodoxy of his denomination. The New York Presbytery was greatly distressed that so brilliant a young man should hold such frankly heretical beliefs, and questioned him all afternoon before ordaining him.

Following his graduation from the Seminary he withdrew

from the quiet decorum of the fashionable Brick Church to the storm and stress of the American Parish in one of the most run-down sections of East Harlem. There for six years he and Mrs. Thomas labored among immigrants of all races whose contacts could not but mold an international mind. During the mild depression of 1913-14 scores of unemployed would flock to the parish house for doles of fifty cents a day. In other settlements the relief seekers were directed to roll bandages for use in the European war that had rudely broken into the orderly development of society. But because of the shortage in material the bandages were unrolled at night to be rolled again on the following day. This, to the Thomases, was absurd. They organized centers in connection with Union Settlement at which the unemployed were put to work making basketry and moulding pottery.

In this East Side parish, Norman Thomas learned the tragedies of unemployment, of old age and sickness, and saw the corruption of a city government that existed for patronage and favors in taxation. He began to doubt the capacity of settlement work to touch the roots of these human tragedies.

Then came America's entry into the War. Thomas had made his own resolve. He would not fight. Nor could he with any vestige of conscience see the church proclaim the gory massacre as God's war. The spectacle of ministers quoting the Gospels in their cries for blood—even the blood of those who refused to murder their brothers—tortured him; and the crusade for democracy led by the foes of democracy was too palpably a sham for him to remain quiet.

Morris Hillquit was then running for mayor of New York on the Socialist ticket, and Thomas wrote him a brief note offering support. A few conservative parishioners had muttered unseemly remarks about the young minister's pacifism, and this espousal of Socialism was the last straw. Thomas gracefully stepped down from the pulpit.

With a few friends he established *The New World* (renamed *The World Tomorrow* a few months later) and became its first editor. He served for four years. Looking back over his editorials in that period of hysteria and fear, one is thrilled by their forthrightness, their eloquent incisiveness, and their shrewd forecast of events that history has since revealed in their stark shame. Department of Justice agents trailed him, tapped his wires, and dozed outside his house at night. Sometimes they came to his office to question him, only to leave flabbergasted by this jovially earnest, persuasive, and seemingly reasonable man. A few years later he had occasion to chuckle with several United States Senators who told him of a mass, almost six inches high, of illiterate reports on his "seditious" activities. Postmaster Burleson, high priest of red-baiting, sought on several occasions to suppress *The World Tomorrow*. "Thomas is more insidious than Debs," he growled.

Reports, too, that leaked out of the military and Federal prisons about the brutal treatment of conscientious objectors, again nearly brought him into conflict with the Government. Himself just beyond the first draft age, and in an exempt class in the second draft due to the number of his children, he had no occasion to refuse arms. But he was often in Washington to argue for humane treatment for political prisoners.

Together with Roger N. Baldwin, he helped found the National Civil Liberties Bureau (now the American Civil Liberties Union). On Armistice Day he saw Baldwin whisked away for a year in jail because of his refusal to register for the draft. Evan Thomas, a younger brother, was likewise imprisoned. The Fellowship of Reconcilation, of which Norman was secretary, was the prey of official and unofficial snoopers. If these events were not enough prematurely to grey his hair, they were abetted by the death of the eldest of his six children and a serious illness of Mrs. Thomas from which she has never completely recovered.

"What I like about Norman," said that doughty warrior of the labor movement, Jim Maurer, for sixteen years president of the Pennsylvania Federation of Labor and later Socialist Commissioner in Reading, "is that he came to us when everybody else was running away."

Among some of the old comrades, that act during those dismal days accounts for his tremendous popularity almost as much as does his winning personality. One after another the Socialist intellectuals were fleeing from the movement either at the beckoning of Wilson's eloquence or under the hammer blows of the four-minute men. John Spargo, safely past the draft age, heaped scorn upon those young Socialists whose consciences sent them to jail; William English Walling who a few months before had been calling "comrades to arms" now assailed them as traitors; J. G. Phelps Stokes bristled about in an officer's uniform; even Upton Sinclair almost in tears relinquished his red card. And then out of his pulpit came this tall, earnest minister, to hearten them at their disconsolate meetings —to win even the bitter anti-religionists by his patient humor and his sincerity, to give expression to dissenting views in his new-founded magazine, and to help to organize a civil liberties bureau for those who were persecuted.

On the other hand there was the defection of the rigid Marxists and the romanticists to the left. But Thomas's deep sympathy for the Russian revolution did not degenerate into a sentimental endorsement of the Soviet dictatorship. He said so plainly in his speeches and in *The World Tomorrow*. The American Communists have never forgiven him. Scarcely a week passes without the Communist *Daily Worker* denouncing him as a "sniveling, yellow Socialist faker" or a "socialist-fascist sky pilot."

For a year, following his resignation as editor of *The World Tomorrow* in 1921, Thomas was associate editor of *The Nation*. Then came an opportunity to join with Harry W. Laidler in building the League for Industrial Democracy out of the old Intercollegiate Socialist Society. Dr. Laidler, foremost Socialist scholar whose *History of Socialist Thought* has been translated into Japanese and Chinese as well as into the languages of continental Europe, has often been called the Sidney Webb of America. To say that the team of Laidler and Thomas relighted the flame of young America's idealism would, of course, be an exaggeration, but none can gainsay they have tinted it red. In recent years Thomas has grown immensely popular even in the more conservative colleges; probably no convocation speaker in America is so greatly in demand or receives such attentive audiences.

Save for a few weeks when he was editor of a short-lived labor daily and for the brief time he spends almost every year in political campaigns, Thomas has devoted most of his time to the L. I. D., through which he has had entrée not only to colleges and civic forums but also to the more progressive labor unions. The Emergency Committee for Strikers' Relief, organized by the L. I. D. and directed by him, has raised and distributed more than $100,000 in relief for various strikes. In the bitter textile strikes in Tennessee and the Carolinas in 1929 Thomas's committee was for some months practically the one source of support.

The strike of the wool workers in Passaic in 1926 and 1927 was one of the toughest struggles in American labor history. The local police promulgated the familiar doctrine that strikers have no rights. Throughout a long winter the strikers hungered, were beaten and ridden down by mounted police and bowled over by icy streams from fire hose. Thomas was in Passaic frequently addressing the solid ranks of mill hands. When the sheriff of Bergen County announced that no more public meetings could be held in the adjoining town of Garfield, Thomas determined to make a test case. The American Civil Liberties Union rented a vacant lot, and word was sent out among the strikers that he would address them. Lacking a platform he mounted the stump of an old apple tree and began:

"This is the first stump speech I've ever made from a stump. We have come here to test our rights as American citizens to hold a peaceful meeting for a legal and legitimate purpose. Yesterday was the birthday of Thomas Jefferson. You may have heard of him. His name is being celebrated in Passaic by a shameful desecration of the cause of liberty for which he strove so valiantly."

A police whistle shrilled. "Lock that bird up," bawled the sheriff. Through the crowd, swinging rifle butts and clubs, went his deputies to the none too ample platform. Thomas was yanked from it and hustled away in a waiting police car. Hours later his friends located him in a remote jail where he had spent the night in the absence of $10,000 ready bail. The story of the arrest appeared on the front pages of nearly every newspaper in America; affidavits proving the illegality of the arrest and the prohibition of the meeting brought an order from the judge lifting the sheriff's ban on all gatherings. There were no more interferences.

In the meantime the 1928 Presidential campaign was looming as the most disheartening for the Socialists in a quarter-century. Where the party organization had survived the onslaughts of the Communist defection, it had generally decayed after the Progressive débâcle. The national party secretary did not even have a complete list of the few Socialists in political office. Contact had ceased with many locals; in most states the party no longer enjoyed an official place on the ballot. Thousands of one-time active members had lost interest following the death of Eugene Debs. Here was the standard-bearer's rôle of a once threatening minority party actually going begging! Thomas did not want the nomination. He had had a strenuous year speaking for the L. I. D.; his desk was piled high with matters that demanded his attention. He needed a vacation. And he wanted to write a book setting forth a socialist theory suited to conditions of American life. His own choice for Presidential nominee was Jim Maurer, a forceful and shrewd campaigner, popular in labor ranks. But Maurer was learning the ropes of city government as the new Commissioner of Finance in Reading.

Maurer, however, consented to be Thomas's running-mate, and against tremendously discouraging odds they set out to win on a sober discussion of economic and social issues an electorate vigorously debating religion, rum, and the pronunciation of r-a-d-i-o.

Candidates Hoover and Smith, when they traveled, rode in private trains, with entourages of a hundred or more publicity agents, reporters, and glad-handers. Candidate Thomas traveled sometimes in an airplane, but most of the hot summer nights were spent in a Pullman berth three inches too short. His entourage consisted of August Claessens who helped local comrades arrange meetings and who took the collection, and alternately McAlister Coleman or Edward Levinson who explained to cub reporters that Mr. Thomas really was a candidate for President, and that he did not believe in anarchy or vegetarianism, and that he seldom wore red ties.

His electoral reward was little more than a quarter-million, the lowest Socialist vote since 1900! He was, of course, complimented, even by the papers that had ignored his speeches, on the high level of his campaign. "I appreciate the flowers," he laughed to some friends, "only I wish the funeral hadn't been so complete." His later campaigns, for Mayor and for Congress, have been less funereal.

Remarkable vitality that he has, Thomas sweeps through life too fast. A quarter century of living in Manhattan has subtly instilled in his veins the virus of the hectic urban swirl of today's times. Like Napoleon he has the facility of doing several things at once; it is no uncommon occurrence to find him dictating to a stenographer, conversing with a caller, and signing letters at the same time. His weekly editorial column in *The New Leader,* his books, and his frequent magazine articles, are nearly always dictated in a rapid, vibrant lecture-platform voice as he strides about the room. The manuscripts are seldom revised, save for stenographic corrections. He accepts too many lecture engagements to speak always at his best; visiting some college for one day only he may consent to make as many as six addresses, while those intervals that most men would reserve for rest are consumed by genial banter or delphic counsel with the flock of students who tag after him. That night he will be sleeping over clicking wheels to repeat on the next day in some city four or five hundred miles distant the same arduous schedule. Tired, he sometimes lacks cohesiveness in his speeches and occasionally the winsome qualities that appeal to those who may not at once be ready to follow his leading.

Yet, this is not to say that he is ever ineffective on the platform. Even when he is jaded he wins hearty applause through his dramatic power, his well-turned phrases, and his unfailing humor. Nor does the rapidity of his dictation seriously impair his literary style which has in it many of the qualities to be found in modern skyscraper architecture: an inspired conception, a richness of materials, and a simplicity of structure that avoids ornament for ornament's sake, yet that is not without a stark beauty suggesting power, precision, a magnificent sweep toward unity, and a noble reaching out toward higher realms.

The Socialism of Our Times, which he edited, reveals much of his philosophy:

"Pure pragmatism has never been a philosophy of power to guide men's acts. Opportunism or the doctrine of doing the next thing may at times be politically expedient but it is never an organized creed for the multitudes. . . . The American Revolution was won less on the detailed grievances set forth in the Declaration of Independence than on the daring generalizations with which it begins. It was the supreme service of Karl Marx that he gave to the vague grievances and aspirations of the oppressed workers a philosophy, a religion, a relationship with cosmic forces. . . . [Yet] modern Socialism is not co-extensive with Marxism or what was popularly regarded as Marxism fifteen or twenty years ago. . . . The great task for us is to continue that intensive study of the cruelties and wastes and wars of capitalism which Marx was the first to analyze after painstakingly amassing the evidence. And the great question is whether and how men can learn to manage the land, natural resources, great aggregations of machinery and public services, which by all their logic should be collective property, for the use of society rather than for the profit of a few private owners.

"The materialist conception of history is inadequate metaphysics in an age when matter itself is being interpreted in terms of energy. It may be bad psychology as well as bad philosophy if it implies an inexorable fatalism in the movement of human society. . . . There is a place in the practical development of human institutions for creative energy of the revolutionary will to which Socialists have always in fact appealed. Yet how much hypocrisy can be avoided if we will recognize plainly the easy way in which men or dominant groups among them have always rationalized their group interests, fundamentally dependent on the way they make their living, into notions of eternal right and wrong! And how many Utopian mirages we may escape by the simple process of remembering that we cannot mold a civilization based on machinery and composed of living men trained in the specialization and interdependence which machinery necessitates as if we were gods beginning life on a new-made world. Whether you like to speak of a society determined or conditioned economically, whether or not you hope under a juster order to diminish the power of economic factors in human life to recognize now the power of these factors is essential to understanding or seeking to shape the evolution of society."

Those passages bespeak solemnity; yet Thomas is solemn only when tinkering with the Universe. He does not play enough, it is true; his few sports are sailing in a small boat with his children in a Long Island bay near the Thomas summer home, puttering in the garden, or milking the cow that is kept during the summer months (which is not, he insists, a play for the farmer vote). But in his social relations there springs up often an enlivening wit that at times becomes a humor of gusto. Indeed, many of his friends think he often deals too lightly with weighty matters, particularly when in a mood for satiric thrusts. Perhaps he must perforce. His vocation as an unsuccessful (to date) political Galahad imposes upon him the requirement of indulgently chuckling at himself and the times. In the closing days of his most recent campaign (for Congress from a Brooklyn district) heartless circumstances rolled over his hopes like waters from a broken dam. The Tammany machine, genuinely frightened, spread excited rumors that he was a Communist, that he was a millionaire in disguise, that he was an advocate of "free love," that he was a Ku-Kluxer, that he was an atheist. An official in the British Labor Government had just promulgated the famous White Paper that stirred Zionism throughout the world, and Thomas's foes were quick to point out to a predominantly Jewish constituency that the Laborites, like Thomas, were Socialists. Indeed, whispered one, Thomas had been closeted with Ramsay MacDonald throughout one morning when the British Prime Minister had visited America the preceding year; Thomas himself was responsible for the White Paper! Some of his associates fumed. The candidate slapped his thighs and roared with hearty laughter at the absurdity of the rumors.

Neither he nor the late Theodore Roosevelt would relish the comparison, yet in at least one fundamental respect he resembles that crusader for Armageddon who in the preceding generation personalized the robust restlessness of emerging America. There is no creed that could hold the social views of both; the belligerent patriot and the pacific internationalist would clash sharply and often if the former were alive today. There is no melodramatic pose about Thomas, no mood for vindictiveness or personal abuse. But a stronger characteristic holds them in the same picture—or better, in the same reel—for many of their dissimilarities derive from different times and the changing social forces with which they engaged. Their appeal has alike been to the masses in a manner that wins the devotion of many of the intelligentsia; alike each has given expression to a current deep in American life—a spirited surging against old bonds, stemming from pioneer days and quickened to the tempo of a mechanical age.

The Thomas energy produced, recently, his provocative book, *America's Way Out,* which won him a better understanding on the part of many who had hitherto considered him only a critical leader of a critical party. And if America will not now try his way to planned well-being, at least it cannot ignore the existence of a program.

Yet except in his adopted city and among student groups Thomas has not yet struck deep in the public fancy. The decade in which he has emerged as a public figure has been one of backwash from the step-by-step, better-and-better democracy of pre-war years, a decade of cynical opulence and bewildering change in the ways of living, a decade in which people have learned to call a limb a leg but have come to blush with Victorian reticence at the mention of ideals and the highest social loyalties. Still, underneath this fluxing foam there stirs today as always the impelling quest for self and social fulfillment which a minister become politician has sought to direct. Stranger things have happened than that within the next two decades Norman Thomas might be caught up in that happy coincidence of a man and the hour that history sometimes calls greatness.

Preacher Without Authority

JOHN HAYNES HOLMES

VIGOROUS and distinguished people who make their lives felt in wide circles of society inevitably gather legends about themselves. These legends spring not so much from fact as from poetry and symbolism, and are sometimes surer than fact in revealing underlying truths.

John Haynes Holmes has not escaped this fate even in these days of literary realism and biographical disillusionment. The particular legend to which we refer relates to a supposed visit of Holmes to a spiritualist who held a seance for his benefit. After the proper solemnities had been observed, the medium announced: "I see Theodore Parker standing behind you, and he is the guiding spirit of your life." Without raising the issue of the merits or demerits of spiritualism, and without either affirming or denying the authenticity of the incident, we say without hesitation that poetically and symbolically it is true.

Behind John Haynes Holmes, as the actual record of family history tells us, we find typical New England radicals with unyielding consciences, taking their stand on the great public questions of their day. The family on both sides were reformers upholding such causes as anti-slavery, prohibition, and women's rights when those movements were not easy to espouse. His maternal grandfather was a friend and supporter of Theodore Parker, one of those who helped to secure a Boston hearing for the great preacher. And to make the family heresy complete, they were Unitarians! So the boy John came honestly by his radicalism, inheriting a social attitude of dissent.

If we were to search for other "spirits" guiding this young man's life we should find not only Theodore Parker, the New England reformer-preacher, but Garrison whose impatient soul could brook no easy escape from decision by the path of temporizing and compromise; and back of him, Channing with his belief in human nature, and his pioneering mark for peace; and back of the New England tradition, all the brave and heroic souls who in the period of the Reformation were *protestants* against an old and decaying order, as well as witnesses for a new day; and back of them the early Christians who were struggling with martyr zeal for the founding of the commonwealth of man—the Kingdom of God on earth; and back of them, perhaps the supreme influence of all, the noble company of Jewish prophets—an Amos thundering against the injustices and iniquities of his people, an Isaiah whose feet are "beautiful upon the mountains," proclaiming peace and good will among men.

But inherited radicalism is not radicalism; it is conventionality. And so after four years at Harvard topped by Phi Beta Kappa, and later an S. T. B. degree from Harvard Divinity School, young Holmes entered the Unitarian ministry not as an act of daring—for New England Unitarianism of that day had become well established as a proper tradition—but rather as the conventional selection of a career of respectability among the intellectually and socially élite. He ascended his pulpit with the gods smiling upon him and the authorities prophesying a brilliant future. He was well grounded in the essentials of a classical education, an eager student who read omnivorously, an orator of unusual force and vigor, and above all, a conscientious workman.

The content of his preaching during those early days at Dorchester, Massachusetts, though progressive, was along conventional lines. If Theodore Parker was his guiding spirit, Holmes was saying what Parker had said during his life-time, rather than going on to proclaim the truths Parker would be preaching had he been alive at the beginning of the twentieth century. Nevertheless, the spark of revolt was smouldering, ready to leap into fire when the proper moment came. The two writers who influenced him most were Henry George and Walter Rauschenbusch, and so stirred did Holmes become by their yeasty ideas that in 1907 the last year of his Dorchester parish, he founded the Unitarian Fellowship for Social Justice. This act not only reflected capacity for leadership on the part of so young a man, but it also indicated the direction which his thought was taking.

The turning point in Holmes's career, however, came with the invitation to become minister of the Church of the Messiah in New York, a pulpit made famous by a long line of eminent preachers who had stood high as theologians in the Unitarian fellowship and as men of force and character in the community. We do not insist upon an "environmentalist" theory of history and biography. Perhaps if Holmes had remained in Boston the inner urge would in time have driven him to his present position of leadership. But we do affirm that his adventure into the new world of New York added the impetus and provided the conditions which made him what he has become.

New York offered a striking contrast to New England. Here was a vast and seething mass of all sorts and conditions of people—rich and poor, foreign and native, Catholic, Jew, and Protestant. Here were extremes of wealth beside extremes of poverty; here social problems cried aloud for solution, and titanic forces were straining to be born. The transplanted

JOHN HAYNES HOLMES

Puritan had his vision enlarged, and he began to realize that there were other functions for the church and minister besides preaching a progressive theology and helping individuals by inspiring sermons. There was the age-old dream of the Kingdom of God to be realized, there were mighty ends of justice to be served. There was a hard and bitter fight to be waged against the forces of entrenched reaction and privilege.

The new preacher proved that he was worthy the succession to which he had fallen heir, and his fame quickly spread. This fact alone was ample proof of his ability, for New York is the grave of mediocre ministers, and a stranger must rise to great proportions to be seen above the multitude or heard above the noise of its teeming life.

Young Holmes soon found himself deeply involved in the struggle for the emancipation of the poor. Steadily his philosophy swung from individualism to racialism, and his emphasis changed from that of the ministry in the conventional sense to that of the ministry as Theodore Parker had made it in his greatest days in Boston. He became a public defender—a champion of unpopular causes, a prophet of the "Revolutionary Function of the Modern Church." He began to see that if the individual is to be "saved," then society must be saved. It is not enough to convert individuals as such; preaching must transform the individual into a social creator who goes forth to battle for the larger good.

Such a conception of the function of the minister and the church brought the young man into conflict with two major forces. In the first place, he began to fight the somewhat easy-going, traditional-minded authorities who controlled the destinies of the Unitarian Church. Holmes believed with all his soul that the Unitarians were especially equipped to perform the work of the new movement. He pointed to their great men as prophets and pioneers, and he challenged those of his day to "go thou and do likewise." In his attempt to bring new life and vigor into the denomination, he was eagerly followed by many of the younger men, but he never succeeded in capturing the denomination's real machinery. Consequently, as long as he was a part of it, he found himself engaged in continual warfare, a fight which cost him many friends, which antagonized officials, and which at times waxed bitter.

The other major struggle of his early pastorate was with those of his own local parish who did not share his new social vision and whose sympathies were not with the revolutionary movement either in church, or in politics and economics. There were many people of wealth in the congregation, and more whose inclinations were in the direction of *status quo*. It was inevitable that Holmes should offend both these groups when, with vigor and energy, he preached against special privilege. As a result, he found himself engaged in a long struggle for the control of his local church, which he wanted to make over into an instrument for social righteousness. But fighting did not weaken or discourage him. Rather, it became the food and drink that nourished his soul. His reputation grew, and in place of the conservatives of the old church of the Messiah, who beat a retreat before the rising tide of radicalism, his pews began to be filled with progressives who came to hear his message. The downtrodden and sufferers of every race and creed found a new voice to make their cry articulate. Jews, Negroes, Socialists, pacifists, dreamers of dreams, and seers of visions—all began to find in John Haynes Holmes a champion. To him they brought their causes, and none were too desperate or unpopular for his sympathetic ear.

His conservative friends became solicitous for his reputation. They did not like the company he kept. They did not like the fierce attacks he delivered against all reactionary forces. They believed that he was being used by people who would do him no good and who would not stand by the church in its hour of need. They urged him to "go slow." Those who regarded the pulpit as the place for pleasant essays couched in balanced and polished phrase were shocked by the growing vehemence of his sermons.

But Holmes believed that the pulpit was the place for strength. He despised all weak dilettantism. He read the lives and works of the abolitionists and thrilled at their heroic courage. He read the words of Jesus who called hypocrites "whited sepulchers filled with dead men's bones," and his soul was stirred with admiration for the straightforwardness of the Nazarene. He pondered the life of Amos, how the son of a shepherd descended from the hills and shook his fist in the face of priests and kings, denouncing them for their meticulous performance of ecclesiastical rites while neglecting the weightier matters of justice and righteousness. These men did not mince matters. Far from it! They did not choose words daintily as if entertaining at a pink tea. Rather they smote with mailed fists and roared with might. There was no indecision in their conduct. They did not palsy their action by trying to keep a perfect balance of judgment. When they had once made up their minds to hew to the line they hewed, and nothing could stop them. We call them great for they are dead and dead radicals are more comfortable to live with than live ones! But they were the guiding spirits of Holmes' life and he could not but be true to them. The calm temper, the judicious mind were not to be his outstanding characteristics. A fighter, even though a pacifist, must throw the whole energy and devotion of a lifetime into his fight.

There is no doubt that when Holmes lets loose against his favorite sins—militarism, capitalism, imperialism, the evils of drink, he becomes extreme in statement and manners. He becomes intemperate and exaggerates to such a degree that he often drives people out of the church, especially those who do not know and understand him, and who are hearing him for the first time. So completely does he let himself go that some critics think he becomes intoxicated with his own oratory and with the radicalism of the crowd. There may be some justification in this view, but it is true to only a slight degree. His passionate outbursts are usually carefully prepared in his study where he writes every word of his sermons in advance. His method of preaching is a matter of deliberate choice. He believes in telling the truth as he sees it with all the energy he can summon. He enjoys seeing people fling themselves out of his church in dudgeon, for is not that the best proof that the shaft has struck home? And what is preaching for if not to strike home?

Critics will retort that the business of the preacher is to convert the unbeliever, and that therefore he should lead his people gently. There is certainly a need for such men and manners. But Holmes does not fill it. He is more apt to drive away and antagonize men and women who do not believe as he does. But for those who see with him, and for those who can exercise their own judgment, accepting and rejecting where they see fit, there is no preacher in America who is more stimulating than John Haynes Holmes. He rouses his audience, body, mind and soul. Listening to him is like taking hold of an electric battery. His sermons shock, and his hearers tingle. It would be hard to imagine anything finer from Channing, Theodore Parker, or any other liberal leader of the past than the best sermons which Holmes preaches when he is deeply stirred over some great public wrong. One of the finest pieces of pulpit oratory ever delivered was his sermon on "The Greatest Man in the World," in which he introduced Gandhi to an America which had hardly heard of the Mahatma. It should remain for all time a classic.

Holmes should be thought of as a chivalrous knight who has chosen the pen and the pulpit as his weapons rather than the sword. To judge him by the conventional standards of a conventional ministry or an institutionalized church would be to do him wrong, to force him into a Procrustean bed. He is to be measured not by a professional measuring rod, but as a man who escapes categories and creates fields and spheres of his own.

This does not mean that he is not a faithful steward to the trust imposed upon him as a minister of a church. Not even his sharpest critic can charge him with lack of attention to his professional duties. He is faithfulness incarnate when it comes to administrative details; he labors in season and out, and no business is so minute as to escape his attention. He has his hand upon all the controls, and he knows exactly what is going on every moment of the day or night at the church. In fact, he almost lives there, attending meetings of committees, boards, socials, clubs, and classes, granting endless interviews and innumerable consultations. His schedule is so full that Mrs. Holmes has been heard to remark laughingly that it is almost necessary for his family to make an appointment to see him.

Another form of labor which absorbs an appalling amount of time and energy is the correspondence he carries on with an astonishing number of people. He has friends in every part of the globe and through them keeps in touch with world affairs; he is besieged by countless zealots, some of them cranks who want him to write reams of advice on every conceivable theme or read poems, tracts, and books which they have written. And he does it! No matter how apparently absurd the subject or how unimportant the writer, he pours himself out in letters which are hardly ever brief or perfunctory, but which reveal careful attention and sincere solicitude.

Big business lost an ardent disciple of the strenuous life when Holmes went into the ministry, for he has no mercy on himself and spares neither his strength nor energy. He lays the lash upon his own shoulders and goads himself as with an all-consuming passion. Many a time when he is exhausted with speaking or writing, he will drag himself by sheer force of will to the office and spend a long hard day when he ought to be at home in bed, or escaping the confusion and pressure of work by a few days in the country. But he despises all forms of shirking and he cannot brook inattention to work either in himself or in others. For this reason he is high-strung and nervous, giving the effect of a human dynamo, restless, eager, impatient, exacting, and not always easy to work with, even though generous beyond measure.

Nor is Dr. Holmes negligent as a pastor. He has always declared that anyone can see him for any purpose whatsoever, and he lives up to that promise. All sorts and conditions of people want to consult him about every theme under heaven, for he is the kind of man who invites confidence. He deals with the personal tragedies of the most intimate sort which are known to all ministers—unhappy marriages, abnormal fears, sex problems, heartache, poverty and unemployment—as well as with people who have chimerical schemes of the most extravagant sort for saving society and reorganizing the world. To all such—poor or rich, wise or foolish—he lends a sympathetic ear, and few go away from the interview without renewed courage.

There are those who feel that Holmes lacks "spirituality," especially in the conduct of his church services. They feel after hearing him that they have been attending a public meeting rather than religious service. They miss the sense of reverence, the quiet communion with the Eternal, and the atmosphere of devotion which they habitually associate with a church. Worship requires a relaxation, a let-down from absorption in worldly things, and Holmes is by nature so tense, so eager, and he speaks with such rapidity and energy that one is not conscious of restfulness in his presence. But this again is largely a matter of deliberate choice on his part. He believes in worship, and hidden in the recesses of his soul is a poet-priest which few people perceive. Nevertheless, he consciously rejects the so-called spiritual aspect, for he believes that it is a conventionality which, as usually practiced, lacks vitality and reality. The rationalist and reformer in him have left little room for the priest.

On the other hand, he is not unmindful of his function as a leader of worship, for he has put much time into the problem and has always been eager to create an effective "order of service." Witness *Great Readings from Authors* which were designed by him and his colleagues as responsive selections to replace the use of the older psalms. Also witness his hymns which he has written as lyric aspirations toward his ideal of worship. His Scripture lessons, drawn from the whole world's literature, are chosen with great care after wide study. His prayers—aspirations, voicing the hopes of the human heart—are in the modern manner rather than repetitions of the old, stereotyped praise and petition. Those who come to his church anticipating an experience of "spirituality" in the conventional sense do not get it, partly because it is not in Holmes to give, but even more because it is not a part of his philosophy of worship. But for those whose needs are distinctly rationalistic and modern, there is a refreshment of spirit and lift of mind which the older churches cannot provide.

All this leads to one inevitable conclusion: namely, that

John Haynes Holmes is such a unique and powerful preacher, such a creative force, that sooner or later he would have to break with the eccesiastical order which had been his background. Like a Luther, he would have to revolt and build an ampler church to house his expanding spirit. Two events, occurring about the same time, conspired to hasten his decision to take this step.

First, the World War shook him to the very roots of his being and disillusioned him as to the place and function of modern Protestantism in the social order. The church and its ministry with few exceptions went over bag and baggage to the frightful business of carnage, and the disciples of the Nazarene became converted to the worship of Mars. This was a terrific shock for Holmes, as it was for all conscientious objectors on religious grounds, and he began to question whether the church of today could possibly serve as the instrument of the building of the Kingdom of God on earth. Had it not become so inextricably related to the machinery of governments and so entangled with the meshes of capitalism that it was impossible to use the old order in building the new? Probably the greatest moment in John Haynes Holmes' life was when he preached his sermon on the entrance of the United States into the war. He publicly declared that he could not support the war and would have nothing to do with its prosecution. He asserted that he would under no condition surrender to the mob spirit, but would keep both his own soul and that of his church free from hatred. He promised a ministry of love and good-will to friend and foe alike. And all during the war he kept that promise inviolate, even though he was followed by Government agents, and hounded by 110-per-cent patriots. But the experience of those years burned itself into his mind and made him question the very foundations of the ecclesiastical order. Gradually plans and aspirations toward "new churches for old" began to grow in his mind.

The second event was the publication in *The New Republic* of a series of articles on "Religion and Democracy" by Joseph Ernest McAfee, who is now an associate of Mr. Holmes. These articles made articulate the more or less vague yearnings on the part of a certain group for a new type of church. They pointed to the fact that if religion is to function democratically it must break loose from ecclesiasticism and become a part of community life. Holmes seized upon the idea and began to put it into practice in terms of his own church.

The moment had come for him to dramatize the new Reformation. He preached his theses and declared that there must be a break with Unitarianism and the past, and that a new church "of the people, for the people, by the people," must be built. It was to be a free fellowship uniting men and women in bonds of love, beyond theological creed and class distinction. The new institution was to be founded not on speculative philosophy but on man's passion for truth, justice and mercy, untrammeled by the prison-house of systems which have their day and cease to be.

Again Holmes found himself with a fight on his hands, for there were many sincere men and women in the church and in the denomination who opposed a break with the Unitarian fellowship. They believed strongly in remaining loyal to the tradition which had built the old Church of the Messiah, and to the pioneers who had provided the funds which made it possible. It was the timeless struggle between loyalty to the past and confidence in the future, and Holmes is always to be found on the side of the future.

He took hold of the new idea of a community church with his usual unbounded energy, preaching it with all his heart and soul, writing it in books and magazines, and laboring for it among friends and foes. The result was that in 1919 the Church of the Messiah passed out of existence and in its stead was established the present Community Church.

Few socially-minded travellers to New York fail to visit Dr. Holmes' church, for in many ways it has become a demonstration center of a new type of religious institution for a new day. A community service department, a good-will court, a community forum, a medical dispensary, a mental hygiene clinic, a bureau of adult education, a school of religion for children—these are but a few of the ways in which Holmes and his able staff of trained assistants essay to carry out the Scriptural admonition, "By their fruits ye shall know them." An association of men and women, unhampered by theological or ecclesiastical control, the Community Church is pledged to "freedom of thought and speech; to hospitality to all citizens of the country, without regard to sect, class, nation, or race; and to the usage, without fear or favor, of that spirit of universal love which shall some day bring in upon the earth the ideal society of men." It is "an institution of religion dedicated to the service of humanity. Seeking truth in freedom, it strives to apply it in love for the cultivation of character, the fostering of fellowship in work and worship, and the establishment of a righteous social order which shall bring abundant life to men."

In view of these ideals it is not surprising that the Community Church is cosmopolitan in membership, comprising as it does men and women of 34 different nationalities, including "Protestants, Catholics, Gentiles and Jews, theists, atheists, and humanists, and a few Buddhists, Mohammedans, Hindus, Bahaists and Zoroastrians. The visitor to his Sunday services will find Chinese, Mexicans and Indians in the pews, men and women of the proletariat as well as the white-collar class, professors from Columbia sitting side by side with East Side laborers, while among the ushers are Negroes and Jews as well as Anglo-Saxon Nordics."

Inspired by the success of the New York project, Boston has established a Community Church of her own, and in addition to his other labors, Holmes preaches there once a month, besides giving generously of his counsel.

Of Holmes, as of nearly all men who achieve greatness, it must be said that the man is bigger than any of his formal accomplishments. The latter in his case are legion. His editorship of *Unity*, which he carries on with the same boundless energy that he gives to every task, would entitle him to rank as a competent journalist, were he in position to devote himself solely to that field. As it is, the readers of the magazine recognize in his virile pen a tremendous force for every movement toward peace, justice, and social righteousness. His paragraphs have a pungency, a zest, a verve which would make him a noted "columnist" is he chose to become such.

As a writer of a long list of books, he has proved himself a capable biographer, and an anthologist of vast reading; while in the field of social religion he has attained wide influence by means of his pen, and his *Palestine Today and Tomorrow*, one of his more recent books, shows keen observation and understanding of foreign affairs.

Civic affairs and race relations occupy important places in his life. His interest in the former was clearly attested by his chairmanship of the City Affairs Committee of New York, a group of public-spirited citizens who have battled in season and out for decent municipal government and civic progress. His concern for racial good-will and brotherhood has led him to render determined service to the Negro, on whose behalf he was in 1909 one of the founders of the National Association for the Advancement of Colored People, and to labor tirelessly in the field of better Jewish-Christian relations. He frequently exchanges pulpits with his friend, Rabbi Stephen S. Wise, and New York church- and synagogue-goers are frequently treated to provocative sermons on "If I were a Christian" and "If I Were a Jew," delivered respectively by the rabbi and the minister. The first honorary degree of Doctor of Divinity was conferred upon Holmes in 1930 by the Jewish Institute of Religion. And when the Community Church, having outgrown its historic building, was obliged to erect a new structure, the congregation upon invitation from their Jewish friends, held their services in Temple Beth-el, during the period of construction.

Holmes' efforts in behalf of civil liberties would alone distinguish him, for he was one of the founders of the American Civil Liberties Union, and stoutly withstood the post-war hysteria by braving the lions in their dens and more than once offering himself as a test case to be arrested in defense of the right of free speech for pacifists, laborers, and radicals. Needless to say, such activities have placed his name on every blacklist issued by patrioteers.

Beyond these many accomplishments, beyond all this whirl of dynamic action, the man himself stands out—universal in sympathy, bigger than class or creed, a hard fighter, a loyal and generous friend, inspirer, stimulator and energizer to all who come into contact with him. Through him indeed

"The voice of God is calling
Its summons unto men."

Labor Must Learn

A. J. MUSTE

BROOKWOOD LABOR COLLEGE stands up on a high hill, four-square to all the winds which blow across a rolling country-side.

A. J. Muste, the head of this colorful college whose undergraduates are coal-diggers, railroad men, textile workers, mechanics, tailors, stands up six lean feet in his socks.

And around him there are blowing fierce winds of controversy these days. For some, he represents a baneful influence over youthful workers. For others, he is a shining figure against a drab background of smugness, defeatism and surrender which tired radicals, retired liberals and place-holding labor officials have joined hands in painting. For some of the Socialists, with whom he will not join because he deems them insufficiently class-conscious, he represents the sniping of impatient, even jealous, left-wing-labor discontent. To others, regarding his latter-day rebellions with philosophic tolerance, he personifies that valuable insistence on radicalism which is a needed check against the all-too-easy drift of any movement aiming at votes. Whatever your opinion of "A. J." may be, you do not come away from him without feeling that you have been in touch with something tremendously alive and challenging.

"A. J.," said an Illinois coal-miner who had been listening to a talk by the Chairman of the Faculty of Brookwood, "loads his turn every trip."

Praise from the laconic, crotchety men of the pit, is praise indeed. And not only miners still in Brookwood and those out in the fields again after graduation, but graduates of the college who have led picket lines in Kenosha and Elizabethton, taught labor classes of their own up in New England and down in Pennsylvania, edited labor papers and generally given momentum to a decidedly sluggish movement—these are agreed that "A. J. is a square shooter."

It means something to be a square shooter in the labor movement today. It means, for one thing, being shot at from both sides. From the hierarchy of the American Federation of Labor. From the Hell-for-leather Communists. And just when the air is thick with critical bullets, you will find A. J. grinning a most winning grin and shooting right back, straight and hard.

It's not new for A. J. to be in a fight. He is only forty-six years old but he has battled his way to victories of which the oldest labor leader might be proud. Those early fights were for the right of the workers to organize. There were the surging strikes of the textile workers in Lawrence, Paterson, Utica, and more lately, Passaic—all of which he saw and a large part of which he was. Anyone who figures Muste as "one of those pink intellectools," anyone who gathers from his easy-going, peace-time manner that he is a bit soft, is sorely mistaken, as many an old-time labor official and many a hard-boiled employer have discovered.

Today he fights for the right of the workers to learn. The grounds of the battle may have shifted, but A. J.'s spirit burns as fiercely as when he led his "damned Hunks" through the Lawrence streets back in 1919.

How came this scholarly-appearing ex-minister, keen student of history and economics, to the vanguard of those who are fighting for a different sort of labor movement from what

there is in America today? How does it happen that the call
to Progressives, inside and outside the movement, to marshal
their forces for a labor revival is sounded by Muste and those
who have stood by him in the building of Brookwood? "How
come" A. J. Muste?

The story begins back in the home of a coachman for a
family of Dutch landed nobility, the home of A. J.'s father,
Martin Muste, in the little Netherlands town of Zieriksee.
There Abraham John Muste, the oldest of four children, was
born in 1885. The town lay on an island in the midst of
dykes and canals. For six years Abraham John sprouted in
the placid, sturdy life of the rather straight-laced Dutch Reform community, sailing paper boats on the canals at his door,
helping with household chores and carrying cooked cereals
from the baker's to the homes of the few wealthy people in
town. Then came word from his mother's brother in the
States that in a place called Michigan and an oncoming city
called Grand Rapids there was plenty of work and some money
to be had. Also Grand Rapids was a good Dutch Reform
settlement. The Mustes sailed for America.

A. J.'s mother was taken sick on the voyage and the child's
first impressions of America were gained in a long month in
a government hospital under the shadow of the Statue of
Liberty in New York harbor. It was there that he heard an
official talking about Abraham Lincoln. And as he had a
natural interest in anyone with that first name, he started right
in to find out about this Lincoln. From then on for many
years, Lincoln was his beloved hero and he collected everything he could lay hands on that told about the life of the
Rail-splitter.

The family from the Netherlands had chosen a bad year
for their migration. Times in 1891 were hard in Grand Rapids
and the country over. The father finally got a job in a saw-

mill on the log-choked Grand River (and incidentally at the age of 73 A. J.'s father still works with his hands). He was paid $6.25 a week. A. J. soon went to work in summer time packing tie-plugs in a furniture factory. In the winter he attended a Dutch Reform parochial school. There was high thinking and plain living, those years, for all the workers and their children in Grand Rapids. Much of the man's simplicity of manner and taste dates from the days when a family of seven (for by now another child had been born) must needs scrape along on the most meagre of wages.

By the time A. J. had reached the eighth grade, his future had been settled for him. The eldest in a family whose head was intensely religious, he was being zealously groomed for the ministry. It was accepted that he was to be a preacher and ways and means were devised to send him on a scholarship to the preparatory school for Hope College at Holland, Michigan, twenty-five miles from Grand Rapids. He gathered up his books on Lincoln and went, according to the best Dutch Reform tradition. Seventy per cent of his classmates were headed for the ministry. They were fed the Bible and the classics in copious quantities. Young Muste whizzed through the prep school in three years and entered Hope College at the age of sixteen.

For all his studying, which must have been prodigious, he found time to captain the basketball team of the college which won the championship of Michigan for two seasons (A. J. would want to be sure that any biographer of him puts this down), he played baseball and football, he was the first man from Hope to win the State oratorical contest, and was Valedictorian of his class at Commencement when he was twenty.

He was paying $1.25 a week for his room and his food to a boarding-house keeper who miraculously was making a profit

A. J. MUSTE

out of this and he was supplementing the income from his scholarship by acting as assistant in the college library.

And it was then and there that A. J. first began looking a bit quizzically at the orthodoxy which was all around him. He had access to books that were not in general circulation and there was Darwin and his "Origin" to begin with and other writings which seemed to Muste to ruffle the placid mental waters of Hope. He was graduated with the makings of a theological rebel, at any rate, already in him.

There was an opening for a Greek teacher in the floridly named Northwestern Classical Academy at Orange City, Iowa. There A. J. went, drawn not so much by the lure of the $700 a year salary, as by the fact that some twenty-five miles away lived Anna Huizenza who had graduated from Hope Prep at the time that A. J. was leaving the college and who within a short time was to be Mrs. Muste.

A year at the Academy and then to the New Brunswick Theological Seminary and further contacts with dogma, with the result that in 1909, in his Commencement speech, young Muste was thundering against "obscurantism," announcing that the seminaries were turning out "mediocre preachers" and for the first time in the history of such exercises at the old church in New Brunswick arousing a sedate audience to applause.

While on a scholarship at the seminary, he preached in the summers at the Middle Collegiate Church at Second Avenue and Seventh Street in the heart of New York's East Side and although his concern was still mainly with theological doubts, he was beginnning to rub shoulders with the city workers and their problems.

For a while after his graduation in 1909, he was head of the little chapel of the Old Collegiate Church at Fort Washington Avenue and 181st Street. Whenever there was an opportunity he went down to Union Theological Seminary whose liberal atmosphere he found particularly congenial. There were a keen lot of questioning youngsters in and about Union at that time. In the seminaries they were talking about the duty of Christian ministers to align themselves with the labor movement, then militant and almost spectacularly emergent. Muste read *The New York Call,* followed the crusading progress of 'Gene Debs, and although he had been hot for Woodrow Wilson at the beginning of the campaign of 1912, was among the million who voted for 'Gene on election day.

Two years later he went into his pulpit and told his somewhat bewildered congregation of young white-collar folks that he could no longer subscribe to many of the creeds of the church and that as a consequence he was resigning.

He accepted a call from the Congregational Church in Newtonville, a pretty Boston suburb, and in 1915, A. J. and his wife (he was married in 1909), looking forward to a scholar's paradise with much reading and comfortable liberal conversation, set out for Massachusetts. It was permitted to be liberal, even radical, within polite bounds of course, in those years from 1912 to 1916. Was not the President himself talking about "The New Freedom" and hinting at the need for industrial democracy? Labor was becoming more and more insistent and finding sympathetic audiences in all walks of life. *The New Republic* was making a bright beginning. The younger men in the churches were reading Walter Rauschenbusch and the other Christian radicals, the Socialist Party seemed on its way to becoming a real labor party, the War was still overseas.

Nevertheless the rumblings of that conflict had a way of breaking into the Newtonville study, and by 1916 its tall young occupant was moving rapidly towards a more dangerous position than any theological heterodoxy might land him in. From the first, he was definitely anti-war. He was one of the Boston founders of the hopeful Fellowship of Reconciliation. He was attending meetings of the Socialists with a membership card of the Party in his pocket. He was hobnobbing with Scott Nearing and James Oneal who was then Secretary of the Massachusetts Socialists, and some of his wealthy parishioners were cocking worried eyes at him. To be sure, the majority of his congregation, because of a personal affection for their young minister, were inclined to accept without much protest his outspoken denunciation of the war. But when we went in, and the casualty lists began coming back and the young men of Newtonville went off to the training camps, then it was different.

The situation soon became intolerable for a man with as high-powered a conscience as A. J.'s. Opposed with all his heart and brain to the bloody business, he could hardly offer the fathers and mothers of the boys overseas the kind of religious consolation which they craved.

In the Fall of 1917 Muste again resigned from a church which he could not conscientiously serve.

This break was far more serious, from almost any angle, than the first. It meant the loss of friends who could not understand A. J.'s refusal to conform, a certain amount of social ostracism and of course, most serious of all, facing the slim chances for a minister, a Socialist and a pacifist to make a living in a world at war.

The Quakers came to the rescue. In a meeting-house in Providence, A. J. found an audience for his pacifist views and in the basement of a book-shop run by an old Quaker, the only place in town where dissident literature could be had, he found new friends. There the handful who had the courage to oppose the war would meet on Saturday nights with spies from John Rathom's jingo *Providence Journal* among them taking notes. The Mustes (there were three of them now for Ann Dorothy had been born in Newtonville the year before) lived in a house with a big garden which the Quakers had given them. Those were dark days, lightened only now and then by the discovery that you were not alone in a mad world but that here and there were others who thought as you did. Among them was Harold Rotzel, a minister who had left his church in a rich Worcester suburb much as Muste had done and was now Secretary of the League for Democratic Control, a pacifist organization which had peace without indemnities for its immediate demand.

Mrs. Anna N. Davis, Mrs. Glendower Evans and a few other courageous women whose names some day will be written large in the history of the struggle for peace, freedom and plenty in this country, arranged for the Mustes and the Rotzels to share a home in Boston. The two rebel families occupied the top floors and the first and second floors were given over to meeting places. This house soon became the headquarters for all the radicals in the regions round about. How many were the committees formed there, how many programs for a better world drawn up on those first two floors!

Long into the night Muste and Harold Rotzel, a courageous minister, and the late Cedric Long, a graduate of Union Theological Seminary, soon to become a splendid leader in the cooperative movement, and other dissenters would discuss ways and means of returning an entire nation to sanity. There seemed to be so little they could do. Muste was rallying members of the Fellowship who were economic radicals as well as pacifists and the three outcast ministers were discussing plans for becoming lay preachers, going about presenting the cause of the workers. It was all very gallant and very vague.

Then of a sudden something blew up in their own backyard. This was the strike of 30,000 textile workers in Lawrence, Massachusetts. Lawrence had the strike tradition from 1912 when the bayonets of the militia glinted down the slushy streets. In 1912, Giovannitti and Carlo Tresca and Gurley Flynn had flamed through the city and, while the workers were beaten then, the "agitators" had left behind a militant nucleus among the hard-driven, underpaid men and women in all the Lawrence factories. In January, 1919, a wage cut had been announced.

The workers came out on a bitter cold day in February, singing strike songs and determined not to take a cut in wages though they starved. At first the fight was led by a conservative member of the conservative United Textile Workers' Union. He was all for having the workers, the vast majority of them foreigners, go back at the low wage scale offered by the bosses, but with reduced working hours. The piece-workers could see nothing gained by this. A provisional strike committee with foreign-born workers at its head was formed to carry on the strike and the United Textile Workers' organizers left the field.

Such was the situation when the three inexperienced, innocent-appearing, high-hearted Muste, Rotzell and Long, young ministers, arrived in Lawrence to try out their plans of doing something tangible about the things they stood for.

They went to strike headquarters and found a depressed and bewildered group of labor leaders there, out of touch with the main currents of the American labor movement, inarticulate when it came to English at any rate, without funds, without much hope, without much of anything except the determination not to go back to work on the bosses' terms.

They went to the office of William Wood of the American Woolen Company and to their surprise were received with open arms by Wood and the other employers. Word had reached the bosses of the coming of these pacifists. It was

taken for granted that Muste and Rotzell and Long would urge
the workers to return peacefully to the looms. There was a
great deal of tall cussing when it developed that on the contrary the invading trio intended to support the strike.

The town was on its collective toe tips. "The menace of
Bolshevism" was not then an economic cliché. There had been
nationally advertised strikes in Seattle and Winnipeg, and 1912
was not forgotten. The little shop-keepers were scared. The
larger merchants were on the verge of panic. Special police
were being sworn in with instructions to "get the Hunks before they get you." At the Lawrence railroad station, machine
guns were being unloaded.

The three parsons took off their coats and went to work on
behalf of the strikers, addressing envelopes, translating appeals
for relief, distributing circulars about hours and wages, talking
to reporters who had got nothing from the strike committee
except black looks. Ten days of this with the strike leaders at
first a bit uncomfortable in the presence of these white-collared
outsiders and then when it was evident that here were friends
indeed, friendly in their turn.

On the tenth day, the heads of the provisional committee,
with some feet-shuffling and embarrassed circumlocution asked
A. J. to become Chairman of the Strike Executive Committee.

So there was A. J. with the fate of 30,000 workers and their
families on his hands, in a strange town, packed with spies and
police and the paraphernalia of industrial warfare. And all he
knew about strikes and their conduct was what he had read in
papers and books or had picked up at Socialist meetings.

What does one do in a strike? How do you organize relief?
What about pickets? How do you start negotiations? How
do you get national publicity? Where do you get milk for the
hungry kids? How do you spot a labor spy? How do you
start a union?

From the moment that he said "yes" to the strike committee's request that he lead them, he had to answer these and a hundred and one other questions. He needed all he knew of pragmatic philosophy.

He and his two friends went about town setting up soup and coffee kitchens, rushing relief to the neediest cases, starting off the pickets in the cold dawn, listening to reports from the organizers, sending strikers out of town to take up collections at mill-gates, appealing to liberals the country over to come to the help of the embattled 30,000.

Then the police helped. They turned ugly and day after day pickets would come back to strike headquarters with their heads bloody, their bodies bruised from the riot clubs. The strike got on the front pages from Coast to Coast because of this police brutality. Larger sums began to swell the relief treasury.

As is so often the case, the attitude of the police and deputies only served to stiffen the strikers. The workers stood out there and were knocked over and got up again and went back on the line.

The three pacifists looked on this violence with troubled eyes. This was a war which they could not conscientiously avoid. They decided to lead a great parade of 15,000 workers to the gates of the Arlington mills where scabs were working.

The police, on foot and mounted, were waiting for them. Muste was striding along up in front. Cedric Long was just behind him. The mounted police bore down on the two, cut them off from the workers pressing up in the rear, hustled them down a side street and then commenced swinging riot clubs. Long was knocked unconscious by a blow in the back of his head. He was dragged to a patrol wagon and thrown in. Muste went ahead with blows raining on him until he was opposite the door of a barn on the side street. The door suddenly slid open, a hand came out and yanked the young minister into the darkness beyond. A striker, the owner of the barn, was trying to save his leader.

But the police stormed the place and threw Muste into the wagon beside the unconscious Long.

They put the two in a cell and half-drunken cops beat on the bars and yelled their hatred of the prisoners and one of them, a boy from Newtonville who had known Muste, kept asking how a decent guy could have any truck with them damned wops. Muste and Long were bailed out that night and held for trial. Next day they were out on the line again.

The trial was a boomerang from the police standpoint. Under the skillful questioning of George Roewer, the Socialist attorney for the defense, the two young leaders were able to broadcast from the witness chair facts and figures about actual conditions in Lawrence which the papers could not ignore.

Now May was coming and the treasury at strike headquarters was tragically low and the bosses were offering to take back workers at an increased wage. But only as individuals, not as members of the hated Amalgamated Textile Workers of America, the independent union which the strikers had joined and of which Muste and the others were official organizers.

The offer sounded mighty good to men and their families who had gone hungry for many weeks. But still they would not go back until they had orders from their leaders calling the strike off.

In the sixteenth week of the strike, on a Friday night, Muste called his committeemen together. The situation was reviewed. Was it fair to keep men out of employment any longer with a depleted treasury and most of the sources of relief money exhausted? Reluctantly, with heavy hearts, the leaders decided to call the strike off at a meeting on Saturday noon. At the same time they persuaded A. J., very much against his will, to leave town before the announcement was made. There was no foretelling what form the resentment of defeated men might take.

Early the next morning A. J. started for the train. This was the bitter end of all his hopes for bringing a more abundant life to the workers of Lawrence. In his first contact with the brutal realities of life he had been beaten. It didn't work. You used all your intelligence and courage in a just cause and that cause was lost.

He stopped to look at the unusual spectacle of a large automobile standing before a strikers' relief station. At the sight of him, a man climbed out of the car and hurried over.

"You're A. J. Muste, aren't you? L——" (he named the spokesman for the operators) "wants to see you."

What was this? Persistently the operators had refused negotiations with any "outside agitators," chief of whom they named Muste. A. J. tried to conceal his excitement and fenced a bit. Where was L——? In Andover waiting for him. This was on the level. Could he come right away? A. J. got into the car and drove to the home of the head of the operators at Andover.

There the Big Boss received him and there, while A. J. spread his long legs from a comfortable chair and looked quizzically out from under his clasped hands, L—— grew perilously purple of face with his denunciations of "apparently intelligent men, ministers of the gospel, and all, who would side with foreigners and anarchists." Bolshevism was also mentioned.

At the end of half an hour Muste uncoiled himself and asked pleasantly if that were all that L—— had to say. If so—

"No, no. Sit down. Now you know our situation. You know that we're going into a new season and that the market has improved since the cut and we must get the boys back to work. Now what exactly is it you fellows are after?"

Some time later a despondent man at the telephone at the strike headquarters in Lawrence, putting on his hat to go to that last meeting, heard A. J.'s voice at the other end. There was a bit of a thrill in it.

"We've won," said A. J., "make that a victory meeting."

Muste had come away from Andover with recognition for his union, a fifteen per cent wage increase and hours cut from 54 to 48.

It is, no doubt, the remembrance of the climactic morning that makes him a trifle dubious of the advice of pessimists who tell him the fight he has recently been waging against powerful forces of the labor world is doomed to failure.

Since those Lawrence days he has gone through rough and tumble strikes from the successful one of the broadsilk dyers of Paterson, New Jersey, where he and Robert Dunn and Evan Thomas carried on gloriously, to the long bitter struggle of the Passaic workers with its ignominious conclusion. As General Secretary of the Amalgamated Textile Workers' Union, he helped in the conduct of the Utica strike in the Fall of 1919, when they had Paul Blanshard, another strangely perverse ex-parson, in jail. And he was on the inside of a long strike of the Amalgamated Clothing Workers.

From all of which one might gather that A. J. is little more than a grand, good agitator with a peculiar genius for organization. Not so. All of these industrial clashes are incidental and to A. J., more often than not, tragically needless phases in the development of an indigenous American labor movement.

He takes no pleasure in strikes. He gets none of the sentimental kick which some of our young intelligentsia derive from the sight of men marching to the picket line. He knows what's going on in the homes those men have left. And he knows what it is to be hungry, for there were many days in Lawrence when he himself went hungry.

No, A. J. is no labor opportunist. He knows what he wants. Only recently in a summons to Progressives, printed in *Labor Age* and other labor papers, he called on the young men in the unions to set about the titanic task of organizing the thirty million unorganized workers in this country, to give over empty flirtations with "The New Capitalism," to build a strong labor party and always, *always* to learn and keep on learning.

When in the Spring of 1921 he went to a conference on workers' education at the home of William Fincke (who too had gone into the labor world from the ministry), he had before him a vision of a self-reliant and militant movement led by men and women come up from out of the ranks and taught how to think. Already he felt that a genuine labor union should not be led by any mere intellectual but by the workers themselves. Workers acquainted with the history and tradition of their movement and devoted to causes larger than but inclusive of the pure and simple unionism of higher wages and shorter hours.

So he was in the mood to undertake as difficult a task as one can imagine, when the organizers of that conference came to him and asked if he would be the Educational Director of America's first residential labor college.

Bill Fincke, whose recent death was a major tragedy for all who knew that brave spirit, had some fifty-three acres of ground and a fine old farm-house near Katonah in lovely Westchester County, New York. This he and his wife proposed to turn over into a labor college to which the unions should send their most promising young men on a scholarship basis. Fincke's friend, Toscan Bennett, would help with the financing, Muste would take care of the teaching and the labor movement would contribute the pupils.

So Brookwood Labor College was born and Muste entered once more into an academic life after the years of *Sturm und Drang*. Or so it might have seemed for a few fleeting moments at the beginning. That first year there were only the main building and two cottages in one of which the Mustes lived. A. J. taught history and economics, Eli Oliver taught research methods, the devoted Sarah Cleghorn gave up the writing of beautiful poetry to teach English to manual workers. They had seventeen students—miners, machinists, carpenters, garment workers—and all sorts of advice from all sorts of people. The official labor world looked at the experiment up on the hill with a tolerant, if slightly patronizing gaze.

But Brookwood, because of the sheer novelty of such an institution in America, got publicity. And presently in local unions in the coal-fields of Illinois and among the garment centers of Philadelphia, New York and Chicago and out through the chapels of the printing trades, went word of this place where a man could study about things that mattered and go back and help the boys at home in the practical matters of everyday unionism.

That was ten years ago. Today there are many who will tell you that Brookwood is the one most hopeful beacon on labor's horizon. Certainly Brookwood bulks large in any consideration of the future of the movement. For labor is emphatically at the cross-roads in this country. If there is much more of the present journeying up the road to the right under the subtle guidance of the National Civic Federation and its Acting President Mr. Matthew Woll, who is at the same time Vice-President of the American Federation of Labor, why then the A. F. of L. simply becomes a clearing-house for a group of organizations no more meaningful than fraternal bodies, with job protection and life insurance as their objects. If, on the other hand, the oncoming men and women from the ranks

show any capacity for constructive leadership, are in earnest
about extending the movement beyond hours and wages with
the goal of a new social order as their ultimate, then surely
labor will take its place as a significant factor in American civilization.

The desperate attempts of its enemies to kill Brookwood indicate its actual importance. Through the stormy years
full of heart-breaks and despairs and occasional triumphs, too,
Muste and the men and women associated with him have established the Brookwood tradition that it is not so important to
teach young laborites precisely what to think as how to think.
Little by little, as the plant has expanded with better equipment, a large dormitory back of the main building, several
more smaller buildings; as there have come on to the faculty
men and women who combine practical experience in the labor movement with teaching ability; as the original seventeen
undergraduates have now grown to forty odd; as, best of all,
Brookwood men and women have gone from Katonah back
into the movement and proved themselves in the most critical
situations—little by little then, Brookwood has arrived.

And with the arrival of Brookwood graduates, tough-
minded, curious, with the good and welfare of the rank and
file very much to the fore, there has been an uneasy whirling
of the swivel chairs of labor's Old Guard. It is not difficult to
understand the consternation caused by these dynamic youngsters, "rarin' to go." You climb to power from the pits, the
foundries, the presses, you make "radical" speeches *en route,*
you run around the district shaking hands and slapping backs.
And there you are, before an unfamiliar desk, with a brisk
secretary at hand to give out your statements to the waiting
reporters and accept invitations to discuss the labor movement
at dinners of Rotarians, Elks and Chambers of Commerce. It
is all quite thrilling. Now you eat good food regularly, ride

on Pullmans, sleep at the best hotels and develop a waist-line. You see less and less of your rank and file. A good deal of your time, like the time of any place-holder, is devoted to building up a machine that will keep you in power. Provided the skilled men retain their high wage scales and you can pin the Bolshevist label on your opposition, you are quite likely to sit pretty for a long time.

Then comes a young upstart from that labor college who knows as much about labor history as you do and who has the energy and courage that you have somehow lost. He wants to start something. Wants to get a lot of outsiders, foreigners and the like, into your nice, compact organization whose members pay their dues regularly, stir up no fuss at the cut-and-dried conventions and regularly can be counted on to re-elect you. What to do?

Well, this is what was done. Finally, the Executive Committee of the American Federation of Labor made a secret investigation of Brookwood, acting, it was stated, on the complaints of five students who alleged that they were being taught atheism, Communism and other disturbing theories. As a result of that investigation, word was sent from A. F. of L. headquarters to all affiliated unions that Brookwood was under the ban of the official labor movement and that neither pupils nor money should be sent to the college.

At the next A. F. of L. convention Matthew Woll, Vice-President of the A. F. of L. and Acting President of the National Civic Federation—an unholy alliance if there ever was one— bitterly attacked Brookwood and precipitated his now famous row with Professor John Dewey, a firm supporter of Brookwood. Mr. Woll said that Professor Dewey had dangerously friendly dealings with the Soviets. Later on, William Green, President of the A. F. of L., an Odd Fellow, an Elk, and a Baptist from Coshocton, Ohio, issued a statement in which he announced that during a labor celebration at Brookwood a picture of the late Samuel Gompers was draped in red.

Still later the Workers' Education Bureau of America, whose Secretary, Spencer Miller, Jr., had at one time been an instructor at Brookwood, refused any longer to recognize Brookwood as an integral part of the workers' education movement in this country. This Bureau is, of course, completely dominated by the Old Guard and has purged itself of all progressive elements, including James Maurer, one of the pioneers of the educational movement and for years President of the Bureau.

Under such circumstances no one could become righteously indignant if A. J. had chosen to close down Brookwood, turn his back on all the pettifogging labor politicians and go back to his beloved books. The Communists apparently are as anxious to kill Brookwood as is the National Civic Federation. But, far from quitting, A. J. has carried the battle right into the reactionary ranks and there are many of the Old Guard today who wish "they had never mixed into this Brookwood mess." All across the country, young men and women and veterans in labor's struggle for freedom as well, rallied around the standard bravely flying from the Westchester hill. It is not impossible that the long-delayed awakening of labor in America will come in response to the sort of challenge which Brookwood poses.

So that is "how come" A. J. In these days of doubt and hesitation, when so many of our so-called intellectuals are washing their hands of the labor movement or preaching the gospel that the true religion is indifferentism and that the New Capitalism will automatically usher in the Good Life—in such a time the drawling voice of A. J. is a clear trumpet call.

Prophet of Israel

JUDAH L. MAGNES

IN September 1894 Judah Magnes walked into my college
boarding-house in Cincinnati, introduced himself to our
little coterie, and announced that he came from Oakland, California, to pursue the course of study which would qualify him
to become a rabbi in Israel. He was a welcome recruit for, in
addition to the ordinary and generally accepted qualifications
for a rabbinical career, Magnes came with a reputation as a
crack baseball pitcher on his high school team. He looked the
part—tall and of athletic build. His winning smile soon en-
deared him to all of us and before long he became the leader
of our college world. He did not seek this leadership. It was
simply that we came to depend on his judgment for many
things and to seek his advice when difficulties beset us.

As a student he was not among the grinds. He supplemented a rather mediocre university course (they were all universities in Ohio in those days) with a vast amount of reading
on every conceivable subject and even organized extra-curricular groups for reading and discussion.

The only incident in his university days which offered some
forecast of the Magnes of the future occurred in his senior year
when he was editor of the college annual. A stupid dean attempted to impose a censorship on the material which was to
go into this senior publication. Magnes resigned without hesitation and invited the faculty to edit the book. The student
body backed him up whole-heartedly and, as a result of the

JUDAH L. MAGNES

rumpus which ensued, the so-called university won a president who began his tenure of office by dismissing the senescent faculty. From that day the University of Cincinnati began to be a real institution of learning.

Did Magnes dream that one day would find him at the head of a great university? In 1898 he received his A. B. degree when he was twenty-one years old. His rabbinical course of study at the Hebrew Union College kept him in Cincinnati until 1900 when he received the degree of Rabbi and Teacher. He was the valedictorian of his class.

Magnes was an earnest student of Bible and Talmud, Jewish theology and philosophy. Scholarship for itself, however, did not interest him. The theological foundation for a system of American Judaism which would lead to ultimate assimilation failed to attract or excite him. Judaism as an ethical or sociological program held no fascination for him. He was interested in the living Jew. Before he could quite realize it in his own mind, he was already a Zionist.

During our undergraduate days Masliansky, the great popular orator, came to Cincinnati, addressed a large assembly of Russo-Polish Jews in the Yiddish vernacular and the student body at Hebrew Union College in the classical Hebrew of the Prophets. For Magnes, as for many of us, it was an exciting experience. Yiddish was lifted out of its lowly and degraded position of linguistic inferiority. Did not Masliansky thrill us and move us to tears in Yiddish? Hebrew ceased to be the dead and classic tongue of sacred scripture, to be studied grammatically and subjected to syntactic analysis. Using this ancient Hebrew tongue, did not Masliansky express Jewish ideals and aspiration to a living Jewish audience? The net result of this experience was that Magnes flung himself into the study of Yiddish without which he felt it was impossible to understand the Jewish soul. At the same time he began to devour modern Hebrew literature on subjects not necessarily concerned with religion or theology.

Fortunately, upon graduation and ordination, Magnes was not forced to accept a pulpit but was able to go to Germany to pursue graduate work. He took his studies both at Berlin and Heidelberg with a seriousness that earned him the degree of Doctor of Philosophy from the latter university. He did more than study philosophy and semitics, however. Paulsen, Simmel, and Thiele on the one faculty and Gunkel and Delitzsch in the other were to Magnes not merely the dispensers of more or less useful knowledege and the partisans of either conservative or liberal views—they were above all personalities. Types and individuals hitherto unknown to this young Californian in his own home and in the provincial, Ohio city revealed themselves to him daily and enriched his knowledge of human beings and their reactions. Wherever he found himself, in the classroom, at the opera, in the theatre, he studied his fellow men and added to his store of that kind of knowledge which prepared him for his career of leadership.

The European Jew was a revelation to him. The Jewish youth, especially, appeared to him as more vital and purposeful than his brother in America. Among the students he discovered two distinct groups with sharply drawn, antagonistic programs—the one frankly assimilationist, the other militantly national. Here was a clean line of cleavage without any sign of compromise. Here was no vagueness, no indecision. The conflict of ideas often led to the battle of sabres. In his letters to his classmates at home, Magnes described a number of such affrays between the two factions. How different from the conditions prevalent in American Jewry where one section was indeed drifting toward assimilation, but without any conscious program beyond some empty pulpit phraseology, and where the party

still loyal to Jewish ideals was pitifully inarticulate and ineffective.

Magnes found himself spiritually at home with the loyalist group. He developed a passionate desire to know everything about the Jews, and to satisfy that longing he arranged to spend his vacation in the company of a fellow student on a tour of the Jewish towns and villages of Galician and Russian Poland. In one of his letters to the writer, Magnes explained the purpose of the journey. "I lay great hopes in this trip. I believe that I shall benefit from it vastly more than a trip through the Schweiz or into the art galleries and historical centres of Germany. We intend giving all our energies to work with Jews. How can we get the best result if we do not know our Jews? . . . The theatres and the concerts and the English poets— and I was about to say the German philosophers—have for me only a minor interest at present. I imagine I shall emerge from this state of mind some day. . . . One thing I should always like to possess—the feeling I now have, namely, that Jews and their interests have more worth for me than anything else in the world—more worth than all the governments, literatures, etc. Not that the Jews and their interests are superior to anything else in the world—perhaps they are inferior. What I mean is that I would rather give up my all for Jews and their cause than for anything else, no matter how exalted."

Certainly this adventure intensified his feelings. He emerged from the East-European ghettoes completely re-orientated. Magnes could not find spiritual satisfaction in mere Jewish Nationalism of the political and secular kind. For him, Jewish nationality and culture rooted in Judaism as a spiritual attitude toward life, as a religious message and a daily discipline. No doubt the zeal and genuineness of the mystics whose lives he had studied in their native villages contributed to his conversion to a rigorous orthodoxy. He had

seen and he had lived the real thing and the teachings he had
heard eloquently expounded in Cincinnati that Israel's mission was to play the prophet in every land to a hostile and un-
sympathetic world became empty platitudes. Only by living
his own cultural and religious life could the Jew hope to contribute anything worth while to the general human culture
and civilization. Zionism became Magnes's creed, but it was
a Zionism that had as much to do with the ideals of the
Prophets and the wisdom of the sages as with statecraft and a
legally guaranteed Jewish homeland in Palestine.

With this kind of spiritual equipment Magnes returned to
America. To accept a pulpit in one of the less important Reform Jewish congregations then available was out of the question. As a temporary stop-gap he became an instructor in the
very institution which had given him his rabbinical training.
A year of this work convinced him that he did not belong. He
had too many things to say and he required a platform from
which he could expound his views. To be sure, he found himself among the Zionists and very soon became their gifted orator. But the Zionists counted for little in American Jewish
life and his audiences were among the despised visionaries and
dreamers.

It happened that just at this time one of his classmates and
close friends was about to give up the ministry after a two
years' trial in order to return to his Virginia home and prepare
himself for a career in law. Through his influence Magnes
succeeded him as rabbi of a fashionable Reform Temple in
Brooklyn. Here he enjoyed the luxury of living his personal
life according to the strict tenets of orthodox Judaism, while
preaching national Judaism to a congregation which most
likely had no inkling of what it was all about. But one thing
they did understand—that their erstwhile empty pews were

being filled by strange men and women, not of their social set, and suspiciously of East European origin.

It was too true. The Williamsburg and Brownsville ghettoes constituted the major portion of the audiences to whom Magnes preached. This the congregation was quick to understand and it gave them no satisfaction. East European Jews are all right, they may have argued, for are not all Israel brethren? Nevertheless, they preferred that these ghetto Jews keep their distance and be satisfied by a less direct contact with their more "cultured" co-religionists of German origin. Let them accept charity and institutions for their rapid transformation into Americans, but let them stay in their own synagogues. No need to invade these costly temples in which Jews were already boasting of an emancipation and a liberalism which would in due time transform them into near Unitarians. In short, the congregation regarded their rabbi's audiences as more disquieting than his doctrines.

In addition to his rabbinical duties Magnes threw himself into organization and propaganda work as secretary of the Federation of American Zionists. In his office, situated in the heart of New York's East Side, he became more than a Zionist leader. To his neighbors he was a veritable prophet, oracle, sage, and deliverer. Every day his office was filled with a motley crowd of petitioners who sought advice and material help for every kind of personal problem, who brought him schemes for the deliverance of Israel and for the salvation of mankind. His name became well known to the thousands of Jews who read the Yiddish newspapers.

His Brooklyn congregants, however, were not among these readers and they might have remained blissfully unaware for all time that the gifted rabbi, who charmed them every Sabbath with his forceful personality and pulpit style, was leading a double life. The Kishineff pogroms and the other similar attempts on the part of Czarist Russia to solve the Jewish problem by killing off those Jews who would not enter the Holy Russian Church or emigrate provided the climax in the relationship between the young rabbi and his congregation. Magnes now became the fighter as well as the orator. Isaiah became Judah Maccabee. In New York and in many other Jewish centers he succeeded in raising large sums of money for the purpose of providing the Russian Jewish self-defense organizations with arms and ammunition in order to defend themselves against future attacks. He organized and personally led a parade of Jews up Broadway and Fifth Avenue in funeral procession as a demonstration of sorrow and indignation. The bells of Grace Church tolled forth their sympathetic notes, a noble gesture of Christian sympathy for stricken Israel. Magnes addressed dozens of meetings in large and small halls and on street corners when no other place was available. He brought the cause of Israel before the American public, and his name began to figure prominently in the columns of New York's dailies.

Self-sought publicity was never in Magnes's mind. No one ever doubted his sincerity. With him, the idea was ever uppermost. Far from seeking fame or position, he proved on more than one occasion that he was ready to sacrifice himself and his material well-being. The cause of Israel which thrust him into the limelight made his career as rabbi a troublesome one. His congregation did not mind his Zionist theories. They did resent his activities. He had become an agitator, and in the bourgeois mind any agitation is immediately classed with socialism, anarchy, and nihilism. Indeed, if bolshevism had existed at the time it would have been included. By the latter label he was to be stigmatized some ten years later. There was unrest in the Brooklyn congregation. He was given orders to behave and to confine himself to his pulpit. Magnes resigned.

His friends rallied in his behalf, and the resignation was withdrawn.

However, the very activities which irritated his congregation
served to make Magnes rabbi of the largest and most influential congregation in America—Emanu-El of New York City.
The late Louis Marshall happened to attend one of the mass
meetings addressed by Magnes. The level-headed lawyer was
attracted by the gifted young orator, although he could hardly
have agreed with the doctrine that was expounded. There followed a period of negotiations during which Magnes was by
no means overly enthusiastic. His own heart must have
warned him that the proposed alliance could not, under the
circumstances, last very long. Some of his friends and admirers, notably the late Professor Solomon Schechter, pointed
out to him that it was his duty to accept. Their argument ran
something like this: True, you won't succeed in bringing these
Jews back to rigid orthodoxy, nor will you convince them of
your Zionist fantasies, but you may help to delay their ultimate
and complete assimilation for a generation or so.

Magnes graced Emanu-El's pulpit as no rabbi of that great
temple did before or has done since. A few big-minded men
appreciated him then as they do now. But to the majority of
the members he spoke a strange language and again as in
Brooklyn, he attracted an even stranger following. Magnes's
interests were with the Jewish masses, with the proletarian
Jew. Judaism could not live without them, nor would Zion
be re-peopled by millionaires. Magnes could not and would
not preach polite sermons in sonorous phraseology. He did not
essay pulpit book reviews, dramatic criticism, and the usual
drivel of the popular preachers. He accepted the Reform dic-
tum that Judaism was Prophetism, and he turned the texts of
the prophets of Israel into sermons which dealt with the social and economic injustice of the day, with the grim poverty

of the masses, with the hopelessness of their lot, with the real mission of Israel which was not only to proclaim peace but which was to combat the forces of hatred and strife. The real Magnes emerged, an enigma to his congregants. Admired and even loved for his sincerity and his personality, he was feared for his dead earnest way of blurting out unwelcome facts and for what was implied in the whole scheme of his thought and words. The crisis and ultimate severance of relations came about over a set of concrete recommendations for a change in ritual and liturgical procedure which Magnes submitted to his congregation. The trustees of Emanu-El rejected them *in toto,* whereupon Magnes resigned.

At this stage of his career, it is felt by many that Magnes missed his great opportunity. Hundreds and even thousands were ready to follow him into an independent religious movement based on Jewish nationalism and the high humanitarian ideals of the Prophets. Had he led a movement of this kind there is no doubt that he would have given American Judaism new direction and purpose. Perhaps he was too tired and disheartened to attempt any further efforts to save the assimilationists for Judaism.

Thinking that the avowedly traditional Jews offered a more likely field for his activities, he became the spiritual leader of one of the oldest orthodox Jewish congregations in New York. There he suffered an even greater disillusionment. Smug, self-satisfied orthodoxy was no whit better than the reform brand and was equally convinced that America was the Jewish Palestine and that the word of God might come from the Rabbi but must first be sanctioned by the Board of Directors. He was through with congregations for all time.

The next few years found Magnes organizing the Jews of New York on a secular community basis through the Kehillah of which he became the head. Into this Kehillah he brought together all the diverse Jewish groups, temples, synagogues, schools, lodges, labor unions, social clubs, and Zionist societies. Their failure to agree on a common and broad Jewish platform was responsible for the breakdown of the Kehillah after a few years of stormy existence. The net benefit which Magnes left the Jews of New York was the beginning of a standardized and modernized system of religious education for Jewish youth. He was also helpful to large bodies of Jewish workingmen and to their employers by introducing and popularizing arbitration in the frequent labor disputes prevalent in the Jewish trades.

The World War lifted Magnes out of the restricted sphere of Jewish life and produced a valiant champion of human rights, a foe of reaction, hysterical nationalism, blood lust and world madness. Superficially, he ceased to be a Jew and became a citizen of the world. Actually he was never more Jewish. For, in espousing the unpopular cause of peace, in espousing the hypocrisies of chauvinism, in his plea for national sanity at a time when to be sane was to be suspect, Magnes spoke with the voice of the Jewish Prophets. In all his speeches he interpreted the real Jew and preached the message of Zion to the peoples of the world. He suffered together with all the fearless and brave men and women of the war period. The Department of Justice paid its compliments by covering him with its agents, watching for the damning phrase. Rumors of his impending arrest were rife more than once. He shared honors with the outstanding liberal minds in America on the lists of the proscribed issued by the patriotic societies. He was called pro-German, pacifist, and bolshevist in turn. The safe and sane among the Jews grumbled and openly fulminated against this *enfant terrible* as a troublemaker who was compromising the good name of the Jew and casting doubt upon

Jewish loyalty. Many shook their heads and said that it was too bad that this brilliant man's career ended in disgrace and futility.

The war, however, provided Israel with the unexpected boon of Palestine as a restored homeland and incidentally afforded Magnes the opportunity of realizing himself fully in this old new land. Characteristically, the first institution which the Jew planned and perfected was the Hebrew University in Jerusalem on Mount Scopus, and immediately after the war Magnes withdrew to Palestine. The American sponsors of the university were in the main Magnes's friends who believed in him, and whose loyalty remained unshaken even when in their hearts they could not follow and approve his reasoning and his public utterances. They gave evidence of their confidence in his integrity and ability by entrusting to him the work of organizing the new university. When this seat of learning was dedicated by Balfour in April 1924, Magnes became its chancellor.

Far from being buried in the university and thus being rendered harmless as some fondly hoped would happen his influence has grown. During the Arab-Jewish conflict he came in for well-nigh universal abuse because he counseled peace with the Arabs as against dependence on British imperial force or interference from any government, be it Conservative, Liberal or Labor. In view of the occurrences of the following months, even this stand must now be viewed as both prophetic and sound. Magnes, the Jew, can never forget that he also is the humanitarian, that the God of Isaiah is the God of mankind.

A recent visitor to the Near East who has always regarded Magnes's views on social questions, on national and international problems, on war and treaties as dangerous and unsound to say the least, reported upon his return to this country that

Palestine has already produced two great Jews—Pinchas Ruttenberg, the engineer, and Judah L. Magnes of the Hebrew University. He added that if Palestine possessed twenty such men, neither England nor the Arabs could prevent Israel from realizing its noblest aspirations in the land of its fathers.

Education in Action

JOHN DEWEY

EDUCATION is often a tedious, uninspired business. Not a few schools are still places where courses of study, text-books, methods, and teachers, are simply dull. But in one American city after another today, in Germany, in England, notably in Russia, and as far away as China and Japan, a new spirit is astir. For this no one person is wholly responsible; but if any man has done more than others to quicken and enlighten the changed attitude, it is John Dewey. Wherever education calls itself progressive, his name is known and honored, even by those who are not in accord with the philosophy out of which his offerings to the new education were born.

Observers see children in these new schools moving around freely, acting out plays, running stores, wielding paint-brushes, chisels, saws, hammers. One child may be reading a book while three others are discussing a problem assigned to them by their classmates as a committee; still others are busy building a boat. Where is the teacher? Where is the unbroken quiet which once marked teachers as "good disciplinarians"? What has become of the rooms we used to know where boys and girls sat for long hours each at his own desk from which it was crime to move without permission?

About two centuries ago Rousseau dreamed something like this. Another social reformer named Pestalozzi attempted to carry out some of Rousseau's ideas. Then Froebel caught the inspiration and within certain limits applied the thought to children of pre-school age. In America, the Workingman's School, established by the Ethical Culture Society of New York in 1878, took Froebel's principle of free coöperation among the children and carried it up into the grades. Elsewhere in our country, while the public schools were still sunk in the old formalism, here and there progressive schools (chiefly under private auspices) were letting in a bit of fresh air.

Then in 1899, under the imprint of the University of Chicago, a little book appeared which is now listed as a classic. *School and Society* told the story of a three years' experiment at the University Elementary School, and set forth the views of one John Dewey, then Professor of Pedagogy. The book gave heart to the discontented; it offered edge and direction to the movement for a modern schooling; it fired the imagination with prospects of close, fruitful linkage between children's school lives and the better life all about them. More than any other single writing, it hastened the pedagogic revolution which we are now witnessing and which still has ample work to perform.

As might have been expected, the new movement found expression at first in the private and experimental schools. It is now a commonplace for conventions of the Progressive Education Association to be assured by superintendents of public systems: "We are sold on these ideas. You have shown that they work. All that remains is to get our communities to vote the necessary money and to free the teachers."

In Russia, especially, this modern spirit is strikingly evident. To lift the multitudes from the ignorance in which state and church had willingly kept them has long been the hope of revolutionists, and the Soviets are making its fulfillment one of their major performances. Schools everywhere and for everybody! And modern schools—not the old-fashioned places where weary children sat reciting to weary teachers, but schools where children conduct their own business, carry out projects as heartily as any youngster in the latest American experimental venture, understanding what they are doing and coming back next day eager to learn more. Because a new social order is being initiated in that land, the schools have the advantage of a clean start and a fresh opportunity to connect education in a creative way with life itself. It is mainly to John Dewey that they have turned for light.

What lies back of the new education? To appreciate Dewey's contribution, it is necessary to consider the man and his philosophy of life. His biography is a record of degrees and other honors conferred, chairs of philosophy occupied, books published and causes espoused—in all of which there is very little front-page stuff for the dailies. He was born in Burlington, Vermont, among the folk whom Dorothy Canfield has interpreted for us in *Hillsboro People*. Theirs are not the homes in which one looks for orators, painters, dramatists, singers, revolutionists. Indeed one of the first impressions these persons create on visitors from New York, is that they must be either very slow-witted or congenitally tongue-tied. Who are the fools, natives of Vermont do not say in public if at all.

This one of her many distinguished sons still looks shy whenever he gets up to speak. But he has spoken bold words on the unpopular side of public questions. And the list of books which he has written is long and impressive. One reason for the influence he has exerted is suggested in the passage where David Hume pictures Nature as saying to a philosopher: "Let your science be human. . . . Be a philosopher; but, amidst all your philosophy, be still a man." John Dewey meets the requirement eminently. When his seventieth birthday was celebrated in October, 1929, a flood of hearty tribute poured in upon him; and characteristically enough, along with the expressions of respect for his services as a thinker, people dwelt upon a certain genuineness and human brotherhood. In the minds of many there were recollections of unusual kindness. Whether at Michigan, Minnesota, Chicago, or Columbia, no professor was ever more generous to the stray cats that wander in and out of a university campus. That some of these won blue ribbons, is due to his trustful encouragement.

A striking act of respect was accorded to him at a public meeting a few weeks after the birthday celebration. He was to speak at a public meeting in behalf of Norman Thomas, Socialist candidate for Mayor of New York. When he entered to take his seat on the platform, the immense audience rose and applauded with a warmth which left him visibly touched. If tributes still count at his time of life, this honor from plain people meant no less to Dewey than the degrees which great universities in all parts of the world have conferred upon him.

In 1929 he delivered the Gifford lectures at the University of Edinburgh, an honor awarded previously to William James and Josiah Royce. *The Quest for Certainty,* in which these lectures appear, is a dangerous book. No one observing this retiring thinker would suspect him of being a destroyer. But such he is. He wants to release philosophic thinking from bondage to conceptions framed centuries ago in response to life as understood then, but out of harmony with the new world of the present. Though philosophy is an attempt to grasp the meaning of life as a whole, in the main the business of philosophers has been centered upon a single quest which Dewey regards as barren—the effort to understand the perfect reality back of all the changing appearances in the world. It is, he thinks, a search for a mistaken kind of assurance. Because human life is uncertain, men have sought security in two ways. One is practical, the other religious, or philosophic. The former way tried to get certainty by such arts as farming, hunting, building, weeding, making tools and weapons. This is the method which, by understanding nature in order to use it, has literally revolutionized the conditions of man's living, increased the span of his years, and filled them with satisfactions utterly unknown to earlier times. And yet, remarkably enough, this practical attitude has been held, until recent times, in only slight honor as compared with regard for the beliefs of philosophers about the unchanging, absolute, universal, eternal, reality behind all changing things. Intellect was rated as immeasurably higher than practical knowledge for busying itself in grasping this secret of all secrets.

With such a quest for certainty, Dewey will have nothing to do. He terms it frankly a mere compensation for men's failure to handle successfully the risks of existence here and now. He challenges them instead to cope intelligently with the actualities of daily life. For philosophic study of the absolute, he would substitute search for methods of control. Assuredly he wants the world to be understood, but in the practical sense of learning how to change it for the better. "Truth is to be won by the adventure of experimenting."

For thirty or more years he has been elaborating this "Instrumentalism," the philosophy which says that the heart of our best knowing is doing, that all ideas must be defined at bottom in terms of things done, or to be done. "Typically American," many have said. But Dr. Dewey remains good-humored. The doing which he praises is certainly not brainless doing. If American Pragmatism (the name used by William James) has been associated with dogmatic, unreflective doing, this is not Dewey's fault. He wants a doing which is more thoughtful, more intelligent. And he insists that the greatest of harm has come not merely from treating thinking as if it had no connection with acting, but even regarding it for that reason as somehow more praiseworthy.

JOHN DEWEY

When, in like spirit, he pays his respect even to the thinking done by plain men, women, and children, the charge that this is democracy carried to its extreme gives him little concern. He is not unaware that people differ in intelligence. But he questions whether the pure intellect which tradition honors is as untainted as its devotees suppose. Philosophers are also human beings, with their own senses, dimensions, affections, passions. Aristotle, for example, was not merely pure intelligence. He was an upper-class Greek with the prejudices of his class against the lower orders. He thought that pure intellect made it unmistakably clear that the non-Greeks were barbarians and deserving of nothing better than subjection to their Greek superiors.

Dewey delights in showing how through the ages this alleged pure reason gave the sanction of a seeming eternality to what was after all only the vested interest or the custom of a given time and place. Philosophers and preachers have not been exempt from the weakness of the old woman who, on being asked by a friend whether she had ever journeyed in an airplane, replied, "No, and I don't intend to ride in one. I stick to railroad trains, the way the Good Lord intended his creatures to travel." Slavery, disease, the subjection of women, come to mind. Today "the will of God" is against socialism or pacifism, or any other such disagreeable proposal.

Because feelings, habits, volitions play so important a rôle, Dewey wants them held up to the light and given as rigorous a study as men ever offered to so-called pure reason. He is no more ready today than he was in the earlier stages of his growth to minimize the importance of abstract thinking. But he has come to see how false it is to offer special privilege to any such isolated mental operation. People (including philosophers) feel and do as well as think. Their doing and feeling also tell us much of great importance. Every center of experience, he says, should be heard from. Although all, of course, are not of equal value, at least give all a hearing upon their merits. In short he wants men's brains to stop doing what a certain Negro preacher, according to Ingersoll, called "scruting the inscrutable." Spend them instead upon examining all the stuff of human experience in order to reconstruct that experience on constantly nobler lines. Such is his religion—"an idealism of action which is devoted to the creation of a future." He believes ardently that a spirit of this kind will be invincible.

For all these reasons, Dewey is an active champion of more than one good cause of betterment. He has eyes that twinkle with kindly merriment; but they can blaze, too, at sham and cruelty. Gentle philosopher that he is, he protested strongly against injustice to Russia, and to Sacco and Vanzetti. He is Vice-President of the Teachers' Union; and it is like the man that the most revered educator in America is willing to lend his name to a group whose members are mostly of alien antecedents. He refuses to accept war-making as a final, unchangeable attribute of human nature, put there by God and changeable only by God. In his earlier days he was a dweller at Hull House where, in company with so many other social pioneers, he attempted to bring a ray of light into Chicago's "jungle of wretchedness."

He is actively interested in getting a better politics. He holds that there is no longer any vital distinction between the Republican and the Democratic party. When it comes to practice, both do the same things at the behest of much the same type of master. He wants to see a third party arise, and he is Chairman of the League for Independent Political Action, recently formed for this purpose. Most philosophers are not likely to be found on such committees. Politics is a messy business. To organize a new party, a man cannot lock himself up in his study and devote himself to "thinking." He must go to meetings, bother himself about raising funds, interesting likely supporters, answering critics. All these details are precisely those practical instrumentalities which traditional philosophy has been above; but Dewey is consistent in treating them with the respect they deserve. His own example illustrates his teaching that it is not enough for philosophy to be interested in the ends of life. It must use its brains to work out appropriate means. Otherwise it will be like an engineer who despises the stuff and the energies of nature on the ground that they are merely material.

In the same spirit he is keenly interested in promoting a new economic order. His warm human sympathy shows itself in his feeling for the part played in a man's welfare by such bitter actualities as the wages he gets, the food, clothes, shelter, recreation, which he can buy, the working conditions which make his day's job (when he has one) a dumb or hated per-formance, or a liberating affair. He speaks very plainly here. He fears "that there is an irrepressible conflict coming as real and as deep as that to which Lincoln called attention." We live in a civilization controlled by interest in private profit. But our criticisms, our religion, evade all this. They keep to the tradition that these bodily material concerns are no busi-ness for the superior part of man. How long it took to get economics into the colleges—even conservative economics!

Who is interested in the intelligent direction of our economic life? Business men themselves? Politicians? These people know what they want for their own advantage. Let the phi-losopher lead in studying what is best for all together. Let the intelligence which goes into science or which heretofore spent itself in arid metaphysics, be given to this intelligent studying and planning. Otherwise, we shall drift blindly at the mercy of routine or of the will of those who have their own axes to grind and know how to go about getting them ground. "Apply the intelligence which has made our industrial machines and revolutionized the conditions under which people live today to banishing waste, unemployment, strife, extremes of wealth on the one hand and dire want on the other."

Here is where education takes on the full meaning which it has in Dewey's philosophy. To the question "Can human nature be changed?" he answers, "We never can tell what the 'nature' of anything is until we learn by experience all that we can make of it."

So it is that he has done such notable pioneering in trying out the latent possibilities in the young. Often teachers are reminded that childhood is essentially plastic. But immediately they are told to use this fact in order to make the children act as their elders do. Not so, is Dewey's plea. Because the child is plastic, try to make him do better than they have done.

For the same reason that he refuses to give "pure" intelligence a favored place in the thinking of adults, he wants a schooling where the whole child, not merely his skill in arithmetic or grammar, will be at home. Remember how grimly the older educational philosophy mistrusted the natural impulses of the child. The desire to handle things, to take them apart, to move around, to explore, to ask questions, was often a nuisance to the elders, who found it all too easy to regard these manifestations as therefore diabolic in origin. What legitimate place had these natural impulses in the school-room where learning was to be got solely by attending to books? Today we know better. These human propulsions are not necessarily marks of depravity. Everything depends on the direction they are given. Use them in order that on the solid basis of experience, children may learn how to build better experiences—the kind which lead to an ever broader and deeper understanding of good life.

Boys and girls still study from books. They still learn arithmetic, geography, history. But they are no longer subjected to meaningless drills and verbal memorizings. They are no longer led from one isolated bit of information to the next. A single day's excursion brings them back to the class-room, with many problems in arithmetic, geography, history, composition over which to work and in which they see enough sense to make them work heartily.

Do they learn as well? They learn better. They learn with the help of their once-despised natural activities, not in conflict with them. School life is now so interesting that they cannot keep their minds off their work. They study with all heart, not half. They want most of all to be doing things. The school now gives them the chance; and it is through these problems with an intrinsic appeal, real problems of every-day community life, not chiefly artificial problems set by the teacher out of a book that they learn. And they care less for the silly pranks which in other schools are often the only outlet for cramped energies.

In a recent number of *The New Republic,* Dewey severely criticizes the usual run of college graduates in America on the ground that their college training does so little to interest them in the realities of the social order into which they move when they graduate. The reason, he holds, is largely that college life is still wedded to the academic tradition of aloofness, where mind is not supposed to occupy itself with such sordid business as unemployment, or the realities of present-day politics. Hence he holds that our American graduates as compared with those of other countries manifest a kind of infantilism. Our higher education "evades serious consideration of the deeper issues of social life; for it is only through induction into realities that mind can be matured. Consequently the effective education, that which really leaves a stamp on character and thought, is obtained when graduates come to take their part in the activities of adult society which put exaggerated emphasis upon business and the results of business success. . . . There is little preparation to induce either hardy resistance, discriminating criticism, or the vision and desire to direct economic forces into new channels."

Sharp as this criticism is, it indicates again what high hopes Dewey places in an education which never loses sight of the organic relation between thinking and doing, and especially of the crying need for endlessly better doing.

Not all who admire the man and work with him share his entire philosophy. His views on the quest of the absolute keep him outside of any church. In the popular sense, he is without religion. There are, however, other conceptions of the good life than the hedonism which he accepts. Though his following is large and influential, his authority as a thinker is by no means unchallenged. The style of his writing can hardly be called polished. While the difficulties in understanding him are ascribed by disciples to the profundity of his thinking, the less sympathetic put the blame upon confusion in the thought itself. On many points of prime importance, able minds disagree with him sharply.

But even those who view religion and ethics with other eyes, respect the philosopher who, for all his quiet demeanor, is hot against the follies, the vice, the stupidity of this age of industrialism—especially the indifference which lets these ills continue. In so far as truth can be bought only by the adventure of experiment, these persons are one with him and his disciples in his practical hopes, and grateful for his insistence that "human nature" includes all the unexpressed potentialities—all that a better statesmanship, a better economic order, a better life-long education in the remaking of experience may help men and women to become.

Forty Years at Hull House

JANE ADDAMS

HALSTED STREET at its hottest. . . A sweating wind from the southwest carries the fervor of all the prairies into the stockyards and pours out again laden with the indescribable effluvia of a myriad of doomed cattle. This is in the full track of it. . . Clanging street cars . . . wretched wooden shacks packed in between glaring-fronted stores. . . Swarthy men crowding into smoke-filled cafés that bear strange names across their dirty windows . . . H. Akropolis . . . Kaffenaion H. Lakonia . . . Pantopoleion To Athenaion. And in among them a new generation of cafés labelled "La Chihuahua," "El Liberador," "La Puerta de Vera Cruz"—full of still swarthier men.

Mexican restaurants always bear the sign *Mesas para familias*—tables for families. But the Greeks eat and drink in exclusive masculinity. The Mexican invasion is the newest thing on Halsted street—that and the gypsies. The largest winter colony of gypsies in the world, it is said, camps along Halsted street. The figures doubtless are as reliable as anything else connected with gypsies. Came the Irish, the Jews, the Italians, the Greeks, and now the southern Latins, or at least the Aztec remnants, speaking Spanish and singing softly to the conqueror's guitar. One national wave washes over and submerges the ebb of another.

Halsted street's interminable thoroughfare crosses Harrison and Blue Island avenue in a star shaped cluster, all incredibly dirty with dingy traffic going six ways. A deaf mute clothing worker was killed there by thugs as he was protecting two girl strikers during the long battle in which the Amalgamated Clothing Workers finally routed the sweatshops. They organized in Hull House.

One perceives the shift of population by the titles of the newspapers that billow and drift high in every alley. They change from Yiddish to Italian, to Greek, to Spanish, with occasional Russian, Lithuanian, Polish, and Hungarian for a sprinkled spice on the journalistic hash. Formerly one could follow changing races in the neighborhood by the airs played on ever-grinding phonographs, but that has largely been abolished by the radio squawking the same tune from twenty different stations.

Halsted meets Polk. Wooden shanties give place suddenly to a reddish brick bulk, filling a whole block with its imposing height. A brick archway leads inward. A paved court is being used for a handball game. Along a low brick wall roosts a row of children comparatively clean. They shout in friendly fashion as the visitor stops and scans the place.

"This is it—this is Hull House, mister!"

Over the door is a painting of an old-fashioned brick house set in the middle of a pleasant field. It has a square white wooden cupola, and broad porches with wooden pillars. Willow trees surround it. There is a summer house, a well house, and a garden. Such was Hull House when it was built, seventy-two years ago, far out on the prairie.

When it was fifteen years old, it saw from a not too safe distance the glaring horror of the Great Fire. When it was thirty-three years old a pair of girls, newly graduated, and fresh from a visit to Toynbee Hall in London, came to live in it. They were Jane Addams and Ellen Gates Starr. They are still there. They will always be there. Come life or go life, those two will hover forever, over and within Hull House, over the swarming myriads who eddy around and through it, over the city into whose spiritual structure their souls have been wrought.

I saw a picture once of Saint Genevieve keeping watch over Paris at night from the window of her cell high on the windy hills above the Seine. So will these two watch over Chicago, not from a height, but from deep within.

In September, 1889, the two young women moved into the old building which, after it had ceased to be a home, had been used as an asylum for the aged by the Little Sisters of the Poor, a factory and later a boarding house. The story of their early days is known round the world through Miss Addams's book, "Twenty Years at Hull House." The later days are described in the recent volume covering her "second twenty years."

As she sat in a rocking chair in the famous entrance hall that had been the front parlor of the old country house, I asked her about her present-day work.

Her reply to my query was interrupted constantly. Every few minutes she would rise to answer a telephone call, or to interpret the halting inquiry of some bewildered, foreign-speaking woman caught in a mesh of official incompetence, with gas cut off or lights dark on a misunderstanding.

While we spoke, processions of visitors filed through, eyeing her curiously—boys and girls from public schools, students from universities, members of some of the unbelievable number of clubs and associations which make their headquarters there.

"Well, of course," she said in that remarkably girlish voice with its clear lift belying her years, "our greatest pride here is our adaptability. Races change, their needs vary. We must meet all. In the early days we had so many Jewish young folks, bright as whips, sharks at debate and literature. One of our boys in those first years captured the national interscholastic debating contest. We were proud as peacocks. But now our folks are Mexicans and Greeks. They care little for debate. The Greeks like athletics, the Mexicans love music. The Irish, too, have moved up. Each race has its own characteristic good points and its bad. Hull House helps every race according to its need."

Ellen Starr and Jane Addams opened Hull House as a friendly welcoming door in the midst of a huge madness which then was Chicago. Their ideal was "a house easily accessible, ample in space, hospitable and tolerant in spirit," situated in the midst of the large foreign colonies, which so easily isolate themselves in American cities. Not for five years did they incorporate. At that time the object stated in the charter was "To provide a center for the higher civic and social life, to institute and maintain education and philanthropic enterprises, and to investigate and improve the conditions in the industrial district of Chicago."

It sounds formal and academic. But what battles have raged around that peaceful open door! Only three years before the opening of Hull House, the Haymarket bomb had been thrown. All foreigners were supposed to be anarchists, all anarchists were supposed to be madmen thirsting for blood and destruction. To treat foreigners as human beings—still worse, to be friends with them—was esteemed a blow at the foundations of state and church.

Immigrants from the peaceful villages of Europe came flocking in myriads. They were drawn by lurid posters of steamship companies who packed thousands in one hold, dumped them here, and went back for more. In long processions of two and three thousand at a time they would disembark from the Ellis Island ferry, loaded with bags and bundles, fright in their eyes. The lure of immediate employment drew them Chicago-ward. Here they found themselves kennelled in sweating, festering filth, with every hand against them and every eye full of suspicion and hate. They found no justice in the courts, no friendliness anywhere.

Gradually word spread that there was a welcome at Hull House. The aliens came, timidly at first, then with more self-assurance. They learned the language and customs of their new country. They brought out of holes and corners in their minds almost forgotten handicrafts learned abroad— weaving, basketry, rug-making, woodcraft, pottery.

All this is well known. What is not so well known, however, is that of all the settlements anywhere, this company of residents has remained practically unchanged in all that time. They have not come and gone, broken up into cliques of self-important career-seekers. They have remained true to the first vision. One reason is that none are paid except technical workers. The residents earn their living elsewhere and spend their leisure time at Hull House. It is a labor of love. They remind one of that famous monastery Abelard founded at Brest where the monks spent eight hours of every day praying and singing, and then went back each man to his own wife and family outside the monastery walls.

To call the roll of the first residents at Hull House, many of whom still are there, is like calling the register of all great deeds within the past four decades. Julia Lathrop is one of them, first head of the Children's Bureau of the United States. Florence Kelley is among them, pioneer of the heroic battle for mothers in industry; Grace and Edith Abbott, founders of the Immigrants' Protective League; Caroline Urie, who brought the Montessori system into this country; and Alice Hamilton.

It is difficult to realize that it was as late as 1910 that Alice

Hamilton made the first survey of industrial diseases. She was named by Governor Deneen a member of the first commission on industrial diseases appointed by any state in the Union. The facts she uncovered in Illinois were so ghastly that the then Commissioner of Labor, Dr. Neal, asked her to undertake a similar survey for the United States at large. There was at that time no Department of Labor. There was only a Bureau which was a section of the Department of Commerce and Labor, itself a novelty. Dr. Hamilton investigated paint poisoning, phossy jaw—that hideous thing which eats away the bones of the living workers—lead poisoning, and sweatshop diseases. The horrors she photographed and forced before the unwilling, incredulous eyes of the American people startled them so profoundly that the whole great movement for industrial safeguards seems to have been based thereupon.

Robert Morss Lovett is a resident there. Dean of undergraduates at the University of Chicago, professor of literature, editor of radical magazines, he braved the screaming frenzy of war madness with a bright, engaging smile, presiding cheerfully at meetings where death was threatened to speakers by the patrioteers.

To list the whole glorious company would require a catalog. But the wonder arises in the mind of one who has known settlements elsewhere: "What has held these people together for so long?"

Let Miss Addams answer. She is known the world over as a propagandist for peace. She founded an international organization for peace, and is an officer in most others. Yet during the war she steadfastly refused to have peace meetings at Hull House because her fellow residents were belligerent by a large majority, and she would not commit others to anything on her own convictions, however profound.

"You see," she said with a smile, "those were strenuous days. Not everybody knows it, but Hull House residents were far from being unanimously pacifist. Even Miss Starr was belligerent, and she is no mean antagonist in a debate. In fact, most of the residents were for the war. So were the trustees. At one meeting, one of our heaviest subscribers announced that he would never again give a cent to Hull House as long as I was connected with it because of my views on peace. Of course, I offered my resignation. But Charles L. Hutchinson said, 'Hull House has received a great deal of money on account of Miss Addams, and we have taken it. If she loses some money for us, we will just take that, too.' So nothing more was said of my resignation."

Eight of the residents volunteered. The Boys' Band, composed of forty-two young musicians, went to the front. They were taken into the occupied territory, and received with great acclaim. Soldiers from the district were given their last meal before they left for camp at Hull House.

These things explain perhaps how Hull House has been able to hold so long its great company of valiant souls, slacking neither their valor nor their comradeship. It is the complete respect with which widely severed convictions are regarded by every member of the group. They differ violently but with great fellowship, like knights who battle in the tourney but drink to one another's prowess before and after.

When Jane Addams won the Nobel Peace Prize in 1931, her name gave a luster to the award which it has not always possessed. But, deserving as she was, her biggest prize will always be the success of her beloved Hull House.

Hardly anything civic takes place in Chicago without Miss Addams's presence. She addresses a national crime commission, speaks at the public school pageant, and addresses the convocation of the University of Chicago almost on the same day. Everyone knows about Miss Addams. But not everyone knows about her Round Table.

The specific contribution made by Ellen Gates Starr falls under three heads. One is the spice of her personality. Where Miss Addams is calm and judicial, Miss Starr is pungently witty and strongly partisan. She enlivens any situation like paprika on a salad that might otherwise be too smooth. Another is a passionate love of beauty; the third a fierce democracy. Her trade is bookbinding. Her love is for all things beautiful, not because it is the proper thing to admire works of art, but because love of beauty is wrought into the very structure of her being. Frail she is—her slightness strongly contrasted with Miss Addams's sturdy build—and quizzical of eye except when she flames out with some sudden indignation. But her greatest contribution to the saga of Hull House is her absolute refusal to accept less than the best from the poor. The attitude of condescension from the privileged to the underprivileged—"of course, one can't expect too much from these people"—she meets with a shrivelling blast of scorn. "These people can do as well as we can, and a great deal better if they will set their minds to it"—that is her consistent attitude.

Among the bitterest opponents of Hull House have been the churches. Evangelical pastors of those early days considered themselves affronted to have as neighbor such an institution without a definite religious, not to say denominational flavor. Hull House and all its works were denounced as atheistic and immoral. The churches passed, however; Hull House remained. Later there came a bitter controversy with the Roman Catholic clergy. A company of Italian players put on a play about Galileo. They were ordered by the editor of the archdiocesan paper, *The New World,* not to permit the play "or they would regret it." Miss Addams read the text carefully, found nothing objectionable in it, and replied that the play would go on as scheduled. Whereupon Hull House was denounced as being a school for inciting the murder of priests. There is another editor of *The New World* now, and such things have long ago ceased.

The place is a cross-roads of the continents. One meets famous folk from all over the world. I was much amused by an editorial protest in a New York paper against the policy of the Soviet Government in showing visitors only the bright side of life in Russia. How many American cities, I wonder, take their visitors proudly through their own slums and back alleys? Chicago does. Most people worth troubling about visit Hull House.

Francis Hackett complained, riding in a taxi away from the institution, "How filthy you keep your streets!" I tried to explain that Hull House was not located where it was on the same principle that one locates a country club. But in vain. He must have his clean streets. Margaret Bondfield, Lady Cynthia and Oswald Mosley, Sheehy Skeffington, the Filipino commissioners—one meets almost everybody at Hull House some time.

Dr. Hamilton tells of trying to find a settlement in Paris. The Frenchwoman to whom she was appealing could not understand what she meant. At length a light dawned. "Oh," she said, "you mean our Hull House!"

The specific thing which sets Hull House apart from others, which has carried its name around the world as a generic title, is this atmosphere of chivalry, so hard to describe, so much harder to achieve. Think over the melancholy wreckage of the fine young battalions of idealists who manned the settlements in New York, for example, as late as twenty and fifteen years ago. How is it that this company preserves its ranks so staunchly unbroken? The reason is their profound conviction of the worth and sanctity of the opinions of other people. Few Socialists, no Communists have it; few reformers, few doctrinaires, few radicals, few uplifters. Only heartwhole democrats, who believe the Kingdom of God is a republic in which the Sovereign dwells equally within each citizen, can possess it.

Jane Addams will in time, I suppose, be regarded as a legend; like Arthur's Round Table and the Paladins of Charlemagne will be the knightly group that surrounds her. There are so many Castles Perilous they have stormed and overthrown, so many Black Knights they have laid low, so many oppressed and hopeless captives in dark dungeons they have set free. And while it is not fair to let the specific and separate histories of those about her be eclipsed by her fame, it is certain that the spiritual mortar which has held them cemented so strongly together is the fairness, the steady courage and the knightly courtesy of Miss Addams.

"Twenty Years at Hull House" has become a school classic. Issued in a neat brown volume, it contains copious and scholarly explanatory notes, with pages and pages of "study questions" for careful reviewers, and a system of numbering the lines on each page of the text for instant reference. It gives one a queer feeling to read this book after one has known the forceful, lively characters whom it portrays—as though one spoke with the shadows of the mighty past, or as if one saw one's friends already embalmed among the traditions.

In this book Miss Addams sets forth her own beginnings with unreserved clarity. Her mother died when she was a baby. Her whole childish life centered in her father, a just and upright Quaker, gifted not only with severe rectitude, but with a profound and scrupulous respect for the mental and moral integrity of others. He advised her in a moment of great doubt concerning the doctrine of foreordination, that it was above all things important "not to pretend to understand

JANE ADDAMS

what one did not understand, and to be honest with oneself inside, whatever happened."

It was a lonely childhood the founder of Hull House passed in Cedarville, Illinois; yet her early days were spent amid the clashing horror of the Civil War. Born in 1860, she was but five years old when Lincoln fell. But her father had known Lincoln well when both were legislators in the Illinois Assembly. And the light of that great name lies over much of her early life.

At the age of seventeen she entered Rockford Female Seminary which became Rockford College the year after her graduation. She was one of four who received a degree of A.B. on the very day the institution was declared a college, empowered to grant such titles. This was in 1881.

For eight years thereafter Jane Addams travelled, part of the time studying medicine. For six months she lay recovering from a serious operation for curvature of the spine. It was this deformity, she relates, which when she was a child made her shrink from appearing in public with her father, lest he be chagrined by having it known that this "ugly duckling" was his.

In London, during a visit to the horrible East End, when she saw a Saturday night auction of decayed vegetables, the life-shaping conviction first took form. This conviction was crystallized later during a bullfight in Spain—the conviction that in this ardent devotion to book learning she was atrophying whatever capacity for accomplishment she might possess, and that it was time to act. "Somewhere," she remarks, "in the process of being educated, the first generation of college women lost that simple and almost automatic response to the human appeal, that old healthful reaction resulting in activity from the mere presence of suffering or of helpfulness.... They were so sheltered and pampered that they had no chance even to make the great refusal."

The history of art lost its beauty, and the princely biographies she had been studying lost their appeal against the background of hopeless human misery. One day in April, 1888, she disclosed to Ellen Gates Starr the project of a definite center in which to apply their college learning to human need. Miss Starr responded wth eager sympathy. "By the time we reached the enchantment of the Alhambra," Miss Addams writes, "the scheme had become convincing and tangible."

There, under the arched tracery woven of stone for the pleasure of Moorish kings, the resolution to found the future Hull House came to its maturity. Five months in Toynbee Hall, London's first settlement, for Miss Addams; then the great adventure was begun—forty years ago. And already it has set its mark upon the ages.

But the distinguishing characteristics of this settlement, its unshakable tolerance, the fundamental respect its members have for one another's firm beliefs, date back, it appears, to the quiet study of the old Quaker miller of Cedarville where a little girl was bidden by her father to hold "mental integrity above everything else," and who kept that faith with him.

What child of "this generation"—ominous phrase!—holds a parental ideal sacred? Such a thing is "pricelessly Mid-Victorian"—a "hallmark of the booboisie"—contrary to behavioristic individualism!

Perhaps it is for this tragic reason that the story of the genesis of Hull House and the clear sincerity of its tradition strike us as already one with the great past. From the clash and horror of the Civil War something of intelligent responsibility was inherited. But from the World War, what but the bitter snarl of cynics and the yapping laughter of sneering infants, aged in the cradle, has descended to its heirs?

Forty years—the period is big with meaning in Scriptural tradition. Forty years from Egypt to the Land of Promise, forty years of desert wandering. Perhaps the steady light of that loyalty to moral integrity which Hull House embodies and enshrines may guide us through.

Galahad of Freedom

ROGER BALDWIN

A YOUNG man sat on the edge of a cot in a cell in
Tombs prison, New York, busily writing away by the
light of a drab dawn.

He was Roger N. Baldwin and he was working on the
speech he was to make that day (it was October 30th, 1918)
before being sentenced by Judge Mayer in the Federal Court
for violation of the Selective Service Act. Against the war
which was then drawing to a close Baldwin had stood four-
square, refusing to take his physical examination when he
was called up for the draft.

"I ask the Court for no favor. I could do no other than
what I have done, whatever the court's decree. I have
no bitterness or hate in my heart for any man. Whatever
the penalty I shall endure it, firm in the faith that whatever befalls me, the principles in which I believe will
bring forth out of this misery and chaos, a world of
brotherhood, harmony and freedom for each to live the
truth as he sees it.

"I hope your Honor will not think that I have taken
this occasion to make a speech for the sake of making a
speech. I have read you what I have written in order
that the future record for myself and for my friends may
be perfectly clear, and in order to clear up some of the
matters to which the District Attorney called your attention. I know it is pretty nigh hopeless in times of war

ROGER BALDWIN

and hysteria to get across to any substantial body of people, the view of an out and out heretic like myself. I know that as far as my principles are concerned, they seem to be utterly impractical—mere moon-shine. They are not the views that work in the world today. I fully realize that. But I fully believe that they are the views which are going to guide in the future.

"Having arrived at the state of mind in which those views mean the dearest things in life to me, I cannot consistently, with self-respect, do other than I have, namely, to deliberately violate an act which seems to me to be a denial of everything which ideally and in practice I hold sacred."

Such was the conclusion of his memorable speech. The judge looked at the straight young figure before him and remarked, "It may often be that a man or a woman has greater foresight than the masses of the people. And it may be that in the history of things, he who seems to be wrong today, may be right tomorrow. But with these possible, idealistic and academic speculations a court has nothing to do." Whereupon he sentenced Baldwin to a year in jail.

Federal marshals took him through the streets to a Newark penitentiary while the people of that city were celebrating Armistice Day with much confetti and blowing of horns. "The war was over for them," says Baldwin with a grin, "but it was just beginning for me."

As a matter of fact the closing of that jail door was the logical end of a long spiritual journey that began for Baldwin when he came to New York as this country entered the War. From then on he had given all his time, without other compensation than his expenses, for the preservation of civil liberties. Whereas before he had been interested in municipal reform and social welfare work, now he was an out-and-out pacifist and a philosophical anarchist. And being Roger Baldwin, he took no pains to hide his views from the world. As Director of the National Civil Liberties Bureau he and his comrades kept alive those faint sparks of freedom for the individual which were not stamped out by panic-stricken men. For, as is always the case, liberty was the first of the War's great casualties; and rare and courageous indeed were her handful of defenders. So very naturally Baldwin was hated and spied upon by that great army which skulked behind the lines and did all in their power to make life miserable for the heretics.

One day during his absence the office of the Civil Liberties Bureau, which was an offshoot of the American Union Against Militarism, was entered by that notorious Red-baiter, Archibald Stevenson; desks and files were rifled and a great mass of the Bureau's correspondence removed. One of Baldwin's friends who happened to drop in to solicit his aid for a pacifist office which had also just been raided without a warrant or any semblance of legality, found a cordon of police stretched along the corridor and so many bluecoats about the lower floors that the scene looked like nothing so much as a police department field day. Undeterred, the visitor stuck his nose inside the suspect quarters. There, surrounded by a group of zealous plainclothes agents, was Baldwin, busily pulling open drawers and doing his best to make everything convenient for the searchers after something terrible (which, of course, was never found). Catching sight of a familiar, if bewildered face, Roger looked up cheerfully and called out, unperturbed, "Hello ———, come on in. I'm being raided!" One of the raiders, incidentally, was a college classmate, and after the raid the two went out to lunch together to talk over old (and new) times.

As soon as Baldwin received notice that he would be called

for the last draft, he made up his mind as to his stand. Resigning his directorship of the Bureau in order not to interfere with the work of that organization because of his personal views, he went down to the Tombs to take his medicine.

Baldwin is blessed with a happy temperament. He can see humor in situations that would make the average man develop a full-sized martyr complex. And when he talks about his prison experiences today, it is with a reminiscent smile.

While he was awaiting sentence in the Tombs, he was allowed to go out in the company of Federal men and walk along Park Row. The agents were friendly. They admired the courage of the man and had a sneaking fondness for drawing him out along his rebel lines. But there came a strange agent one day bearing handcuffs and a brief authority. He was a stickler for rules and insisted that when taken out the prisoner be handcuffed. Baldwin suggested mildly that he knew lots of folks along Park Row and Nassau Street who might be a bit shocked to see him lugged along manacled to a keeper. But the man was obdurate. Also he was a little fellow, scarcely coming up to Roger's shoulder. So Baldwin said, "All right, come along with the handcuffs," and no sooner had they arrived on the street than Roger fell into his usual swinging stride, literally dragging the guard off his feet, so that passers-by took it for granted the good-looking fellow was taking a desperado to jail.

As soon as he found his way about the Newark penitentiary, Baldwin's organizing instincts came to the fore. Before many months he had made friends with his fellow-convicts and had organized a welfare body among the prisoners. He is a cracker-jack cook, as those who have visited his New Jersey camp will testify, and he soon made himself very much at home in the penitentiary's kitchen. The Warden there was a Sinn Feiner, who had an undying hatred for England, and no particular love for a war which involved us in a British alliance. He and Baldwin soon got chummy.

Men who were in jail with Baldwin have a way, nowadays, of dropping in on him to talk over the old days. Such a one, an expert pickpocket, arrived one day in Roger's office disgustedly twirling an obviously brass watch by a chain. He solemnly informed Baldwin that "a feller oughta be arrested for carrying around a phony ticker like this." He had extracted it from the pocket of a fellow passenger on his way over from New Jersey, and it was intended as a gift for Roger!

When the authorities higher up found how thoroughly Baldwin was organizing the convicts, they promptly removed him to the State Penitentiary at Caldwell, New Jersey. As penitentiaries go, this is not such a bad place, and Roger worked contentedly enough on the prison farm. He has a real love for soil and is happiest, it would seem, when he is digging down into roots. A number of his friends from New York who went out to see him, came upon him in his overalls beaming and begrimed, and anxious for the latest word as to radical activities in town. Suddenly an expression of dismay came over Roger's face. He shook hands all around, then set off on a dead run for the cell block. Over his shoulder he called out, "I nearly got locked out the other day, and I can't afford to have that happen again."

But let no one think that he received any unusual privileges or favors. He served nine months of his term, with time off for good conduct, asking no exceptional consideration. He served with his head up and the spiritual contentment that a man has when he feels he has done a good job. And in his strong person there was contained that spiritual fire which warmed the hearts of lovers of liberty the country over. Today the American Civil Liberties Union which was, and is still, so largely Roger Baldwin, has won the respect of multitudes of intelligent men and women. Its members are found in the forefront of every battle for the underdog, and it has many an important legal victory to its credit. But in those days, while its former director was digging in the penitentiary garden, what is now the Civil Liberties Union was but a small band of courageous people who fought the good fight under Baldwin's leadership.

There was nothing about the man's early environment and education to indicate the strong Left drift which he was later to take. He was born in the fashionable suburb, Wellesley Hills, Massachusetts, in 1884. His father was a manufacturer, inclined to political liberalism and the reading of the works of Robert Ingersoll. The family were Unitarians. Roger went to the public school in the small community, and then to Harvard, where he received his B.A. degree in three years and his M.A. a year later. He was not conspicuous among the few rebel undergraduates which staid Harvard has a way of sheltering. His interests were drawn to social service work, music, and much hiking and reading. When he left Harvard he had no definite intention of what to do.

After his return from a year abroad with his family, a friend in St. Louis wrote suggesting that there was a job to his liking in that mid-western city. He went out to St. Louis and promptly fell in love with the countryside beyond the smoke-hung city. It was this, he says, as well as greater personal independence in the West, which led him to take the position as head of a large neighborhood house in a congested district. But just one job was not enough to consume all his energy. He took charge of the teaching of sociology at Washington University and, a year after his arrival, he was appointed Chief Probation Officer of the Juvenile Court of St. Louis.

From 1908 until 1910, he was also Secretary of the National Probation Association. Thus he was busy with lectures in the University, with investigating cases of neglected or delinquent children, and with the supervision of some 1,500 boys and girls under the Court's care. He had a staunch ally in Judge George Williams, and the two of them soon made probation work in St. Louis a national standard for social service.

At the age of twenty-five he had ten people working under him, and politicians in the Missouri Legislature began to look askance at his activity. Here was a youngster who was raising hob with political traditions and actually doing the work which he was being paid for. One day a bill was introduced into the Legislature to the effect that probation officers must be over twenty-five years of age. Roger grinned when he read the bill. He knew it was generally supposed that he was younger than twenty-five, and that this was an attempt to throw him out. Fortunately he could show a birth certificate that put him just over the age limit, and from then on he made things uncomfortable for grafting politicians and reactionary legislators.

It was the fiery Emma Goldman who gave Baldwin his introductory lessons in revolutionary radicalism. "When I first heard her speak in St. Louis," he said, "I knew that here was a champion for the things which mattered most to me. The more I saw of poverty and distress—and believe me I saw plenty of it—the more I became convinced that social work alone was not enough. I became at heart a revolutionist, though continuing to work at practical tasks of reform."

In 1910 a group of liberal professional and business men—the progressive element in St. Louis of which the city is justly proud—asked Baldwin to form a City Club and to become Secretary of the Civic League of St. Louis. He had for his backers a board consisting, for the most part, of business men and lawyers who were tired of the crooked politics which had dominated the town, and were anxious for a general house-cleaning. Roger went to work immediately. His duties brought him in contact with practically every phase of local and state politics. In the city his group succeeded in getting through a new charter with popular control through the initiative and referendum. Oddly enough, this latter instrument, so largely devised by Baldwin, whose defense of the Negro is one of his outstanding characteristics, was used by the voters at once to put through a measure segregating the Negroes of St. Louis! Later on the Supreme Court decided that segregation was unconstitutional, but the incident did not tend to strengthen Roger's belief in the workings of political democracy.

It was a very busy young man who read the first dispatches from overseas, telling of the marching of troops through Belgium. When he heard that some other young men in Great Britain were refusing to take arms on the grounds of being conscientious objectors, he was at once sympathetic. Even then he felt that he, too, could have nothing to do with a blood-letting mess. When it became evident that the United States was going into the war, he wrote to Paul Kellogg, editor of *The Survey,* offering his services to help defend objectors and civil liberties. At once Kellogg and others then in the pacifist camp asked him to come on to New York and take charge of the work of the American Union Against Militarism. There were some noted names on the Union's letterhead, such as Eastman, Pinchot, Lovejoy, and Villard, but there was no one to do the day-in and day-out detailed work of the fight against conscription. Impetuously, Baldwin dropped everything, definitely turned his back on the world of social work, and threw in his lot with the rebels. His time was now taken up with trips between New York and Washington, with arranging meetings of protest and doing all in his power to stop the business of forcing men to take up arms. The National Civil Liberties Bureau was the answer to the protest of thousands whose rights were being violated by the war-mongers. That was in 1917, and the Executive Committee with many of its original members still meets every Monday, rain or shine, to consult with Baldwin and Forrest Bailey, his co-director, as to the state of Liberty in this domain.

Following his imprisonment, Baldwin did not return immediately to the Bureau. He felt that he had need of first-hand labor contacts, and for a while he went adventuring. He carried a hod; he mixed concrete; at one time he worked nine hours a night in Herculaneum, Missouri, in the heat of a lead smelter for the munificent sum of three dollars. He took out a card in the I. W. W. and at one time belonged to the Cooks and Waiters Union of the A. F. of L. He was active around headquarters in the great steel strike where Foster sat with his hat tilted back directing the struggle. Baldwin is proud of the fact that he could work his way around the country at manual labor. He mixed with a pretty rough bunch, far removed from the cushioned lives of his former friends, and his experiences in the labor world have given him a certain bluntness of speech which was unknown in the St. Louis days.

His function in life is that of the energetic executive who, unlike most executives in the commercial world, is willing to do a big share of the work himself. Even so, he has not escaped strenuous criticism from friends to the effect that he tends at times to be a bit dominating and hard-boiled. Quick on the trigger, he is sometimes—though not characteristically— impatient with those whose minds must move more slowly. The strangest assortment of people come in and out of his office. No one can keep track of the number of telephone calls that he receives, and at one time it appeared that he was a driving force of practically every committee around New York that was struggling for some measure of freedom. Now he devotes all his time to the work of the Civil Liberties Union, and a small committee very dear to his heart called the International Committee for Political Prisoners. This organization has its difficulties. Foreign governments even though they be proletarian, have a way of resenting the intrusion of any outside influences which might liberate their political prisoners. As a consequence Baldwin in Fascist Italy and Baldwin in Soviet Russia, through both of which countries he has traveled extensively, is not always a welcome guest. He is quite upset at seeing folk put behind bars for their opinions, and to dignified authorities he says so in no uncertain terms.

For a man who is constantly in the public eye Baldwin at heart is strangely indifferent to public affairs. He cares little for meetings and conferences, and yet he is constantly going to them. He does it because there are not enough people of his sort to go around, and when you are a Baldwin from Massachusetts, once your conscience is stirred, there is no stopping you.

Those who know him best know that Baldwin's Utopia would be life in his camp alongside the quiet little New Jersey stream where he goes week-ends, with some good reading matter, and a few friends who can leave the world of affairs behind them. He is not at all concerned with things—hates to be cluttered up, and sincerely loves the simple life which so many liberals praise and so few pursue. He loves nature with the poetic passion of an artist, and knows bird life more comprehensively and intimately than many an instructor in ornithology.

He moves easily through the two contrasting lives of our capitalist system, and has devoted friends in both camps. To be sure, he has his enemies and plenty of them. He is an uncomfortable man to have around if you are thinking up some kind of new skull-duggery for the oppressed. For he is as uncompromising after he is aroused as the judge who sentenced him admitted when he said: "I am concerned only with your perfectly definite, frank statements that you decline to take a step which the law provides. I am directing my mind solely to the indictment to which you plead guilty. You are entirely right. There can be no compromise. There can be neither compromise by you as the defendant, as you say, because you don't wish to compromise. Nor can there be compromise by the Court, which, for the moment, represents organized society as we understand it in this Republic. He who disobeys the law, knowing that he does so, with the intelligence that you possess, must, as you are, be prepared to take the consequences."

Changing the Mind of a Nation

CARRIE CHAPMAN CATT

IT WAS Sunday afternoon in the library of Mrs. Catt's home at New Rochelle, New York. Through many windows a garden of perennials in full bloom invited the eye. Many of the flowers are strangers here, sent by devoted friends in other countries, so that her garden contains the flowers of Iceland, Norway, Czechoslovakia, Holland, and other lands in other continents where she is well known and loved. A flock of birds hovered around the bird bath on the lawn. From the height on which the house stands one looked down on the tops of green trees which stretched away to the horizon.

Inside the walls were lined with books to the ceiling. There were a few pictures and documents under glass. A large flat desk with a swing chair before it, roomy and comfortable furniture covered with green velvet or deep rose, flowers everywhere, gave to the green quiet of the room the pleasant air of being lived in by somebody who worked, liked comfort, and read books hot off the press by the carload.

A group of friends were having after-dinner coffee and discussing the recent League of Women Voters Honor Roll, the list of women prominent in gaining votes for women in this country. Some thought it was good and some thought it was bad. Finally somebody asked Mrs. Catt what she thought about it.

"Well," she began in her deliberate way, as usual at the very beginning, "long before any of you were born. . . ."

She went down the list. She knew them all, those who were gone before she came as well as those she had campaigned with. She told what this one did in Oregon and that one in Louisiana or Massachusetts, how one met a crisis in Kansas in 1894 and another stepped into the breach in New York in 1917. When she had commented on the last name on the list, she waited a moment, then resumed with a change of manner.

"If I had been born in Turkey, I would have worn trousers and a veil, and sat around on cushions on the floor without having to think. Presently a man would have come along and said, 'Come out of that harem!' and I would have said, 'Yes, I'll come!'

"Then he would have said, 'Take off that veil and those trousers and put on a hat and a short skirt!' and I would have said, 'All right, I'll take them off and put them on!'

"Then he would have said, 'It's about time you got up a parade and told the world what has happened to you!' and I would have said, 'Yes, I'll do that,' and I would have marched in the parade, and after, I would have got up on a soap box and said, 'Ladies and gentlemen, harems and veils and trousers are no longer respectable in Turkey. From now on, women have got to be up to date and intelligent and do our part in helping run this country. I thank you!' And there would have been loud applause.

"But since I wasn't born in Turkey, and instead in a country that fondly imagines itself to be the most liberal and progressive in the world, I had to spend thirty years of my life fighting tooth and nail, as women had been fighting years before I was born, to win an obvious and elementary measure of justice.

"There is no country in the world where women have had such a desperate struggle to win economic and political rights

CARRIE CHAPMAN CATT

as they have had in this country. In Russia, in Germany, in part of the British Empire, these rights have been conferred almost unasked. In the United States it was a war to a finish and it took seventy years."

There was a gleam in the speaker's eye and the old ring in her voice. Some of us thought of the book she published after the vote was won, *Politics and Woman Suffrage,* in which she analysed the extraordinary opposition to the movement.

Carrie Lane in a way was a nonconformist from the first. She was born in Wisconsin, moved with her family to Iowa when she was seven years old, and was brought up on a farm near Charles City. Her parents had the idea that girls in infancy should be seen and not heard, but this was imperfectly conveyed to their daughter. She was first in war and first in peace in the district school. When her brother Charles chased her with a snake, she caught a snake and chased him, and although he was three years older than she was, he recognized the grim purpose in her blue eyes and ran.

She read Bob Ingersoll before she went to high school. She taught a country school to earn money to go to college, and for light reading perused Darwin's *Origin of Species.* She earned her way through Iowa State College at Ames, washing dishes at nine cents an hour the first year, and as Assistant Librarian in the college library after that at ten cents an hour. She wanted first to be a doctor, then decided to study law. After graduation in 1880, she went into a lawyer's office to assist and read law in preparation for a course in a law school.

She was offered the principalship of the High School in Mason City, Iowa, and afterwards was the first woman to serve as Superintendent of Schools there. Then she married Leo Chapman, owner and editor of the Mason City *Republican.*

A bill was pending in the Iowa Legislature giving municipal

suffrage to women. This was in 1885, the year she married. Young Mrs. Chapman quite independently organized a small group of friends to canvass Mason City, asking every woman to sign a petition in favor of the bill. Less than a dozen declined. The appearance of this remarkable petition out of a clear sky in a town where there was no suffrage club astounded the state suffrage association. As a result, she was invited to come as a delegate to the next state suffrage convention, where she met Lucy Stone and established her first contact with the organized movement.

Shortly afterward, Mr. Chapman died and the young widow engaged in journalism in San Francisco for a year. This year was a critical experience. She discovered that women had a hard row to hoe competing with men in the business world. It was bad if they were homely and it was worse if they were good looking.

In 1887 she came back to Iowa and began lecturing. She had two ideas in mind. One was to earn a precarious living, the other was to begin to change people's minds about woman's function in society. Of course the leaders of the suffrage movement in Iowa—and it was well organized there—seized upon her. She did her first work as an organizer for the state suffrage association that year, and she never got out of harness till August 26, 1920, when Secretary of State Bainbridge Colby proclaimed the Nineteenth Amendment a part of the Constitution of the United States.

The story of her steady ascent in a dozen years from a humble organizer in a rural state to the leadership of the movement is picturesque enough. In 1890 she was of enough importance as a speaker to be invited to the national suffrage convention in Washington, D. C., where she made her maiden speech from the national platform. She was paid $100 for expenses and speech, which she immediately turned over to the fund for the pending campaign in South Dakota. Here in Washington she saw for the first time all the leaders of the cause assembled on the same platform, for it was the year when the two national suffrage societies combined. Elizabeth Cady Stanton, Susan B. Anthony, Lucy Stone, Julia Ward Howe, made a distinguished group, women famous on both sides of the Atlantic, and Carrie Chapman's heart beat high as she beheld them greeting each other, laughing at droll stories, pointing out familiar faces in the gathering audience.

But the leaders were old. (There was a great celebration of Susan B. Anthony's seventieth birthday.) Gray heads predominated in the seats of the delegates. There was that campaign coming on in the summer in South Dakota. Mrs. Stanton was sailing for England. Mrs. Stanton was always sailing for England right after a convention. Her campaigning days were over. She was concerned more nowadays with lambasting the church than with getting votes for women. Lucy Stone's gallant spirit was still willing but her body was breaking. Julia Ward Howe was a name to conjure with, but about as much good as Ralph Waldo Emerson for South Dakota. It would be better to let her stay in Boston, and have the campaigners get their audiences out on the prairies to singing "John Brown's Body," and when they were well warmed up tell them the woman who wrote the words was a good suffragist. It would get more votes than Julia ever could herself.

But there was Miss Anthony. She was seventy years old, but she was going out to lead the campaign in South Dakota. She was still as straight as a lath and people would listen to her homely, pungent, inimitable sentences as long as she would talk, and she would talk till she dropped. She was warned that she was too old for South Dakota. "Better lose me than lose a state," she replied.

Young Mrs. Chapman went back from that convention with a troubled mind. In June she went out to Seattle and was married to George W. Catt, a rising young hydraulic engineer on the Pacific Coast. It was agreed that she should be free to go into the South Dakota campaign that summer, and she went.

It was her first referendum campaign. To this day she winces at the recollection of its bleak and grinding tragedy. Drought had burned up the crops of the new settlers. Their animals were thin and hungry. The boom had collapsed. There was no money. Despair haunted the plains.

The Farmers' Alliance and the Knights of Labor had urged Miss Anthony to come in person to conduct the campaign and had promised to support the suffrage amendment "with all their strength." When she got out there, they had decided not to support it. Mrs. Catt was assigned a section of the state to cover and went at it alone. There were long rides in the springless farm wagons, clouds of dust, meetings in country school houses attended by women and children after a long day in the fields under a scorching sun, nights in crude board cabins where the guest shared the family bedrooms, altogether a miserable business for a bride who had a charming fresh little bungalow and a sympathetic husband over in Seattle.

For weeks she kept at it. Miss Anthony told the young workers there might be no money to pay even their expenses and that those who wished might go home. Some went. Mrs. Catt stayed. In November the suffrage amendment was defeated and she returned home. On the train, soon afterward, on her way east with her husband, she was taken ill and had to stop at San Francisco where she lay at the point of death for some time with typhoid fever contracted in South Dakota.

But this experience made a raw recruit into a new leader.

Never again did Mrs. Catt play with all the cards stacked against her. She started at building up a working organization in all the states where there were possibilities of success. She became chairman of a new Committee on Organization in the National American Suffrage Association in 1894, advocated and carried the idea of having conventions of the national association in alternate years in leading cities throughout the country instead of invariably in Washington, and in 1894, with Miss Anthony, made a speaking tour of the Solid South in preparation for a convention in a southern city, Atlanta.

Campaign followed campaign, with a lonely victory in Colorado, 1893, then one in Idaho, 1896. Wyoming and Utah were admitted to statehood with woman suffrage in their constitutions. Elsewhere it settled down to a nibbling for school suffrage, municipal or bond suffrage, with here and there a state referendum defeat for a full suffrage amendment. But the suffrage forces were growing with every defeat.

When Miss Anthony was eighty years old, she retired from the presidency of the national association, choosing Mrs. Catt as her successor. Mrs. Catt had been the directing energy for several years, and closely associated with her had been Mary Garrett Hay, Secretary of the Organization Committee.

Four years of grilling work as President of the National American Woman Suffrage Association followed. The Spanish-American war like every war ushered in years of dead reaction and depression, spiritual and physical. But there was no pause in Mrs. Catt's creative energy. In 1902 she called a conference in Washington, with foreign suffragists, to consider forming an international association, and in 1904 the first Congress of the International Woman Suffrage Alliance was held in Berlin, at which time Mrs. Catt was unanimously elected President. She continued in that office up to the year

1922 when she was with great reluctance permitted to resign from active leadership of the Alliance.

In 1904 failing health and personal disaster in the illness and later the death of her husband compelled Mrs. Catt to retire from the presidency of the National American Woman Suffrage Association. Fourteen years of continuous mental and physical strain had taken their toll. She left the organization with money in the treasury and workers in the field and a courageous and disciplined membership. She had carried it out of the age of propaganda and into the age of political strategy.

At this time she was living in New York; she had been there since 1892. With the release from the demands of the national presidency she had time to ponder the case of the metropolis, and the Empire State. It was not an exhilarating subject to dwell upon. Without carrying New York City, no suffrage campaign could carry the state. Without carrying New York state, no campaign throughout the country for a Federal Amendment stood the slightest chance. The old enemies, Tammany and the up-state Republican machine, with eyes riveted on each other and both their backs turned on her, stood squarely in the way.

Tired and full of trouble as she was, the sight of those two self-absorbed obstacles to progress acted as a counter-irritant. Twenty-two years had passed since she had secured that petition for municipal suffrage signed by all but ten women of Mason City. Patiently she turned to the project of lining up the women of Greater New York, a somewhat larger job, for the attack on Albany.

The first move was to combine the suffrage clubs in the Interurban Council of Woman Suffrage Clubs of Greater New York. The next was to organize every Assembly District in the five boroughs. Then in October, 1909, she executed one of those brilliant demonstrations of strength for which she is noted. She called a woman suffrage convention which met in Carnegie Hall, at which 800 regularly elected delegates were seated, representing *every voting precinct in Greater New York*. At this meeting, the old suffrage clubs voted to merge in the Woman Suffrage Party of New York.

The new organization was modelled exactly after the dominant political parties in order to measure swords with them, and it had but one plank in its platform. The change in the attitude of New York politicians was marvellous. No one of them would have dreamed of getting up a political convention of that scope in Greater New York. The press rushed to the headquarters of the party, and kept right on rushing for the following eight years, when the party, having achieved its end, disbanded.

The party idea spread within two years all over the country, and the national association adopted it as a campaign measure. But the strain of organizing the New York party hastened a complete breakdown of Mrs. Catt's health. By 1911 she had recovered sufficiently to go to Stockholm to attend the Congress of the International Suffrage Alliance as its President, and afterward to start on a trip around the world. This trip was designed to be a relaxation for a convalescent, but the following excerpt from a letter dated South Africa, September 30, 1911, would have astonished the physician who sent her abroad:

"I have been in South Africa two months. I have made 25 speeches, attended 6 formal receptions, 10 formal luncheons, at least 20 informal ones, numberless teas; lunched three times with wives of Cabinet Ministers, spent 8 nights on an insufferable sleeping car, visited diamond mines, ostrich, goat, sheep, cattle, fruit and wine farms; have received many reporters, callers, etc., and had 3 picnics; spent 5 days at Victoria Falls on each of which I walked to the point of exhaustion; visited 7 missionaries and 3 zoos, read 9 octavo books on the history and conditions of South Africa. I have had a good many letters to write as we close our labors with a suffrage convention, National, the first in South Africa, which I am working up. I have not been so well in years."

She returned home in November, 1912, just as Oregon, Arizona and Kansas had won the vote, a glorious homecoming. There was a mass meeting in Carnegie Hall with a pageant to welcome her. She was so emaciated that her clothes had to be pinned on, but her spirits were in fine fettle, and she was at once swept into the leadership of the oncoming fight for a suffrage referendum in New York State.

In the midst of that crucial struggle, a dramatic incident ushered in the beginning of the end. "Frank Leslie," now an aged and almost forgotten woman, died and left her estate of upwards of $2,000,000 to Mrs. Catt, to be used as she thought best for the cause of woman suffrage. About half of the estate vanished in commissions, lawyers' fees, contests of fraudulent claims, etc., but "Frank Leslie" did manage finally to get $977,000 across to Mrs. Catt of the fortune she had earned in the publishing business.

It took two and a half years to settle the lawsuits, and the final report of the Leslie Commission, in 1929, in that section which deals with fraudulent claims on the estate, beats any detective story. The money became available in March, 1917, just when our entry into the World War impended, and the Liberty Bond orators were combing the country for funds for the Government. The suffrage cause would have fared hard but for "Frank Leslie," and but for her the Federal Amendment might have run a far longer course than it did run, before it was anchored in the Constitution.

The Woman's Party, with its program of holding the party in power responsible for the delay of a Federal Suffrage Amendment, provided an outlet for those whose zeal demanded a militant attitude. Its unerring sense of the value of publicity was its chief contribution to the cause. The fact that its doctrinaire program led it more than once to campaign against old and prominent supporters of the suffrage cause, seeking reelection to Congress, merely because these candidates were Democrats was something which a lot of explaining never made clear to the average voter. Mrs. Catt and the large majority of suffragists had no sympathy with this program, feeling that suffrage could not successfully be made a party issue. Certainly the end justified her judgment.

The three years from 1917 to 1920, during which she conducted first the drive on Congress to submit the Amendment, and second the drive on the state legislatures to ratify it, are the climactic years of Mrs. Catt's life. She lived on trains, in hotels, in conferences. She probably knew more governors, legislators and other public men than did any other person in the country. No request of hers was ever denied by President Wilson, and that too when he was carrying the burden of the War and the subsequent peace negotiations. Doubtless one reason she always got an appointment to meet the President when she asked for it was that she always stated for exactly how many minutes she would require his attention, and never overstayed her time.

At last, in August, 1920, after blistering weeks in the hot town of Nashville, Tennessee, she led the final assault of the seventy years' war. It was spectacular enough. The full story never has been told and probably never will be. The Tennessee Legislature was bitterly divided and harassed by an unprecedented barrage of propaganda for and against ratification of the Federal Amendment granting woman suffrage. Thirty-five states had already ratified; thirty-six were necessary in order to write the amendment to the Federal Constitution.

A presidential election was coming on that fall and if women were to vote in it Tennessee must ratify at once. The Tennessee suffragists were well organized and on their mettle. The National Committees of the Republican and Democratic Parties and the two candidates for the Presidency urged ratification. President Wilson took a hand, sending repeated exhortations to favorable action. On the other hand, the Antis flocked from near and far and lobbied with the energy of despair, their backs finally to the wall.

At last, 36 members of the Legislature rose up in the night and fled over into Alabama in the effort to destroy a quorum and block final formalities. But the rest of the legislators voted without the fugitives, and on August 26, 1920, Secretary of State Colby in Washington received the Tennessee ratification and immediately proclaimed the suffrage amendment part of the Constitution of the United States.

Then what a shout of glory went up all over the country, what bell ringing, what jubilation, what profound emotion words could not convey! Mrs. Catt, more dead than alive, had but one desire, to get back to her farm and its sleeping porch on the slope of a beautiful valley in Westchester County, N. Y. But New York, the Empire State, a citizen of which she was, had no idea of letting a great Conqueror pass through Manhattan like a thief in the night.

When she got off the train at the Pennsylvania Station, a crowd was waiting. There was the Governor, Al Smith, there were representatives of the National Committees of the political parties, there were all the "Old Guard" with the old banners, antiquated now, there was the 71st Regiment Band,

and amid flowers, deputations, congratulations, wild excitement, the last suffrage parade marched through the streets of New York to the Waldorf-Astoria where a victory celebration was held.

And that is where most people would have been glad to stop work. A well-known woman said recently, "Carrie Chapman Catt is the only person I know anything about who as soon as she had 'finished her career' started right in on a new job."

Not only that, but she started with a new zest. The vote for women never was anything but a tool to work with to her. She begrudged the precious years spent in gaining it. She was glad she could have a little time at last to engage directly with the chief menace of civilization and foe of the human race—war.

Was it hope for her beloved cause of women's freedom that led Mrs. Catt, zealous campaigner against war, to swallow the liberal interpretation of the late conflict and swing into line? Many a Jew backed the War not only from loyalty to the crusade as proclaimed by President Wilson but through a desire to further racial progress by demonstrating his people's capacity to aid the nation powerfully in a crisis. Many a Negro did the same. And women leaders were not wanting who frankly saw in the War the chance for which they had been longing. At any rate, Mrs. Catt accepted a post of importance in the Women's Committee of the Council for National Defense. With her, however, mental disarmament after the War began at home, and has proceeded apace.

The Conference on the Cause and Cure of War which she called in Washington in 1926, which has met each succeeding year, which now comprises delegates from eleven of the largest women's organizations in the country and has their chief officers on its Board, of which she is the General Chairman, represents the latest phase of Mrs. Catt's activities. To the work of the conference she brings the contacts and experiences of her full life, and in it she satisfies that inexorable and ceaseless demand of her soul for something worthy of its highest endeavor.

For Mrs. Catt is not content with having changed the mind of this country about votes for women. Nor would she be content should she live to see war abolished. She would want to keep right on till the world were wholly decent. Yet it might bore her then. Anyway, once when Mary Garrett Hay was feeling low in her spirits and inclined to pity the two of them as lifelong slaves and drudges, Mrs. Catt remarked, "Well, Mollie, if we hadn't done what we did, what *would* we have done?"

Economist of Tomorrow

PAUL DOUGLAS

HOW can a professor of economics be a mystic? How can one immersed for years on end in jungles of scaly statistics, festooned with twisted graph-vines, dwell happily on the "contagious power of good-will?" How can a man lost in a swiftly growing maze of towering white limestone Gothic buildings, gifts of the pride of enormous wealth, retain his ardent championship of underpaid wage workers? And— how can the brilliant champion of Soviet Russia remain on the faculty of John D. Rockefeller's university?

The answer to all these questions is simply Paul H. Douglas, who stands out like a landmark above the contemporary run of professors of economics. John R. Commons, light of an earlier day, is growing old and weary. Richard T. Ely, since he made a million (more or less) in real estate, has devoted years proving to cynical undergraduates that there is no such thing as unearned increment. Carver is an analyst of the past—let posterity shift for itself at the hands of benevolent wealth!

But Douglas is looked upon, both by labor and by seekers after justice, as the man who combines a scientist's technical skill with the burning spiritual passion of a mystic—as today's genuine prophet of the ancient creed "Peace on earth, good-will toward men."

It was hard to locate Douglas. In the University of Chicago's amazing campus, which changes overnight like a great white cloud billowing up into new peaks and hollows under a driving sun, he was hiding as in a bomb-proof shelter, evading calls and telephones to complete imperative research on the tabulation of pay-rolls.

Great holes are being dug across college lawns that might have been green, providing a tunnel for a new underground central heating project; limestone blocks, terra cotta tiles, brick and sand are piled up in every direction taking shape, even while one looks, as new towered barracks to house schools of infinitely diversified and specialized learning. Summer school students find their classrooms suddenly heaved up on jack-screws and transported across streets and around corners, to make room for new memorials of great wealth.

This fabulously rich University of Chicago is becoming a labyrinth, a rabbit warren of savants. For many years its stationery proudly bore the words "Founded by John D. Rockefeller." It has taken those words off its letterheads. And to escape the suspicion of influence by the power of that name, it is leaning over a little backwards, in the effort to stand up straight.

This, perhaps, is one reason why a Socialist can fit into the picture so elaborately framed by a constant succession of gifts of millions. Douglas figures in the university as a pungent sauce, to put a little edge on the insipidity of wealth too easily obtained.

It had been twelve years since I first saw Douglas. Then he was professor of economics at Urbana, where the University of Illinois gathers in its tens of thousands from the broad rolling prairies. He was thin, Lincoln-like in his black angularity, and still more Lincoln-like in the mournfulness of his eyes and general appearance of being lost in a strange, sad world.

Ten years after, I had seen him as chairman of the annual

banquet of the Walt Whitman Fellowship. Never was there such a change. He cracked jokes and peanuts with equal facility and infused a note of jolly tolerance, which was sorely needed to savor the professional pessimism of Darrow and the cocky impertinence of callow poets eager for a little self-advertising by cheap disdain of the sage of Camden.

What caused the change? It would be interesting to know. Was Douglas so overjoyed and complacent with the result of the War? Did he feel that everything was for the best, in this best of all possible worlds, where starvation grips so many in hopeless toils and where the poison gas is already being brewed for the next war to end war?

After many telephone calls and a number of fruitless visits I ran him to earth in a strange new burrow, surrounded by a corps of students who were helping him unpack. He had been moved from his former nook in a building now being tossed casually across the street, and was about to be enshrined—of all places!—in an Oriental Museum. He left his students to their task, to talk about his hobby—the Family Wage.

There is something pleasant, something spiritually stimulating in the attitude of these students toward him. He is not, one gathers, merely a pedant who instructs, or an examiner who marks papers. He is rather the captain of a band of adventurers essaying great deeds. It is a comradely deference they offer. And Douglas, the once cadaverous and doleful, who used to look awkward and ill at ease in company, has become jolly and almost plump. He looks straight in one's eyes. He presents the appearance of having so lost himself in a greater cause that he is always at home.

Perhaps it is because he has become a Quaker and attained serenity of soul in the company of that little band of Friends who meet over in Hull House. It was after the war that he joined the Quakers, having been brought up an Episcopalian. The doctrine of the Friends supplied the inward spiritual grace for the outward and visible form of his economic machinery.

"In the Quaker tenets," he said, "for the first time I realized the contagious power of good-will. If like a biologist, one views life as a struggle between bacteria, still one must admit that ill will is divisive and destructive, and good-will is uniting and constructive. The problem of life, then, is to increase the 'bacteria,' the infective centers of friendliness. It is not the approval of formulas but the radiating of good-will which is ultimately the creative power.

"This I believe to be the central doctrine taught by Christ: that this radiating of good-will makes one a participant in the creative processes of life."

Douglas is chary about technical religious phrases. He does not like to be called a mystic, nor to discuss the immanence of God as compared with the perception of his transcendence.

"Several years ago I did feel very intensely such religious implications," he said, "but in the last two years I am afraid that my enthusiastic zeal in these lines has steadily declined, although intellectually I am as convinced as ever. However, in such matters it is the spiritual rather than the intellectual concept which is the important thing.

"In brief, I do have great faith in the power of friendliness and good-will to touch other people and to change many of their attitudes. But I am more and more inclined to believe that this comes from within man himself rather than from forces outside. I believe the solution lies in the creation of a social environment which will give a material basis for the development of this human friendliness. That will be far more effective than the Tolstoyan appeal of a few individuals."

PAUL DOUGLAS

Feeling thus about good-will and its contagious power, Douglas is not particularly proud of his war record.

"I was at first, of course, strongly opposed to the War," he said, "but after the Brest-Litovsk treaty, I began to believe that Germany must be defeated. Still I did not volunteer for service. I became an adjuster of disputes for the Fleet Corporation.

"If Germany's brutality had horrified me, the graft I found here nauseated me. Contemptible little grabs, reaching up to high places in the government, such as graft on photographs and little percentages that mounted up to great sums, were receipted for by great names.

"I stopped some of the graft myself. In unsuccessful battling against other contracts, I was brought face to face with the extremely close tie-up of this petty thieving with noble political sentiment in exalted spheres, with staggering salaries for figureheads and bonuses that ran up into incredible totals. Peace as a philosophy seemed more than ever attractive. I began studying the Quakers. And I joined them."

This is a striking development of contemporary science— this up-surge of mysticism. After all, the central Quaker doctrine is the Inner Light. Fabre found that entomology led him into the presence of a supreme Creative Mind before which he bowed in awe. Josiah Royce and William James proclaim that the austere symbolism of mathematics requires a fundamental mystical faith. Now comes a professor of economics who finds the same experimentally true. It looks as though science has doomed materialism.

Douglas explains this. "In economics, it is necessary to be coldly scientific. The task I regard as most significant is the study I have been making for the past eight years of real wages in the United States. It is a comparison of money paid with its purchasing power. With that I rank my investigation of the relative effect of labor and capital upon production."

But having discovered these things, and made these charts, what shall be done with them?

Economics in its Greek original is a highly poetic word: the Law of the Home. "Real Wages" sounds like a dry subject; in reality it is the condensed history of all the pitiful, tragic, desperate struggles of a myriad mothers in homes that are supported by the labor of day to day struggles to keep enough bread and butter on the table and enough fire in the stove so that it will be possible to live.

Having then through this "coldly scientific" investigation ascertained the pathetic facts, is one to leave it at that? Are these results to be thrown casually into a pile or left neatly stored up in books for any who will to make use of them?

Here is where mystic and economist join, as steam vivifies the machinery which gives it purpose, and as the tables in an electrician's handbook of ohms and amperes provide the light that is shed upon a family circle.

This driving power of active and infectious good-will harnessed up to an actual knowledge of conditions prevailing in the homes of American workers, make Douglas a profoundly convinced and yet cheerfully optimistic non-violent revolutionist.

It is not the philosophy of despair which he propounds. It is not the doctrine of increasing misery on which he builds his faith in the ultimate Cooperative Commonwealth. It is on the philosophy of militant good-will, rebellious against conditions which thwart it and make of it a mockery.

In his hands the study of Real Wages becomes the chart of a sympathetic physician tabulating the rise and fall of the temperature of a beloved patient. No longer is economics the "dismal science"; it becomes rather the chronicling of the laboring of a pulse under the lash of a dread disease. To one deeply concerned in the sufferer's life and health, such tables of figures become vibrant and tense with desperate importance.

How can one preach good-will to a father striving to provide for a family on a wage insufficient to insure comfort or even decency? How can one proclaim war an evil to a worker who finds that in war-time his welfare is eagerly looked out for and his wounds healed, whereas in peace his industrial captains merely throw him wounded aside? And what is the use of preaching political democracy to men who have lost the right of any voice in the real business of life—the making of a living?

Douglas is not a slogan coiner. He is not a facile constructor of programs, like John Spargo, who could toss out at a moment's notice a mathematically precise time-schedule along which every proper revolution should proceed, and who grew furiously bitter with the Russians because their revolution ignored both his time-table and his track. Douglas deals only with actualities.

"My object in life," he said, "is to try to find out precisely what is: to work on concrete facts. The big necessity is to get an agreed basis of facts to which even those who differ as to remedies will subscribe, and then, on the basis of these facts to try and plan a course of action which will relieve the situation."

What proposal does he offer on which to build a concrete move for the betterment of things? His deepest interest, and to his mind the most important human question, is the Family Wage. Political issues are meaningless except as they bear on the dominant problem—the well-being of the man and woman with children. Democracy, either political or industrial, is only a means to an end—the security of the family.

Every home is a temple of the Incarnation; every family a Holy Family, in this religion of good-will, to which he brings his offering of the tables of wages as his sacrifice.

The fundamental idea of this proposal is to make the family, and not the individual worker, the unit of calculation on wages. To the basic needs of a man and his wife must be added an allowance for each dependent, and this is to be paid regularly to the wife and mother, to insure her ability to care for the children.

"I thought I had invented the plan," said Douglas, with a wry smile. "I thought that like Columbus I had discovered a new world, in the realm of economics. After it was all worked out, I found it was in full operation in France where four million workers live under it. England's Labor government is considering it with warm sympathy. Australia has enacted a law making it compulsory.

"How about this country? Well, in the state of Indiana I persuaded one corporation—Hapgood's canning company—to adopt the system. It has been in operation there for three years and seems to be giving complete satisfaction."

We shall hear more, much more about this Family Wage system. It removes one basic cause of the unemployment of men; it takes away the biggest cause for entry of women into industry; it transforms marriage from a terrible liability into an asset; it makes the advent of each child in a workingman's family an event to be expected with joy and confidence.

How would it work out? Something like this. Suppose there are 100 factories in a certain community. They employ, say, 100 workers apiece, or 10,000 in all. These workers would not have 30,000 children, as might be supposed from the accepted standard of a "family of five." They would have from 12,000 to 13,000. By actual count it is found that the average in any worker's family is 1.3 children dependent at any one time. The others are grown up and able to fend for themselves, or else are not yet born.

In this town, each dependent child would constitute a charge upon industry of $200 a year. That would mean a charge of $2,600,000 a year, divided among 100 firms.

Under the Family Wage system, each employer would pay into a central fund his proportion of this charge. His proportion would be based either on the relative number of men he employed, or his share of the total wage bill. If, for example, it were based on the number of men employed, each employer's share would be $260 per man per year, whether married or single.

This sum would be paid not to the man but to his wife, or the woman who cared for his dependent children. If a man were unmarried or were childless, he would not get this extra sum. That would go to the family which had more than the normal number of dependents.

But now, how could industry be persuaded to accept so high-minded a scheme? It should not be much more difficult than the successful campaign for accident insurance, or for old age pensions. The principle of it has already been recognized as in the income tax law which grants exemptions for each child and dependent.

Family Wage might be adopted voluntarily by agreement between employer and employed, as in France. It might be enforced by law, as in Australia. But in either case, the necessity for it must first be popularized and publicly accepted.

"The biggest step forward," says Douglas, "would be to have the churches adopt the Family Wage as the standard for paying their clergy. It is no new thing with them. Missionaries always have been paid under this system. From the beginning of the Wesleyan movement in England, the conferences paid extra allowances for children.

"Adoption of this system would enable the richer parishes to contribute directly to the well-being of poorer ones. It would abolish much of the scramble for highly paid pulpits.

"Already the teaching profession is adopting the Family
Wage. Wells College has it now. Bennington, the new wom-
en's college in Vermont, has pledged itself to adopt the plan."

The Family Wage system, Douglas believes, would take
from poverty its greatest curse. It would insure to the nation
an unbroken chain of contented homes where every child
would be welcome and would be provided for.

It might be objected that $200 a year is no heroic sum on
which to raise a child. Ask any mother, maintaining a family
on a laborer's pay, how great a difference an assured income
of 55 cents a day for each child makes! It would not only
be a difference in things bought; it would transform her whole
mental horizon. It is not poverty but the fear of it which
adds terror to the lot of the poor.

In the summer of 1927 Douglas went to Russia as a member
of the American Trade Union delegation to the Soviet Union.
James H. Maurer was chairman of the delegation. It is no
secret that Douglas wrote most of their report, which is a
powerful indictment of our government for stupidity in refusing to recognize the Soviet Union. It might be thought
that such a book as this would surely result in compulsory
retirement from the faculty of the Rockefeller University. Not
a bit of it. He was not even chided.

"What is your real opinion of Russia?" I asked.

"Our visit strengthened my faith in Socialism," he replied
instantly. "I had begun to doubt, before going there, whether
it would be possible to get production and savings under a
Socialist system. I found that the Russians are devoting as
large a proportion of their national income to the production
of further capital as does any capitalist society. They are
accumulating steadily the material basis for production.

"Work in Russia is going on at a good rate of speed. Abolition of luxury adds to the comfort of the working class. All

this is on the surface. But the big fact, the spiritual fact behind all this material evidence, is that there is a real community of belief, a national ideal and moral unity, which is the solid basis of the new Russia.

"In this community of ideals, there are three main facts. In the first place, close behind the city worker stands the cooperative life of the villages, which has been bred in them through many generations. City workers are nowhere very far removed from the farms.

"Second, they have really a new religion—the building up of a People's Society. It is the strong motive underlying their acts and attitudes.

"The third factor is that the government is very wise. It is careful not to put too heavy a strain upon their communistic faith. Two-thirds of the workers are actually working on a piece-rate basis. In the building trades, three-quarters of the workers are on this piece-rate basis, although it has been held that the building trades cannot be operated on such a basis. They make haste slowly toward their ideal; but they keep headed in that direction.

"We hear much in this country about the rigid system of the communist dictatorship. In Russia they are not so anxious about their political rights as some of us think they ought to be. Their real rights, that is their economic rights, are much better protected than in any other country.

"Thus no Russian worker can be discharged from employment without consent of his own representative. They are free from fear of unjustified dismissal, which constantly haunts workers elsewhere.

"Workers' representatives are also members of the governing bodies of the nation's industries, and help to determine policies. Managers of factories and workshops must be satisfactory to them. They are free to criticize factory administration at any time, and on any point. They fix by collective bargaining the pay and conditions of their work. Managers are compelled to explain major problems of the business to them. Their help is actively solicited in improving production. Mills, mines and natural resources of Russia are theirs, to make of them what they can.

"As production increases, they and the peasants receive the full product, without any deduction for rent or profits. There is no parasitical leisure class, to waste without earning, and to stir up envy."

Here you have the well-rounded basis of Douglas's belief. No co-operative enterprise can operate without the "co." Joint action, self-disciplined and mutually respectful, can come about only through some profound and mutually held faith. In Russia the object of this faith is known as the "People's Society." In earlier days it was known as the Kingdom of God, where the sovereign resided in each citizen.

I remember how, not so long ago, every Socialist mass meeting orator threw all his emphasis upon the class-struggle—no compromise—down-with-the-capitalist theme. Speeches bristled with long lists of horrors and wound up with impassioned appeals to the workers to throw off their chains and claim the world.

Douglas has a different appeal. He is just as thoroughly convinced of the impossibility of the capitalist system, just a little bit better versed in statistics of the iniquities of the profit system. But these do not sour and embitter him. He is interested in spreading the gospel of contagious friendliness, of infectious good-will, of the mystical peace that comes with communion with the spirit of Christ, as a means of healing all these woes.

His group of devoted students catches this spirit. Undergraduates go out into business. Graduate students go into teaching. Both ways the message spreads and spreads into a powerful impetus: "Friendliness is infectious. Good-will is catching. They will end the slavery of man to machinery and bring about a co-operative commonwealth, if we build up a fellowship based on fraternal humanity!"

"Wings For God's Chillun"

BURGHARDT DU BOIS

WILLIAM EDWARD BURGHARDT DU BOIS exemplifies all three conditions of the adage: "Some men are born great, some achieve greatness, and some have greatness thrust upon them." He had in him as a child the fundamentals of greatness; not the type that results from the pomp and trappings of kings, but the essential elements. Up there in that quaint Massachusetts town of Great Barrington where he was born, the little bronze boy, black-haired and beak-nosed, sensed early a difference as of barriers between himself and his white school-mates and braced himself to rise above them.

There really *is* an alchemy in mixture of bloods which makes a man this and not that. And in this lad the stubborn persistence of his half-Dutch mother, the logic and daring of his father's French ancestry and the fire and endurance inherent in some grandparent's dower of pure black blood made him what he is and has since become. He had the mind to perceive, the will to attempt and the tenacity to persist.

In an environment which, while it did not oppress black folk, certainly did not seek to advance them, the lonely, proud little boy yet glimpsed somehow worlds beyond his immediate ken to which education was the pathway. All about him were dark workingmen, artisans, servants—free, humble, and happy for all he knew. But he could not conceive of such a life for himself. It was in those days a notable achievement for a

Negro boy to accomplish high school; but "Willy" Du Bois, as his play-mates unbelievably called him, saw for himself college,—not any college but Harvard!—and beyond that fields and fields!

His father, Alfred Du Bois, handsome, visionary, charming and fickle vanished following the will o' the wisp of varied pursuits. He opened a barber-shop in another town, then drifted into the ministry, thence into silence and the little boy and his mother knew him no more. Mrs. Du Bois, a great-great-grandchild of "Conraet" Burghardt and his Bantu wife, turned her thoughts from her errant husband to center them on her brilliant son. She worked for him, she taught him the responsibility inherent in relationship, she let him work for her, she loved him, she chided him, she worshipped him. He owed her, he tells us, everything and when after his perfect high school commencement she lay down to unending slumber he knew he would not break his silent pact never to fail her expectations. Money was lacking to send him immediately to Harvard so he was sent to Fisk in Nashville. "To learn something of his own people," said the kindly troubled townsfolk, hardly knowing what to do with this fiery, inconsiderate lad whose destiny in the nature of things was surely lowly, but whose ambitions were so strangely high.

I do not think that "Willy" Du Bois in those days had any concept of the greatness and worth of his own racial group. He had only known the untamed sinews of his own heart and his firm belief in himself. He had in that self a natural well of pride which had kept his own head high,—but now of a sudden he espied and understood the *raison d'être* of that inherent pride. He came of a deathless group, he felt, which Antaean-like fell only to rise each time stronger. A group possessed of deeply-ingrained faults but possessed also of the qualities which "make and keep men great."

He saw that beauty could be dark and still be beauty. He had never envisaged such loveliness. Indeed he had never associated the idea of beauty with any but the cold pale folk of his native New England town. He had the eye to appreciate this new aspect. But more important he possessed too the understanding to perceive that the mere presence of more than half these boys and girls whom he was meeting with such delirious joy represented immeasurable patience, plodding, self-sacrifice on the part of parents who perhaps would not even live to see the fruition of their dreams. A race to cherish, to live for, perhaps to the point of self-immolation.

He was seventeen when he went to Fisk. The next eight or nine years were fraught with wonder. He completed the college course at Fisk, he took another A. B. at Harvard, he discovered that the Slater Fund would with reluctance bestow a fellowship on deserving young colored men to assist them to study in Germany. The reluctance of those trustees meant nothing to him. He had been penniless and accordingly self-reliant too long to be halted by anything so tenuous. So presently he found himself roaming the streets of London, adoring Paris and Vienna, thrilling to Rome and Berlin. He came back to America with a doctorate, started teaching at Wilberforce University in Ohio and in 1896 married there.

He was a very young man then, already distinguished though without the grave majesty which was later to become the insigne of his personality. But he was instinct with fire and vitality and dowered with an unquenchable hatred for injustice which thrust him forward and made him keen to be at the business, at any cost, of battling for the oppressed. For Du Bois, an instinctive aristocrat, arrogant, fiery, in earlier days even rash, has always been the defender of democracy. He cannot endure the enchaining of the slave. It galls him, it frets him. With his personality, his training, and that two-edged sword which is his intellect biting and cleaving its way through all problems, it is doubtful if he would ever himself have encountered the grosser forms of prejudice. But there were and are others not so luckily circumstanced. These he needs must champion. And if the unfortunates nearest him happen to be of his own blood and kind,—so much the better. So much more comprehendingly can he fight. But fight he must. He has been for twenty-five years America's great Intransigeant,—a man born to lead difficult causes.

One must be either deeply devoted to Du Bois and what he represents or be divorced from him completely. He cannot leave a negligible impression. For many seasons now he has been the center of controversy between staunch, admiring friends and irritated, baffled adversaries. For he can and often does irritate. A man as just, as logical and as often correct as he, is bound to abrade and sting before he heals. For this very reason his own people owe him an incalculable debt. In a group given too much to humility and deprecation the demands of this proud and fearless fighter are as from heaven. He has given wherever his name is known a new slant on the rights of man. He really believes they are for everybody and he writes down and pleads and cries his belief until those who withhold give way for very shame.

Du Bois left Wilberforce and went for a year to the University of Pennsylvania. Here at a salary of $600 he made a study of Philadelphia Negroes. Thence for twice that sum he went to Atlanta University where he remained for thirteen years, a teacher of sociology.

Here in the heart of the South he came really to know colored people and their problems. Here he taught,—more than the social sciences,—and wrought and wrote so that his name became known all over the country. Always he taught the futility of compromise, of the condonation of wrong. He demanded and urged his own to demand the whole loaf. Here he weathered the Atlanta Riot of 1905 and here he lost a son and gained a daughter.

When in 1910 he left Atlanta for New York to accept the editorship of *The Crisis,* official organ of the National Association for the Advancement of Colored People, he had already achieved greatness. He was at once the despair of all retroactives and the delight of all lovers of fair play; the challenge, the oriflamme for all oppressed struggling men, especially men of color. It was as though he said in flaming letters: "What you are I was; what I am, you may become."

His dear dream had been always to edit a paper. He had already written books, the Atlanta Studies, in numerous volumes and *The Souls of Black Folk* (which now after twenty-five years has the quality of a classic), and he had been co-editor of the little paper called *The Horizon,* casually and occasionally published. And now suddenly here was this supreme last chance to pour out his teeming heart and his unshakable beliefs and to couch them in language at which the world once it took notice must stare and gape and ponder and shake its head and stare and gape again. And sometimes both worlds of readers, white and black, were moved to tears.

Du Bois's forte is the creation of the literature of protest. He has been called a poet,—he is one; he is an instinctive *littérateur,* he is a scholar, he is a sociologist, he is a great finder of facts,—but all these qualities melt and fuse into a single molten stream when he is embarked on one of his holy jeremiads in the cause of liberty. In this, his peculiar and especial field, it is not exaggerating to say that he is outstripped by no one,— not even by Cicero or Demosthenes. He is like a man inspired, —actually just that. It is as though fires from above were breathed into him which he in turn transmutes into Homer's "winged words." He is like an angry prophet, "mystic, won-

derful,"—wielding his pen with the terrible keenness and
deftness with which mediaeval warriors were wont to thrust
and parry. The *preux Bayard* never downed a foe with more
sureness and prowess than Du Bois lets fly at the demons of
prejudice and injustice.

Only the heart of stone could hear unmoved the Litany
which he wrote after the Atlanta Riot:

"Straining at the armposts of Thy throne, we raise our
shackled hands and charge Thee, God, by the bones of our
stolen fathers, by the tears of our dead mothers,—surely
Thou, too, art not white, O Lord, a pale, bloodless, heartless thing!"

He has his foibles in writing. Perhaps he read Fitzgerald's
translation of the Rubaiyat at a too impressionable age and so
all unexpectedly he *will* capitalize abstract nouns. Or with a
sudden trite Spenserian touch in the midst of stately, most
purely classic periods he will dedicate an idea to the "Queen
of Faery,"—an irritating and provoking lapse. But then does
it matter? He is clean-cut and hard and impassioned and piti-
less of phrase for all the things that count. He has earned
the right to pursue a whimsy. It is as though a god, pausing in
his stride up the slopes of Olympus, should stoop to gather
bluebells.

The editorship of *The Crisis,*—still his after nearly twenty
years,—entails on its possessor more than the mere position of
editor. It has made him for almost a fifth of a century the outstanding interpreter of colored Americans to white Americans
and the discoverer of colored Americans to themselves. And
both these positions, obverse sides of the same medal, have entailed endless and unremitting responsibility which must long
since have been the despair of a man less intrinsically destined
to play the grand part.

There are those who say that Du Bois but for his interest in protest might have been a great novelist, a great poet. I do not believe that he could ever have mounted in those endeavors to greater heights than he has already scaled in the emprise that he has made specially his own. But I do believe that it was never his deliberate intention nor his ambition to be considered willynilly by white people as the leader of his group, or by Negroes themselves as their arbiter in certain trying and difficult divisions of ways. Yet both these offices have been loaded on his unwilling shoulders. The white section of America says: "According to the Du Bois School." On the other hand when a Marcus Garvey comes trailing chimeras before bedazzled eyes, colored men remark: "Why doesn't Du Bois say something?"

He has accepted it all with little complaint, with only an occasional murmur of weariness and with no self-pity. He has no time for that. For life has been too perpetually interesting. Perhaps his solitary plaint would center in the fact that the years have sped too fast, too terribly swift for all his hoped-for undertakings,—too fleetingly for him to take the time to enter all the avenues that stretch wide and luring before him.

For he has found that he has but to will and to wish and the dream comes true. That is because with him, "wish" and "work" are synonymous terms. He is not a rich man,—perhaps because he has never wished one-half so hard for wealth as he wished when a stripling for Harvard. He has never yearned one-tenth so sincerely to build himself a palace as he has to construct and develop a series of Pan-African Congresses which shall bring together black peoples, strange, hostile, a little suspicious of each other, as many men would have them be. In 1919 he willed that such a thing should come true and lo! in all the confusion and welter of the tag-end of the World War the thing happened. And now he is envisaging

BURGHARDT DU BOIS

and planning a fifth one. It will, doubtless, be rather small as all the other Congresses have been,—and each successive one larger. But its reverberations will be all out of proportion to its size. And black men and brown will leave Senegal and Sierra Leone and Alabama and Haiti and Martinique and touch hands in London or Paris, or Lisbon or Tunis, as the case may be, and exchange a word on the fate of their brothers in Rhodesia or Cape Town or Georgia. And behind all will be Du Bois directing and teaching and learning and pushing and spurring and tightening the bonds of a brotherhood among dark men which may some day result in world-wide freedom.

I hope you see this dreamer, this dynamo, this finest expression of the inner meaning of American democracy. He is not a tall man but compactly and shrewdly built with nothing lax or loosely hung about him. He is bronze,—a perfect fusion of the streams of blood flowing into his being from black and blue veins. His eyes are hazel, his nose aquiline; he is handsome and more than handsome so that people sometimes turn about on the street to gaze after him. He is so indubitably somebody. His years of unstinted service have given him distinction, arresting and recognizable. His voice is singularly musical and gratifying, informed with culture. He is very proud but not of his books which now must number a score, nor of his position nor of his renown nor his honors,—he is a Spingarn Medallist and he has been sometime Minister Plenipotentiary to Liberia. Nor is he too proud of his magazine which he has built up to a national influence against odds which has to be read by all who desire to be really informed about the cultural progress and the problems of the Negro. About all this he is becomingly modest.

But he is proud as men should be proud because he is cast

in the image of God and he has never denied nor belittled his heritage.

If he is a bit irascible,—and he is—that is the natural flaw inhering in a mind splendidly endowed and superbly trained. If he is arrogant, if he is at first approach haughty, how refreshing and meet to find these qualities in a man who is perforce the exemplar of millions of people in whose blood lurks the virus of a too successfully inoculated humility. If he leans toward justice rather than toward an unregulated mercy how else can he hope to offset a race's tendency toward a tropical laissez-faire?

There is a myth to the effect that Du Bois is bitter; that his whole outlook on life has been warped and distorted by his participation in the battle which he has waged so long. In this there is no truth. Why should a man become bitter when he has known success in his chosen field? Rather he recognized a difficult and dangerous situation, saw that he had the equipment to attack it and went at it as St. George went after the dragon. But no emendation of fable or folk-lore leads us to believe that St. George spent his leisure hours, dight in armor, "having at" his friends and relatives such time as he was not engaged in dragon-slaying. So with Du Bois, as those can testify who have seen him dance a Highland Fling, or eat plebeianly hot dogs at Coney Island, or with quip and jest keep the party going.

Not too often does a man whose work has been along such intangible lines leave so definite a record of his accomplishments. One reads nowadays of the "Renaissance of Negro Literature." This to me seems a misnomer, Negro Literature being still in the making. Howbeit, Naissance or Renaissance there is no question but that *The Crisis* has been the greatest single contributing factor in the growth of significant Negro writers. First of all through this magazine Dr. Du Bois made the Negro theme acceptable, natural and usual. Its pages nurtured assurance and discrimination on the part of the aspiring but timorous colored neophyte. A survey of the numbers of *The Crisis* for the last ten years would show preparation for the present-day output of Langston Hughes, Walter White, Countée Cullen, Franklin Frazier, Jessie Fauset, Georgia Douglas Johnson, Rudolph Fisher, Arthur Fauset, Maria Bonner, Alain Locke and many, many others.

But, of course, the real importance of Burghardt Du Bois, as he is generally known, lies in his elucidation of the ideals of the Republic and his proving of the idea of democracy. Here he functions in two ways,—subjectively in so far as he may be considered the mirror of the possibilities of his people, objectively in so far as he points the moral of democratic institutions to the country at large.

For his own people he is both the Dream and the Deed. By precept and example this man has taught his people to reach beyond themselves, has urged them to dissatisfaction with leavings and crumbs. He has insisted on equality in every walk and relationship of life. His motto has not only been: "We needs must know the highest when we see it"; but also "We needs must take the highest." And having let that lesson sink deep he has shown that it is possible to assimilate the world's culture though one have in one's veins some of the blood of slaves.

But far more significant than this is his justification of the basic truth underlying democracy. He was born not only to poverty but to the stigma attaching in this country to color. Yet after all there were free schools, scholarships, a comparatively free press and men still interested in subscribing to the rights of man. And so urged from within and buoyed up from without by his country's better impulses and first meanings, he has emerged as fine a product as that country can show. He is possessed of all those fundamental characteristics which are supposed to represent our national qualities. He has fortitude, perseverance, courage, daring, the brave heart, the truthful tongue, the understanding heart, the power to insure and endure success. He is Excelsior in flesh and blood.

Excelsior is the note on which to end this sketch. Perhaps that is the most outstanding impression which one receives of Du Bois—a sense as of something upward, outward. Nothing that is low or base can be associated with him. Even his faults are those of the truly great. Some years ago on his return from one of his wanderings—this time from Africa—a group of New Yorkers gave him a banquet. Countée Cullen, then a mere stripling, dedicated to him a poem not so remarkable as some of his later effusions, save for one thing. He imaged Du Bois as a "strong eagle." That *is* Du Bois; an eagle soaring high for his country to follow. And with healing in his wings!

The eagle is the emblem of America.

The World Is Too Small

SHERWOOD EDDY

I HAVE known Sherwood Eddy for eighteen years. I have seen him in action in China where I resided for half a dozen years, in Europe when he was addressing men whose names have shaken the world, and in America when he bore the brunt of severe criticism because of his stand on hot political and social issues. I write not as a journalist but as one who has been sympathetically interested in the man and his achievements. To the professional journalist Eddy would offer a most picturesque subject, one that might be painted in lurid colors, but to me he is an explorer, a searcher after truth and not an individual to be exploited.

The first attribute that I want to set opposite Eddy's name is courage. He is afraid of nothing. He is not standard. He does things differently. He is an individualist. He is creative and frequently plays a lone hand. He draws up new dies and patterns for public thinking. He disturbs the *status quo*. His insatiable curiosity has driven him to intense study of the great problems of the day. When long past fifty I have known him to take a year off from active work and bury himself in a great university in order to get up to date on the current trends in psychology, science and economics. It was during this period that he wrote one of the best books of his career, *New Challenges to Faith*.

He is as restless as the sea. His intense energy drives him forward not in aimless circles but always on a mission for the benefit of mankind. He has a gift for imparting knowledge. He moves men's wills and hearts. He knows theology but never lets it get in the way of his religion.

The charm and intensity of his personality have won for him thousands of devoted friends, just as his uncompromising attitude on vital issues has made him hosts of enemies. His saving sense of humor has enabled him to laugh not only at those who disagree with him but at himself as well.

His contagious chortle, his vigorous athletic actions, his radiant health, his wrinkle-free countenance and lack of gray hair despite his nearly sixty years, his piercing eyes flashing from behind tortoise-rimmed glasses, height about the average, firm grip, strong chin—these are the characteristics that return to me as I try to portray him.

Of American Puritan ancestry, a direct descendant of John and Priscilla Alden and of Samuel Eddy, who came to America in the third Puritan ship in 1630, Sherwood Eddy was born in Kansas in 1871. His parents had migrated to Kansas to help keep it a free state and there is much evidence that the freedom which stirred the souls of these early pioneers has been transmitted to him. His mother, who still lives an active Spartan life at eighty-one, went to school with Buffalo Bill. She later taught school, earning enough to send herself through Elmira and Vassar.

Camping and hunting were Sherwood's delights in boyhood as big game shooting in the jungles of India was his favorite relaxation in later life. But the movement for conservation and humane treatment of wild animal life doubtless did not leave him untouched.

He has told me thrilling adventures which took place when his doctor ordered him into the jungles after a near-breakdown during his first period of service in India. Dressed in green he and the native guide stalked wild animals with success. "I

am not much of a shot," he said. "It was pure luck that I
brought down first on three days running an ibex then a bison
and finally a bear with one shot each." Once he was charged
by an angry elephant but laid the beast low with what he
called a "lucky shot" in the brain. But the movement for
conservation and humane treatment of wild animal life doubtless did not leave him untouched. "I've found adventures with
bigger game than elephants," he reminisced. "Men have always interested me more than big game."

He was graduated from Leavenworth High School and entered Andover and was in due course graduated from Yale
with a degree in Civil Engineering. His mind was made up
to make money in the lumber business with his father. But
the magnetic personality of Dwight L. Moody and the challenge of James McConaughy reversed his plans and he decided
to make men instead of money. He entered Christian work
under Robert McBurney at the Twenty-third Street Y. M. C. A.
in New York City and lived in the famous "Tower Room"
with his chief for a year. Here he got his first test in winning
men for the Christian life.

Eddy's father died in 1894 leaving him an inheritance and
his mother the larger part of an estate. At about that time he
began asking where he could find the biggest opportunity and
hardest task in Christian service. He decided it was the foreign field and signed a pledge to go to India. But before leaving he prepared himself at both Union and Princeton. He
also became a traveling secretary for the Student Volunteer
Movement with his classmate, Horace Pitkin, who was later
martyred by the Boxers in Paotingfu, China. During their
intensive campaigns these earnest young men signed up one
hundred students each who actually went to the foreign field.
Eddy also wrote a pamphlet *The Supreme Decision of the
Christian Student,* which by its sheer logic and force recruited

an additional hundred men for foreign service. That is one
of Eddy's chief powers—his ability to move men's wills. Kirby
Page, who was Eddy's private secretary for years, has told me
that Eddy possessed this faculty to a higher degree than any
individual he knew.

In 1895 he went to India as a secretary of the Y. M. C. A.
without salary. For fifteen years he traveled among the colleges and worked among the outcasts, coming into daily contact with representatives of the eight great religions of the
world. He identified himself so closely with the people that
they said, "He is one of us except his color."

He learned to speak the Tamil dialect as rapidly as he speaks
English. His constant emphasis was the recruiting and training of leaders who could take full responsibility and make
Christianity indigenous. Among the young men he worked
with were Asariah who later became the first Anglican native
bishop of Asia and K. T. Paul now head of the National Y. M.
C. A. in India.

At the time of the Edinburgh conference in 1910 Eddy wrote
his first important book, *The Awakening of Asia*. Followed
his appointment as secretary for evangelism for Asia by the
Y. M. C. A. His first contact with the Far East came in Japan
among Chinese students who had rushed to that country following the Sino-Japanese war and the Revolution. They had
cut their cues as well as their words. Christ as the moral victor
was presented by Eddy, with C. T. Wang, now minister of
foreign affairs in the Nationalist government, as his interpreter.

Called to China by Fletcher S. Brockman, then head of the
Y movement, Eddy brought things to pass in the lives of the
intellectuals that had never before happened. Starting with
the president and his cabinet by request he addressed officials,
merchants, students and gentrymen with as much power as
Paul of Tarsus. Night after night audiences of from one to

six thousand admitted by ticket only crowded the vast halls and heard him proclaim Jesus Christ as the only savior for their country. He carried his message four times across China and also into Korea and Japan. On the last two visits into China he was supplemented by Prof. C. H. Robertson, formerly of Purdue University, who explained the mysteries of science through a unique series of demonstrated lectures while Eddy followed with his fiery addresses on the mysteries of religion.

On one occasion in Foochow when his voice gave out he told his interpreter that the latter would have to carry on. Standing beside him Eddy rasped out a sentence or two and then the interpreter who had been through so many addresses with him that he knew every gesture, story and paragraph, flung himself into the business at hand with such tremendous success that none suspected Eddy was not following his usual course.

Sherwood Eddy is neither an enigma nor a fool. He is neither a Communist, an alarmist, an Anarchist, nor a fundamentalist. He long called himself a capitalist, and even in those days was often blacklisted and maligned by the Daughters of the American Revolution and by the American Legion, two of this country's most patriotic organizations. Why? Because he was a Christian. Because he takes Christ seriously. Because he applies Christian principles to the whole of life and to the solution of its problems—economic, interracial, international.

He believes in free speech and practices it with hortatory vigor. Pre-eminent among American exhorters he speaks always with clenched fists, contracted brow, tight-drawn lips. In almost every land he has exhorted for vital religion, peace and brotherhood. Having no patience with provincial-minded nationalists who constantly shout for preparedness, Eddy has repeatedly stumped the colleges in behalf of peace and international good-will. The American Legion has in several places successfully brought pressure to bear and prevented his speaking, especially in the South. The Legion would have continued its efforts to block him had he not made an issue of their tactics on the basis that American democracy guaranteed him the right to free speech. He won the battle and has continued to speak to greater audiences than ever.

Eddy is an internationalist—not the swivel-chair type who drones out dreary facts for drowsy students but a virile, courageous seeker of truth in a world-wide laboratory. Few Americans have traveled as extensively or as continuously. He is personally acquainted with many of the highest political, industrial, educational, labor and spiritual leaders in the major nations of the world. He has acquired his knowledge first hand by repeated contact with present-day history makers.

He is an envoy of understanding, shuttling back and forth among the nations and races of the world weaving a fabric of peace and good-will. Fifteen years of hard, unrelenting labor among the intellectuals and outcasts of India gave him a rock upon which to stand to proclaim a message of brotherhood. Four extended visits to the Far East followed. Then continuous travel in the United States and Canada as an interpreter of the Orient. But not content with his own one-man efforts he conceived the plan of taking groups of Americans bodily across the seas into Europe in order that they might see and learn for themselves conditions faced by our neighbors.

For ten successive summers he has piloted selected groups of Americans representing business, politics, the press, the ministry and education into Europe where they were exposed to leaders and scholars of London, Paris, Berlin, Prague, Vienna, Geneva. The plan embodies an unusual idea and has been carried out with a degree of ability that makes it unique in the field of international education. Many of the 500 past members of the Seminar have declared that the summer spent with Eddy was worth more than a four years' course at college.

A list of those who have lectured to the Seminar in the continental capitals reads like a *Who's Who* of Europe. Eddy landed as teachers for his peripatetic school prime ministers, presidents, labor leaders, capitalists, university deans, members of the nobility, archbishops, pacifists and war lords. No words are necessary to make clear the enormous significance of such contacts with the activity of Europe by American minds of many types who return home bearing the inspiration of new international understanding.

One of the most noteworthy services that Sherwood Eddy has rendered in this country was in connection with what has been called the Religious Life Emphasis week starting at Des Moines, Iowa. For an entire week early in 1925, a score of speakers presented Christian ideals, individual and social, to the whole life of that city. From twenty to thirty thousand people heard the message daily. Meetings were held in all the colleges and high schools and were followed by personal interviews conducted by trained interviewers. A mass meeting in labor's own hall, followed by industrial forums and discussions, throughout the week were a feature of the campaign. Dr. George Haynes, interracial secretary for the Federal Council of Churches of Christ in America was received with the greatest enthusiasm and cordiality by the churches, the chamber of commerce and other audiences, white and colored.

No finer endeavor has been made in America to give Christianity a chance in a modern city. A new technique for the promotion of Christian principles was developed. An editor of a great Eastern magazine said that it was the most significant thing that had happened in Christian work in twenty years. *The New York World* said that Des Moines had tried out the practicability of Christianity in the test tube.

The idea started when George Webber, secretary of the Y. M. C. A. and Carl C. Proper, publisher and editor, together with a few friends dared to plan a religious approach to the problems of their city that would challenge everybody. They called in Sherwood for counsel and help and men were moved. A business man came away from one of the sessions saying, "that meeting cost me $10,000" and cut out a doubtful practice in his business.

The whole city was challenged with the gospel without distinction of race, rank or religion, of caste, creed or color. No partisan or sectarian note was struck during the entire week. No criticism was heard from fundamentalists or modernists, klansmen or anti-klansmen, Jew or gentile, Catholic or Protestant. Eddy was the center of a group of leaders whom he called in from the outside, consisting of such men as Dean Thomas Graham of Oberlin; Dr. Henry Crane of Malden, Mass.; Dr. A. Ray Petty of Judson Memorial Baptist Church, New York; William P. Hapgood, business man of Indianapolis; Dr. Alva Taylor, secretary of the Board of Social Welfare of the Disciples of Christ; Reinhold Niebuhr of Detroit and Dr. John R. Mott. As the leader and moving spirit of this group, Eddy was able to deploy his forces in such a way as to bring maximum results.

That the experiment was successful is indicated, first, by the fact that those who have kept in close touch with it say that Des Moines has since lived on a higher plane than at any previous period, and secondly, that nearly a dozen cities in the United States have had similar efforts. These efforts have not been emotional spasms or professional revivals, but they have awakened the consciousness of the entire city to apply the

searching principles of Jesus to home, to industry and to business.

In 1926 Eddy led a party of Americans into Russia—educa-
tors, business men and social workers. They went where they
pleased, used their own interpreters, criticized and commended
the Communists to their faces and saw all there was to be seen
in the time at their disposal. Eddy told Russian leaders point-
blank what he thought of the evils of their system including
their abridgement of liberty, their policy of world revolution,
and their unscientific and unjust teaching of dogmatic atheism
to their youth under eighteen while at the same time forbid-
ding organized teaching of religion.

On the other hand he told them he was glad to find a nation that "stood as a challenge to the rest of the world where-
ever capitalism was ruthless, wherever nations ruled by swollen
selfish capitalism, wherever an aggressive imperialism or militarism threatens any part of the world. Yours is a country in
which at least in your ideal and aim you seek that man shall
no longer exploit his fellow man." He expressed the hope that
his unofficial group might be followed by an official delegation
and that the Russian government might be recognized by the
United States on the basis of President Coolidge's first message
to Congress in 1923.

Upon his return to the United States Eddy discovered that,
regardless of the fact that he had been misquoted and mis-
represented by the press, a group of leaders in the Y. M. C. A.
were demanding his resignation from that organization, the
implication being that he had turned Communist. And this
despite the fact that for more than thirty years he had served
the association without salary. He offered to refer the matter
to the general board and national council of the association for
settlement. But the question was settled in committee and in
Eddy's favor. I cite this incident to indicate how unwilling

some Americans are to listen to facts about a nation which is trying one of the greatest experiments in social government that the world has ever known. It had rather become the American habit to label everyone a "Red" who tried to be fair to the Soviet experiment. Eddy bore the brunt of the attack fearlessly but the dust that was stirred up at the time has not yet settled.

His book, *The Challenge of Russia,* was hailed widely as a fine, sympathetic, critical, balanced piece of work. It made clear Eddy's non-support of communism as a system and theory while enlarging upon communism's searching queries to the capitalist world. And almost simultaneously, Sherwood once more raised a furore by joining the Socialist Party of America and publishing the event frankly as a corollary of his faith in a Christian social order.

The spiritual struggle through which Sherwood Eddy has passed in reaching his present position on the question of war has been deep and prolonged. His search for truth and reality lasted exactly ten years. To break away from the entire war system, to rise above the whole habit and method of retaliation, of attempted settlement by force instead of reason was contrary to his temperament.

He had not given much thought to the question of war until the European conflict burst upon us. But long before America entered the struggle, Eddy was "over there" as a noncombatant religious worker in the British army, helping to sustain the morale of the fighting men. He took with him ten speakers and forty college men to engage in Y work. He believed in the war and the motives of the Allies and America. He met the first division of the American Army as it entered France. As guest of the British General Headquarters he saw the whole front from Ypres to Soissons. As guest of French officers he went underground at Verdun and was told that 500,-

ooo young men were buried on that one field. He visited the
Grand Fleet and watched our destroyers hunt submarines. He
flew with our air force and saw fighting along the British,
French and American lines. He threw himself actively into
the financial campaigns for various agencies that were helping
to win the war.

But during this awful struggle something began to happen
to him spiritually. He began to have grave doubts and misgivings.

"I can remember pacing up and down within sound of the
guns," he says, "and on the sands of the seashore at the great
base camps, deeply troubled in conscience, and wrestling with
the most difficult moral problem. How could one be at once
loyal to country and Christ? How could he at once serve
Caesar and God? If he followed the Sermon on the Mount
or the example of Jesus, must he be unpatriotic and disloyal
to the law of the land? When I wrote *With Our Soldiers in
France* I had such difficulty over the chapter which I had
written on 'The Moral Grounds of the War' that I finally had
to leave it out of the book."

When the war ended Eddy was still struggling with his conscience. He met with a group of American and German
Christian leaders in Dresden only to discover that both sides
believed they had been fighting a defensive war. The saddest
thing about the conference was that neither side seemed to
have learned the lesson of the war. Both were ready to begin
all over again, to swallow the propaganda, to fear, to hate, to
misrepresent and to kill. But before the conference closed a
change took place, and agreement was reached that as far as
that group was concerned their living motto was to be henceforth "No More War."

"I came to the conclusion," Eddy has told me, "that war
will never end war any more than filth will end disease or

fuel will end fire. I served notice on the government that I stood with thousands of people who were ready to die but not to kill, ready to love but not to hate. I turned back to a lost secret and a lost leader. I chose the way of brotherhood, co-operation, and love. I took a positive and not a negative position against war and am fighting it on all fronts—economic, international, interracial and in the social relationships, including the relationship between man and woman. I stand for nothing passive but for indomitable love, and I believe I have now found 'the moral equivalent for war.' " And thus Sherwood Eddy fought the greatest battle of his career. He was big enough to change his attitude and practices even with his advancing years. His restless soul has found inward peace and stability.

Probably no living American has traveled as widely among the schools and colleges of America and worked with as many students as Eddy. His fresh and dynamic approach to the problems in which students are interested and his keen desire to share with them the results of his experiences and study have made him *persona grata* wherever he has gone. He believes in youth.

And so it was not surprising to find him engaged in a campaign to aid youth in one of the most difficult and delicate areas of life—the area of sex. He has made a really deep study of the subject, reading hundreds of books and publications and consulting many experts and specialists in this country and in Europe. The result of his investigation was another book, *Sex and Youth*, which attracted wide and favorable attention.

Sherwood's capacity for bobbing up wherever excitement breaks out on the planet found him, in 1931, in Manchuria just when the invading Japanese captured Mukden. Championing the cause of China, he sent documents and sworn

SHERWOOD EDDY

statements to the League of Nations, reported to American periodicals, and hastened to China to help the people to understand how non-violent, Christly tactics could still be vigorous and potent.

Any appraisal of Eddy would be incomplete and misleading if it failed to take into account his faults and failings.

"Confessedly I am superficial," he told me when I raised the question to him. "You can't be a specialist and do the many things that I am doing. There simply isn't time enough for both. I know I have been accused of having too many irons in the fire."

As a crusader, motivated by strong feeling and intense conviction, he is prone to make heightened statements—to exaggerate. His use of hyperbole is not merely a desire to attract attention and arouse interest—it is frankly a weakness.

Being a crusader he is a propagandist rather than a scientific educator. He lacks both the scholarly and judicial mind. His tremendous drive and energy often irritate those who work closely with him. His place is in the thick of the fight where he can give and take in hot debate. He is most useful when he can stir men to argue, when he can challenge them to heroic action. He frankly recognizes that there is a place for detached scholarship and the scientific educational method but he also insists that the reformer and prophet have a place in society.

To many, Eddy is spectacular, which is another way of saying that he is a popular propagandist. Some have pointed out that he lacks appreciation of the hard labor on the part of his comrades who grind out hack work in his behalf. His constant travel program has made his home life irregular with the result that the members of his family have had to bear most of the responsibility in that sphere.

Eddy lives abundantly, though not in the least luxuriously. He inherited a modest fortune, but rather than take his ease and let money dominate him, he has sold his comfortable home and taken a flat built by the City Housing Corporation at Sunnyside Gardens, Long Island City, where he lives among people of moderate means. In all his thirty-five years' service he has taken no salary from the organization with which he has been most closely identified. His modest fortune goes into the building of a new social order—the Kingdom of God on Earth. His plans have all been carried out with the knowledge and approval of his mother and his own family.

Sherwood Eddy's highest aim is "to live simply and sacrificially, avoiding waste and luxury;

"to practice the golden rule in all relationships;

"to practice brotherhood toward all;

"to participate in no secret order or fraternity if it tends to exclusiveness, prejudice or strife;

"to seek justice for every man without distinction of caste or color;

"to make peace where there is strife;

"to seek to outlaw war;

"to redeem the social order; to test its evils by the principles of love and fearlessly to challenge them as Jesus challenged the money changers in the temple;

"to seek a new discovery of God which will release fresh springs of power such as men in the past have experienced when they discovered the religion of Jesus."

A Different Employer

WILLIAM P. HAPGOOD

THE most outright, forthright experiment in industrial democracy yet attempted by any American employer is probably that of the Columbia Conserve Company in Indianapolis—and William P. Hapgood is its prophet. This canning factory is as much a laboratory in social experimentation as was Edison's in electrical discovery and invention. It is demonstrating a faith in the inherent integrity of the average man, even though he is a workingman of the type that is usually paid low wages and worked long hours, and it is demonstrating that the average of the so-called laboring class can, in a school of industrial enterprise, work on a coöperative basis and not only make it pay, but make it pay more.

I say Mr. Hapgood is its prophet. He will not care much for that characterization. His mind works in the open and labels are repugnant to him, above all any that smack of the conventional or pious. He has no dogmas; the words coöperation and industrial democracy mean a process rather than an accomplishment. He is a man of good-will who is experimenting rather than preaching. He does not despise preaching, and he does it well, but he does not like to have it called that; he rejects the word because it puts his talking into a category with so much that is mere rhetorical, impractical doctrine. He is a social engineer engaged in a piece of industrial experimentation. A factory is his laboratory; men, machines and markets are his materials; and his hypothesis is that industrial democracy will work if the preconceptions of the arbitrary, profit-motived system can be replaced with social faith. If this factory has any slogan it is "industry of the workers, by the workers, for the workers."

Billy Hapgood was born with the metaphorical silver spoon in his mouth. His father was successful and he was endowed with a goodly fortune, a Harvard degree, a pair of illustrious brothers, a cultured wife and help-meet, and he needed nothing more than average ability, a cautious business method and the mentality of the Hon. George F. Babbitt to ride fortune easily. His brothers are writers and W. P. used to say it was his job to make the family fortune pay the bills when the "literary fellers" failed to make ends meet. He called himself the "runt pig" of the family in that he was not a scholar and a literary man like his brothers. In Harvard he was one of the champion yachtsmen; his love of nature and out-of-door life could have made a cultured social semi-parasitism quite congenial, and the world to which he was born would have envied him and called him blessed.

He chose a farm, a manufacturing plant, an army shirt and a small cottage, and plays the game with the tools of the field and factory workers. Yes, he is playing a game all right, and it is a big game, but its goals are not surrounded by crowds and instead of cheers there are jibes from competitors. In Indianapolis, business men used to call his factory "the rocking chair" cannery—the council meetings were made comfortable with plain wooden rocking chairs. He was once proposed for a place on the board of the Family Welfare Society but was rejected by the benevolent gentlemen who composed it because he had "dangerous ideas about the conduct of industry." I asked him if he ever went to Chamber of Commerce meetings; he replied that he once did attend but finding he was looked upon as a "nut" he felt more comfortable at home—he was willing to be a "nut" if that is what experimenting in human engineering requires, but he did not feel it necessary to have the implication "rubbed in."

After a forum in a certain western city the chairman said, "We will not all agree with Mr. Hapgood, but we will all say he is a Christian gentleman." "That," said he, "was disgusting. I would rather be called anything else, excepting a scab." Now of course he is a Christian gentleman and with emphasis upon the qualifying word besides, but he resented the classification just because it is the conventional characterization of a certain type of chap, who, while he neither drinks nor beats his wife nor uses bad grammar, may exploit his workers, unite with his fellow lords of industry to beat down labor unions, vote with the corrupt political machine because it stands for "big business" and in general "play the game." If being a Christian gentleman consists in conventional churchmanship, money contributions, graceful living, the peccadillos of etiquette and dress, all supported by an arbitrary system of business organization in which one person orders and many obey, one hires and fires and many suffer, one takes the profits and many take whatever they may happen to get in wages and working hours, then Mr. Hapgood is not even a gentleman, let alone a Christian. But if it means following that way of life, without pretense or ostentation, which the Nazarene carpenter pointed out, then he is both—quite unorthodoxly both.

I induced him to address an intercollegiate group of students once, before his experiment was widely known. It was one of the early groups of the Fellowship for a Christian Social Order. Knowing it as such he began by saying apologetically, "Now, I am not a Christian." After the meeting was over I challenged that statement by asking, "Just what do you mean when you say you are not a Christian?" He replied by saying he did not belong to church, did not believe the creeds and

confessions of faith nor accept the conventional codes of the
time as Christian. Not being either in faith or fact in the fellowship of those who dominate the church life of the time he
felt he was not therefore a Christian. My reply was that many
of us in the church stood exactly where he stood and demurred
that creeds, confessions, conventional codes and institutions did
not make the true fellowship, then asked, "What do you think
about the teachings of Jesus?" He replied, "Oh, that is another
question. I think that the ethical and spiritual teachings of
Jesus have been so adequately proven by nineteen centuries of
human experience that I go to him as authority in those things
just as I would to authority in other lines in which I am interested." Today he talks as freely of "the Christian way of life"
as do any of us.

He and Arthur Nash were our speakers before a ministerial
union one Monday morning. After his talk a pious fundamentalist asked, "What proportion of your workers have you induced to go to church and Sunday school?" Metaphorically
speaking one could see the fur rise, but Arthur Nash arose
quickly, good churchman that he was, and replied, "That is an
unfair question. The Columbia Conserve Company is not a
church or a church agency. Moreover it is not its manager's
business to use it for evangelism. He is engaged in the bigger
job of creating a brotherhood of workers. I wish the churches
were doing more to help in that kind of task." Mr. Hapgood
then said, "We do not interfere or intervene in the religious
life of our people; that is a sacred thing that belongs to them
as individuals." Thus the incident closed.

At the Columbia Conserve the time clock has been abolished, salaries have been substituted for wages, a council of
workers sits in those seats of authority where boards of directors and executive committees usually sit, the workers elect
their own superiors in management, discuss production and

sales policies, fix their own pay, determine their own hours, execute discipline upon themselves and are rapidly becoming in fact, as they are already in authority, the owners of the plant. Every dogma of the arbitrary, capitalistic system has been disproved; every pre-conception has been challenged and found unwarranted. And the experiment has paid in dollars and cents; the profits have not only increased but they have increased amazingly—they were 30 per cent year before last, the largest in the concern's history—and that with the highest wage, the shortest day, the largest output per person, the best quality and the lowest sales price in the plant's record. Every line of the above spells efficiency, but efficiency without drive. The secret lies wholly in that spirit of willingness and eagerness to do well that comes out of coöperation, a chance at self-expression and a sense of partnership. The workers can furnish the same keen interest, the same sense of economy and the same practical desire to see the business succeed that the business man can, and to it they can add, when they become both business man and worker, an efficiency in work that no driver can induce.

Hapgood began the experiment thirteen years ago. He built on faith—faith in the potential qualities of the average man. His motto, like that of Henry George, is "I believe in men." He had no illusions about the difficulties; things have come to pass rather more rapidly than he expected. He began with a council upon which sat three representatives of the owners and seven of the workers. This council was largely advisory but its decisions were acted upon in such good faith that confidence grew and the discovery of an adequate technique for discussion and action resulted in the council's being enlarged until now it includes all the continuous workers who care to qualify by regularly attending meetings. Mr. Hapgood and the other old stockholders have translated their stock into a non-voting category and the common stock, purchased by the workers, alone has voting power. He takes his place as a salaried worker, goes on the road for weeks at a time and council meetings continue on schedule. Profits are pooled and used to purchase the old Hapgood stock, upon which interest only is paid and which is then put into a pool of common ownership. The hours have been reduced from a week of 55 to one of 45, excepting only those few weeks in the ripening season for tomatoes, when, like the farmer's harvest, all hands must work overtime to obey nature's imperious mandate. During that season many temporary employees must be taken on, but their hiring, the fixing of their wages and all else that concerns them is settled in the workers' council.

I have sat in council meetings, have visited the plant, have talked much with the president and others about the business, and the net conclusion to which I come is that Hapgood's function is more that of the skillful teacher than anything else. He is president and general manager by vote of his fellow workers, and so well aware is he that unless goods are sold they cannot be made that he spends many weeks each year on the road with the sales force, and he keeps up with every step in the technical progress in the plant besides managing a big farm. Nevertheless his chief function is that of educator of the workers in the arts of coöperation. He does not teach by textbook nor by the lecture method; he teaches by demonstration. The workers meet, face the issues, discuss them, learn how to differ without feeling, to become tolerant and teachable, to change their minds under evidence and argument, to work out problems through weeks of study, to take chances on their own best opinions, to listen to the advice of the expert without compromising their own independent judgment, and to work together. Above all they get rid of the "inferiority complex."

When asked once what had been his greatest difficulty, Hapgood answered cryptically, "To get rid of the Harvard starch." He had to become a common man himself in dress, deportment, fellow-mindedness and respect for his fellow workers though they had no schooling outside the hard knocks of common experience. But it meant more than that; he had to overcome, as far as it is humanly possible, the tendency to defer to him as the man of education, money and prior rights of ownership. He never will overcome that respect for his judgment which springs out of respect for him as the man who made the undertaking possible, but he absents himself enough to prove that things can run for long periods without him and that there is resident in the working group an ability adequate to tasks of management. The question is often asked, "What will happen when Mr. Hapgood is gone?" Of course, only time can answer, but his own faith grows that things will go on as usual. The tenets of the doctrine of coöperation seem to be getting pretty firmly rooted in conviction, and the success of its practice has in this short time given answer to the fear that the acquisitive in the individual would overthrow the sense of the common good. The individual has found his largest profit in the common good and the acquisitive has been sublimated in self-expression and increased personality.

One of the first things done was to abolish wages and put all the regular workers on a salary basis. Wages are paid by the hour or day—salaries by the month. When the wage earner misses a few hours or a day he loses his wage; when the salaried worker loses an hour or a day or two usually nothing is said about it. Then there is a social differentiation in the distinction between wage and salaried workers. The one belongs to denim and khaki and the other to white collars, and, as is usual, those who enjoy the best advantages demand and receive the best pay and the greater comfort. Along with the abolition of wages at the Columbia came the resolution that when work was slack in one department those who could should lend a hand wherever there was an overplus of work. Several of the office workers quit rather than labor with their hands in the cannery. The treasurer quit because he was in the small minority who believed in the hard-boiled system of arbitrary control. Some went gingerly to the kitchen and packing rooms in order to hold their places but their enthusiasm grew with the morale of the group. Then the council voted to send select young people from the ranks of labor to school to learn to become stenographers and book-keepers. Now the camaraderie is quite complete; social caste is banished; there is mutual respect between denim and linen and the habit of developing talent from among their own ranks is established.

A greater innovation is now nearing accomplishment. It is that of basing salaries on need rather than on ability to *get* under the competitive system. First a minimum was fixed for all; next a differential was arranged to meet needs of family budgets over those of single men and women; then sickness and casualty insurance was added; now a specific provision for children is made, and discussion of the principle of fixing income on the basis of need is nearing acceptance as a principle. Such a move requires a complete break with the industrial world outside this factory. It is revolutionary in economics though exemplary in ethics, but it is being done in no utopian fashion—it has been worked out step by step and its human value has been proven thus far.

There is provision for social medicine at the Columbia and misfortunes are shared, but there is no specific unemployment insurance. Unemployment is simply put out of the reckoning by coöperation. If there is extra work then all work a little extra. Thus a steady income is assured so long as there is money to pay, and so far the more of such practical utopianism they have put into practice the more money there has been to pay the bills.

The big family idea has replaced the big business idea and it works. It works so much better that one of the biggest employers in the land, after examination said, "Why, of course, it's the better way, and it will pay better. But I am so constituted that my pleasure comes out of being the big boss, so I won't adopt it." This declaration more even than money spells out much of that philosophy which clings to the arbitrary, old-time way. There are many who love to "boss," to govern and to manage their fellow-men; who like to say come and they come, and go and they go, and never in my life have I heard a sermon on the incident where a certain soldier told Jesus his house was not a fit place for such an one because he did those things. Even some churches want hierarchies of authority instead of brotherhoods.

In the council at the Columbia decisions are rarely made final by a mere majority. Unless the vote is overwhelmingly one way final decision awaits upon further discussion and the possibility of a greater common-mindedness. Unanimity is a state of group opinion adjudged to be worth a great deal of time and deliberation and talk. Majorities do not make right, nor are they much more often right than wrong. Caution rather than haste has proved to be characteristic of the workers' council, and a mistrust of their wisdom, rather than a conceit, has developed with the years of experience. This makes them good experimenters.

Democracy in this industry has not developed cockiness in those to whom a measure of authority has been given; it seems to have developed a sense of responsibility instead. The greatest task has been to get individuals to accept responsibility. Many a man from the ranks has demurred at promotion and a few have shown an overweening ambition to express themselves in season and out in the council. The theory that to give the workers the right to elect their own foremen and superintendents would destroy discipline has not been borne out. In a dozen years eight men have been discharged by the council for refusal to obey foremen. Others have been "talked to," some reprimanded and given a last chance but only eight have proved intractable. Discipline is not wanting. A trade union usually manages the discipline of its members better than do open shop employers. I once heard Seebohm Rowntree say he would not be bothered with discipline when the workers, properly organized, manage it so much better than he could.

Morale is much higher under coöperation, once time is given to build morale, than under regimentation. Right now the Columbia plant is under study by experts in plant arrangement and management. The council is just as much convinced of the necessity of technical expertness as a board of directors could be and just because they are the workers themselves and the profits are theirs, technical efficiency has a better chance to work; they are willing to obey their own orders. In every way technical expertness, efficiency, economy in use of materials, care of machinery and personal devotion to the task have been bettered under workers' control. It is human nature to exercise greater care and give better service when you have a personal interest than when it is yours to toil and someone else's to claim the usufruct. Right here lies the secret of increased profits. Billy Hapgood says, "If we cannot convert the hard-boiled brothers, we can drive them to it by outdoing them."

Once after addressing a large group of ministers and religious leaders, Hapgood was asked if the new plan was paying more dividends. He replied that it was, only to have the question raised as to whether or not it was then, "Christian." That is, is it Christian to make more money? Certainly not if a few make it at the expense of the many, but certainly "yes" if all who share the toil share the profits and due regard is given to the consumer of the goods. If things done in a right and equitable manner do not pay better under normal conditions then the universe is made up wrongly and the way of poverty is better if only it opens a way to heaven hereafter. But that means the world is a huge mistake, nature is a misanthrope and God a failure.

But William P. Hapgood is not concerned about making money primarily; it is only a necessary means to the high end of making men and women and better homes. He believes in the sacredness of personality and the more abundant life, and he knows from both observation and experience, that food, clothing, shelter, health, leisure, culture, recreation and beauty are requisite to it. There is little of leisure, culture, beauty or recreation possible under the historic system of long hours and low income for the masses of wage earners, and with possession of these only does real living begin—the living that rises above mere existence. To make a factory the instrument through which these lowly, and all too often disinherited in the social order, can be given the more abundant life is to rescue industrialism from the tragedy of drabness, poverty and subornation of mind and spirit, and it is also to rescue religion from a hypocrisy that leads some leaders in the church to promise heaven as a reward for faithfulness to masters and peacefulness under trial.

The Hapgood experiment is a challenge to the assumption of a capitalism that roots in *laissez faire* and a harsh, primitive naturalism. That assumption is that property belongs to whosoever can get it, restrained only by the codes that were made in an elemental period of non-social individualism. They fitted the pioneers, with unconquered nature open before them, but they poorly condition a time when great crowded cities instead of "great open spaces" are characteristic, and when the plow and the axe are giving way to the power-driven semi-automatic machine. The law of the jungle turns the crowded habitations of men into a social jungle, relieved of redness in tooth and claw by the amenities of civilization, but left strident in selfishness and with the acquisitive as the dominant motive in organized life. This capitalism still talks the language of primitive America. It prates of individual initiative and enterprise, knowing very well that only the fortunate and strong can avail themselves of either to any great degree, and that when these exercise their power in a highly organized business or industry the multitude have no more chance at either than do the rank and file of any army.

Hapgood believes in individualism; he is very much of a Jeffersonian democrat. But he perceives also that the average individual has no chance to express his personality in industrial organization if the stock belongs to a few or to absentees, if control is arbitrarily held in a few hands and the masses only toil and obey. So he is working out an experiment wherein the productive power of the machine under an organized factory system will furnish the things for a more abundant life under our modern standards of living, and at the same time recreate for the average man who toils before the machine and under organization that sense of individuality and that chance of self-expression which the less highly organized and less socialized period offered him.

He also challenges the assumption that the possession of property, and thus ownership of the machine, justifies absolute control when it means control of the lives of those who work at the machine. That assumption he deems a hold-over phase of slavery. He who owns the machine owns, for the time being, the man who works at the machine if the ownership of the machine means power to hire and fire, to fix wages and hours and a denial of any right of collective bargaining to the worker. The worker becomes nothing more than whatever cog and lever the inventor of the machine has been unable to supply in his effort to make it more and more nearly automatic. He is willing to install the machine and to have the worker accept its place in the work of producing usable goods, if only the worker can control the organization that owns and controls the machine. That makes him master collectively as an answer to the collectivism of the means of production, just as he was master personally when he produced with the hand tool. The creative tasks of handwork may be taken from the workman by machinery, but it does not follow that the creative must be taken away from him; it only means it is transferred, along with ownership, from the individual to the social. There is an old Anglo-Saxon saying that he who owns the land, owns the law—owns the man. We may paraphrase it by saying he who owns the machinery owns the rules—owns the man.

This experiment is an effort to apply the canons of democracy to industrial organization. Hapgood believes it can be made to work there more efficiently than in political organization because those who work together under it use tools and goods of a more tangible and concrete kind, and are brought into continuous contact instead of occasional. The ties of political democracy are more or less remote and its exercise is so occasional as to allow little real experience in its technique, while those of industrial democracy come under the factory roof and are exercised daily with the very tangible tools of technical efficiency. He finds the correlative of socialization in industrial coöperation. He is not protesting inevitable machine progress nor efficiency in management, but he is protesting the assumption that he who owns the machine can also own the man; he is doing that thing without which ownership tends to increase in the hands of the few, regimentation to increase for the many, and industrial society to become an industrial feudalism.

Hapgood says that in these twelve years he has found more satisfaction than in the forty he had lived before. The casual observer would think he had put in twelve years of the most patience-trying work. Human nature is so intangible, so much a complex of motives, of suppressions, fears, aspirations and undefinable what-nots that those who seek to lead it out of itself and its unquestioned acceptance of whatever is as inescapable, require an infinite patience and a surpassing love of fellow-men. The average man accepts fortune as deserved and misfortune as an unavoidable calamity. Here is an employer—though now he is hardly that in any usual sense—who accepts neither concept; he thinks the luck that brings material fortune may be no more deserved than was that which gave him one as an heirloom, and he is sure penury is seldom deserved. He believes a better social engineering could abolish poverty and should make great personal fortunes impossible. He believes there are undiscovered potentialities in the average normal human being to whom the fates have denied a share in the excess goods by which men live above their fellows. And he is no disciple of softness and sobbiness; he does not weep over the woes of the less fortunate—he is too busy trying to discover a more equitable way of living together. He thinks it is difficulties, not ease, that educate mankind. So much does he think it that he himself works an average of twelve to fourteen hours per day and believes that when the workers own and manage their own plant they may, like the farmer, take joy in long hours because the work is interesting and profitable.

He thinks there is a better way to pleasure than a short day's work and long evening's dissipation, and that is joy in

WILLIAM P. HAPGOOD

work; but he knows there cannot be much joy in work when it is all work for one and all profit for another. Where the less original and more sordid business man takes pleasure in piling up profits and increasing his power to control and adding to his social prestige, Hapgood finds satisfaction in creating out of a group of common workers an exceptional group of industrial coöperators.

Where the conventional rich man gives of his surplus to relieve poverty, living the while himself in luxury, this rich man gives himself, helps the common man to provide for himself, experiments with a way of working together that will abolish all poverty springing out of a denial of opportunity, and takes pride not in a great plant that bears his name but in a group of fellow-men in whom the sense of *noblesse oblige* has replaced petty self-assertion.

To make a brotherhood out of a factory, to extend the bonds of family to a group of fellow workers, to challenge the arbitrary, profit-motived system, to discover a way by which the toilers can express personality, increase their own standards of living and become their own "bosses," is to justify democracy and brotherhood. A democratic society cannot be maintained in an industrial age unless industry is democratized. If the democratic way of life is denied where human beings work together daily it cannot be maintained in those more remote and less tangible social relationships involved in politics and social organization. Indeed those dominant in our industrial feudalism are coming, more and more, to be dominant in civic and social life.

William P. Hapgood is lighting a pilot light for industrial democracy, and though he is not a churchman, he is giving a finer expression to that sense of brotherhood taught by the Carpenter of Nazareth than are churches which allow distinctions of class and culture to condition fellowship, and from whose pulpits the plea of the prophet for the rights of the least of these is never heard. His creed may be found in the words of Walt Whitman:

"I will accept nothing which others cannot have the counterpart of on the same terms."

Labor Can Lead

SIDNEY HILLMAN

NOT so many years ago an American Communist in a fine careless rapture, wrote a story about a convention of the Amalgamated Clothing Workers of America at which Sidney Hillman reported on the efforts of the Amalgamated to help the clothing industries of Soviet Russia. It was a colorful piece of excited adulation and he headed it, "Red Roses for Hillman." Nowadays, of course, it is anything but roses for Hillman from the Communists.

It must be granted that the temptation to dramatize the sudden emergence of this youngest of important labor unions with its youthful-appearing leader is a strong one. But when you sit down and talk with Hillman and his fellow officers about the policies and achievements of the Amalgamated, the pictures of surging picket lines, of May Day celebrations—all the red roses stuff—are subordinated by the very practical blueprints of a modern labor organization, compact and militant and at the same time cooperative and constructive. For the Amalgamated can fight with a drive and punch which many a hard-boiled operator has had reason to rue. And it can step in at peace-times with scientific reorganization schemes for the betterment of the industry which have been gratefully received by many a hard-pressed employer on the verge of bankruptcy.

If just now there is a pause in the quickstep of the drama during the first embattled days of organization, there is plenty of thrill left for the more thoughtful in the manner with which these coat-makers, pants-makers, cutters, vest-makers, spongers, examiners and bushelmen, the workers in the men's clothing industry of the country, meet the every day problems of their trade. The process of building a genuine industrial democracy out of what might seem at first sight the most unpromising of human material in all the world of labor has its fascination for the onlooker.

It has long been the custom of Sidney Hillman to say to his interviewers, "Please keep the personality business out. After all, it is the organization, not any individual, that matters." And there is no false modesty about this. He means it. He does not give himself freely. He is the despair of the more popular school of biographers. Nowhere, in all the vast literature about the Amalgamated, the mere bibliography of which fills a good-sized pamphlet, is there any biography of Hillman. He would be rash indeed who would attempt to penetrate that screen of reserve which Hillman throws around himself with the usual Sunday-section interview questions about the man's hobbies, his private life, his thoughts on immortality, the younger generation and the like. So completely has he submerged himself in the crowded life of the organization which he heads, that it is doubtful if many of his closest associates know very well their unofficial Hillman.

He is forty-three years old and today he is president of an organization of one hundred thousand men and women which is by all odds the most successful and significant trade union in the United States. Under his continuous leadership, the Union, born as recently as 1914, has organized seventy-five per cent of the workers in the men's and children's clothing industry in the major American and Canadian cities. The standard union agreement calls for the forty-four-hour week and a joint commission to study the feasibility of the forty-hour week. Workers are protected under the agreement against arbitrary discharge and the hiring of workers is done through Union Employment Exchanges. Wage rates are fixed by the Union and the employers jointly.

These gains have been won and consolidated in the face of the most desperate odds. At the beginning there was a chaotic, sweated, slum-bred industry, with the workers almost without exception recently arrived immigrants, unable to speak English and ignorant of the customs and conditions of other American industries, helpless victims of exploitation. More-over, there was a sinister onslaught upon the new "outlaw" union on the part of the old-line organizations of the American Federation of Labor to be met and conquered. From the very outset the clothing workers had to stand on their own feet, as often as not to be knocked off them, only to get up and go on. To go on to the laborious building-up of a system of industrial government which has become the model for the progressive world, to go on to educational and housing projects, to unemployment insurance and labor banking until the Union has made itself part and parcel of the every-day life of its members, outside as well as inside the shops.

In the face of this achievement, it may well seem to Hillman that his personal story is of little significance. And it would be, were it not for the fact that there is contained in it, as in the story of every pathfinder, a clue to that baffling thing which we call leadership.

Looking back across Hillman's life one sees the bold out-lines of a philosophy which has moulded and tempered his character and motivated all his activities. In this he is sharply set apart from the run of American labor leaders. Consider, for example, the career of John Mitchell of the miners as told in Elsie Gluck's able biography. All his life long, in spite of what he did for his people in the great anthracite strikes,

Mitchell drifted, a bit bewildered by any shifting of familiar scenes, ready enough to fight, to lead a forlorn hope, but utterly unable to adapt his strategy to new economic environs. As a result, he left very little of permanence behind him except the tradition of implacable warfare. And as a result, too, the miners have today fought themselves to a frazzle so that their last state bids likely to be worse than their first. And all through the labor movement the old-line leaders are following the Mitchell aimlessness without even the saving grace of Mitchell's militancy.

Hillman, on the other hand, has been at work consciously forging an instrument to be handed on to his people after he has gone. To be sure, he has willingly gone out to battle, but his concern has not been chiefly with open and violent hostilities between the workers and their bosses. Always he has had in the back of his active mind, the building into an industry of a stable labor organization which will be indispensable to the running of that industry. "The union," he says, "cannot take the position of an outsider in relation to the industry; it must fight for a place in the councils of the industry, a place of power as well as responsibility. Having achieved that place, the union must proceed to utilize its new position." So the Amalgamated statisticians and research men and industrial engineers (though they don't call themselves that, of course) have come to be fully as important in the life of the union as strike committeemen and picket-line leaders. Men of the Amalgamated have been studying the various and often hidden elements of labor costs. They have looked earnestly into the opportunities for increasing efficiency of operation without endangering union standards. And they have gone farther into fields where labor has hitherto never thought of entering, the fields of overhead costs, selling and purchasing expenses. They have been able to see the industry on which they are dependent, clearly and wholly, which is more than most manufacturers do.

Very naturally this technique, so alien to the pure and simple unionism of the A. F. of L., has raised no end of hob at both extremes of the labor movement. The Communists howl "class collaboration" whenever there is a conference between union officials and employers on ways and means of stabilizing the industry. Many old-line Socialists accuse Hillman of forsaking Marx for Frederick W. Taylor. The tired and prematurely aged men in the hierarchy of the A. F. of L. look upon this slight, bespectacled, young Russian Jew with anxious eyes. He causes them great unhappiness. He is doing the things they are too indolent or too stupid to do.

And in the midst of all this criticism, far too busy to be ruffled for one moment by it, Sidney Hillman goes on his way, remarking:

"The unfolding of a positive and constructive program by popular mass movements is generally slow and painful and has been no less so with the labor movement. If, out of the tangled mass of labor manifestos, platforms and preambles to constitutions of labor organizations, anything tangible and orderly emerges, it is the description of organized labor as the machine for achieving democracy in industry. Stripped of the very special literary quality that still helps to conceal the ideas of labor movements, their goal is the adoption of representative government in industry and through this government, the progressive achievement of a more equal distribution of the wealth and income of the country. The methods of reaching this goal vary from time to time and place to place, but the variations are accidental and temporary; the direction, irresistible and permanent."

These are the words of a man who knows what he is about, whose own direction is "irresistible and permanent."

At the very outset, for example, it was his keen sense of direction which made him decide (at the advanced age of fifteen) that his place was not in the rabbinical school to which his people had sent him but with the revolutionary movement in Czarist Russia. He was born in the little town of Zager in Lithuania, then a part of Russia, and when he was thirteen he was sent to the Seminar at Kovno to be a holy man. But he read Zola and La Salle in preference to the literature which the school offered, and by fifteen he was a confirmed revolutionist.

During the abortive revolution of 1905-6, he and a group of other rebel youngsters took over the town of Zager in the name of the people and were running it through a proletarian committee of which Hillman was the guiding spirit, when the Czar's police arrived. Hillman and his friends fled, assumed other names and were hunted through the country. The youth was arrested three times in 1906. It was during a four months' incarceration in a jail near Dvinsk that he first read Marx.

England, the traditional place and refuge for revolutionists, had no job in the Socialist movement sufficient to absorb the energy of young Hillman, and after a year there he headed for America. He went to Chicago and found work as a clerk with Sears, Roebuck. Distasteful, monotonous, underpaid work it was too, but it gave him the chance to learn English and look around a bit.

Most of his friends were in the clothing business, and after a year with the mail-order house he went as an apprentice into the cutting-room of Hart, Schaffner and Marx, the acknowledged leaders of the men's clothing industry and the one big firm which had refused to enter the Chicago Wholesale Clothiers' Association, an organization of the other "inside" concerns formed in defense against the new, small tailor shops.

Hillman came to the cutting table at a time when a bitter

trade war was being waged between H. S. and M. and the Association shops. In this war, the workers played the unenviable rôle of innocent bystanders and were liberally shot up by both sides.

"Gradually," says a historian of that struggle, "under the competition of more powerful firms the smaller inside shops were driven out of independent business. Many of them turned their inside shops into contract shops and began to work for these big firms on a contract basis. The contractors thus found themselves caught between the upper and nether millstones of the Association firms and their rival, Hart, Schaffner and Marx. They became mere pawns in the fight for supremacy. The first important move in this struggle came in response to a tactical increase in contractor's prices, granted by the association houses, when Hart, Schaffner and Marx suddenly withdrew all work from their contract shops and opened in their place inside shops employing over eight thousand tailors. This step was the signal on the part of both competitors to reduce their labor costs. . . . At the same time Hart, Schaffner and Marx would try to preserve its competitive position by cutting the wages of its workers. This whole process was also made easy by the prevalence of piece work in an unorganized market. Without protection of their piece rates, the workers would be speeded up and then, when their earnings increased, would have their piece rate cut."

Thoughtfully the apprentice cutter looked upon this amazing spectacle of "rugged individualism" at full play. The whole vicious business, bearing down hardest as it did upon the helpless workers, was an affront at once to his humanity and his innate sense of order and direction. With a number of other socially minded youngsters he began to talk about the necessity for having a powerful and continuous organization of the workers to oppose the forces which were preying upon them.

Then of a sudden came the now historic strike of 1910. Among labor and liberal circles, that strike has become a subject for sagas. Around it is a glamor and a glory and, though ostensibly it failed, it represented the dawning of civilization in a barbaric industry. It has been described as "a simultaneous upheaval of over forty-one thousand garment workers, brought on by sixteen girls, against petty persecution, low wages, abuse and long hours; an upheaval unorganized at the start, which later took on the form of a fight for recognition of the union." There were at first no specific demands as the men and women came down from the shops. The only demand was that something be done to make life bearable for the workers. When the sixteen girls walked out of a pants shop of H. S. and M. rather than accept a wage-cut of a quarter cent in rates, no one suspected that within three weeks more than forty thousand would follow and that the entire industry of the city would be affected. But that is what happened; and that mass exodus was the signal for the entrance on the American labor scene of the young apprentice cutter with a well-disciplined mind, a nice sense of direction and an organizing genius that put him at once in the front rank of the strikers.

The logical union for the carrying on of the strike was the United Garment Workers, which had been established in the Nineties as the result of a row between the A. F. of L. and the old Knights of Labor. It existed mainly through the sale of union labels in the overall industry. Its officials had not concerned themselves with the lot of the immigrant workers. "The American Labor movement did not want to know us," said an Amalgamated official the other day, "but we wanted very much to know them."

The strikers went to the United Garment Workers for aid and were received with snobbish indifference. Finally the union was forced by a militant Socialist press to call a general strike, but from then on the conduct of its officials in the strike was open to the liveliest suspicion. Time and again the workers voted down the obviously meaningless "agreements" which these officials proposed. It was such organizations as the Women's Trade Union League and Hull House, and such individuals as Mrs. Raymond Robins, President of the League and chairman of the strike fund committee, Ellen Gates Starr, Katherine Coman, Jane Addams, of course, and Robert Dvorak, hard-hitting editor of *The Daily Socialist,* who brought to the attention of the outside world the facts of the struggle. And to the everlasting credit of John Fitzpatrick and Ed Nockel, of the Chicago Federation of Labor, be it said that here were two "American labor leaders" who were not afraid to come out and stand with the despised "foreigners."

On January 14, 1911 an agreement was signed between the management of Hart, Schaffner and Marx and the workers in that organization which marked the beginning of a relationship unique in the history of collective bargaining in this country and which was to give Sidney Hillman and his associates a chance to test their theories of industrial democracy in the light of everyday realities.

While the bulk of the workers, beaten throughout the rest of the industry, betrayed by old-time labor leaders, blacklisted by the bosses, were begging for reemployment under the old conditions, the H. S. and M. employees were returning to work, 6,000 of them—men, women and girls—under an agreement which set up a new form of machinery for the adjustment of disputes. This provided for an arbitration committee with each side selecting one arbitrator and the two to pick a third. It also established the Labor Complaint Department for the settlement of day-by-day grievances.

Clarence Darrow and Carl Meyer were the first arbitrators, and Professor Earl Dean Howard was head of the Labor Complaint Department. No one knew just how the new machine would work. Those were days of trial and error. The habit of sporadic strikes in small sections was still strong upon the workers. Professor Howard and Sidney Hillman went about patiently explaining that there was a new and better way of adjusting grievances. The Complaint Department was soon up to its neck with cases large and small for adjudication. The great bulk of them had to be taken up to the overworked arbitrators. Finally, when it looked as though discontent would bring on another strike, Professor Howard and Carl Meyer for the employers and Sidney Hillman and W. O. Thompson for the workers devised an instrument which they called the Trade Board. The Board functioned principally through deputies selected by both management and men whose duties were to investigate all grievances and if possible settle them on the spot. On that board Hillman was the deputy for the coat tailors and one of the outstanding figures. Within two years the deputies had adjusted 1,178 cases or 84 per cent of those brought before it. During this time only one per cent of the cases went as high as the Board of Arbitration.

"This Trade Board was created," said Hillman, "so that it was really a new method of adjusting complaints—an adjustment by the workers themselves. It introduces what I call the new principle in organization: that if the workers are to be disciplined for any violation of the agreement, they themselves partly should be the judges."

Inequality of piece prices, a high-handed foreman, varying quality of work demanded, inadequate toilet facilities, division of work in slack times, payment for overtime—with such workaday matters were Hillman and the other deputies concerned. This was their school where all philosophies were put to the pragmatic test, and psychology took on more than an academic meaning. Today its graduates, with Hillman at their head, have brought into the trade union world new concepts of industrial government, at once the despair of the conservative and the shining hope of the progressive.

It was in the course of this work that Hillman met Bessie Abramowitz, deputy for the dressmakers, whom he later married.

In the meanwhile with the H. S. and M. shops as nucleus, a persistent educational campaign was being waged among the other workers in the market, looking towards their eventual organization and a fresh attempt at winning freedom. In Chicago, Hillman and his group were talking twice a week at meetings held independently of the A. F. of L. or the Garment Workers' Union. "The tailors are studying," ran a report on these well attended meetings, "and when another strike comes, another story will be written."

New York had now come dramatically into the picture with the hard-fought cloakmakers' strike of 1913. And New York wanted Hillman. The first Hart, Schaffner and Marx agreement had not been a union agreement in the technical sense of the word, but out of it the union had grown so that in March, 1913, a bona fide trade union agreement was signed by the representatives of the firm and the local unions under the United Garment Workers, the Chicago Federation of Labor and the Women's Trade Union League. So to New York Hillman went to take up the delicate job of Chief Deputy of the Cloakmakers' Union, with the cheers of the Chicago workers celebrating three years of peace ringing in his ears.

This was in the early part of 1914, and he found himself plunged into a situation requiring tact, patience and all his great powers of conciliation. The cloakmakers had just been through a bitter internal row and a desperate strike. While Hillman tackled this job with his customary effectiveness, his heart was back in Chicago. It was evident by now that the time had come for a definite break with the inept officialdom of the United Garment Workers. The old guard of the United and the up-and-coming young men of the Chicago market simply did not speak the same language.

The break came in a red-hot convention of the United Garment Workers held in Nashville in 1914. President Rickert of the U. G. W. succeeded in keeping some one hundred and fifty clothing delegates off the floor of the convention on a technicality. But he had made the mistake of recognizing Rissman and Rosenblum, and these two made life miserable for him by accusing the officers of using unconstitutional and dishonest methods and finally by leading the clothing workers in a shouting and triumphant march to a nearby hotel. Only the subservient overall workers were left. In the new headquarters it was announced that in view of the fact that the convention called by Rickert was illegal, Sidney Hillman of Local No. 39, Chicago, was unanimously elected General President of the United Garment Workers of America with that stout-hearted idealist Joseph Schlossberg of Local No. 156, New York, General Secretary.

This was the nucleus of the Amalgamated. The American Federation of Labor sided instantly and instinctively with the Rickert forces and officially excommunicated the rebels. To this day the A. F. of L. officials pretend to regard the Amalgamated as a "dual union." The executives of the new United Garment Workers called a convention of their followers to meet in New York on Christmas Day, 1914, to begin the needed work of removing "the antiquated and undemocratic forms and methods of our organization." The general of-

ficers selected at the rump convention were here confirmed
and, as an agreement had been made with the Tailors' Industrial Union for their amalgamation with the new group, it
was decided to adopt the name, Amalgamated Clothing Workers of America.

Now definitely on their own, the organizers for the Amalgamated went vigorously into the Chicago market and by
September, 1915, 25,000 workers were on strike. The strike
was called off in December despite the fact that it had received notable support from the public. Mayor Thompson and
his club-swinging police proved themselves faithful allies of
the employers. But important concessions were made to the
workers and, while the union was not recognized, the tailors
went back to work with union cards in their pockets.

Victory came gloriously four years later when the Chicago
market, the last of the big markets to withstand the union,
surrendered *en masse* and at a huge meeting on May 13, 1919,
Sidney Hillman standing on the platform at Carmen's Hall
read the agreement to his people. It meant that the Amalgamated Clothing Workers of America had become a national
organization in fact as well as name and that a handful of
earnest young men mainly recruited from Hart, Schaffner and
Marx had blazed a new trail for the freedom of thousands.

Those who follow labor's world even from the outside are
familiar enough with what the Amalgamated has done since
then. They know of its educational work, of its prospering
labor banks in New York and Chicago, of its unemployment
insurance systems in Chicago, Rochester and New York. Tailors, today, once the pariahs of the labor movement, are living
in New York in up-to-date apartments with garden spaces
around them for which they pay $11 per room, per month,
and all the civic planners are wondering how it happens that

a trade union can do this for its people whereas no municipality has as yet had the courage to attempt such a project.

Today tailors are playing handball, after hours, in the big gymnasium of the Amalgamated Centre in Chicago and cooling off with a swim in the pool. They are reading their own papers edited by as brilliant journalists as can be found on any old-line publication. They are depositing money in their own banks, and their deposits make the minimum wages of 1911 of $6 and $8 a week seem the pay of paupers. Instead of the fifty-four hours of those days, they are working forty-four and looking to a forty-hour week in the near future.

"The clothing workers," says J. B. S. Hardman, editor of the weekly organ of the Amalgamated, *The Advance*, "was not born into this world to baste coats, to press pants, to fit lapels. . . . The tailor was not born to carry on strikes, to live up to agreements, to vote for officers, to be organized into local unions. All these institutions have come into being in order to serve the tailor, the cutter, the presser, to make their lives more reasonable, more attractive, more livable, to make their lives worth living. The clothing workers were not made for the Amalgamated, but the Amalgamated for the clothing workers. The extent to which the Amalgamated has helped the clothing workers enlarge their living is the measure of the organization's legitimate pride. What can be done beyond that is the unlimited field of the Union's ambition." On the whole it would seem that Sidney Hillman's approach is astonishingly resultful.

He speaks of the "open secret of successful organization." Any labor leader is entitled to try it. It consists first in having an objective. His happens to be the more equal distribution of income through organization of democratic machinery in industry. And then you go on to examine the peculiar economic terrain which is yours to cross until you are more fam-

SIDNEY HILLMAN

iliar with its characteristics than any of those who would block your way. Finally you bring your crowd along with you by persistent and repeated demonstrations that you know where you are going and that your way is the way for them. Simple, isn't it? But how few are doing it. And how many are content to announce their goal in wordy phrases and let it go at that!

Hillman is a shy, serious, often sombre man. As he has come to the other side of forty and the strains and stresses of one of the most difficult of jobs, that of labor leader, have begun to take their toll, Hillman has grown more and more impatient of inefficiency on the part of those around him. He is hard to work for because he demands that his official family give everything they have to the building of the Amalgamated just as he has done. As a consequence he has plenty of enemies who will tell you that he has become swollen with power and is rapidly cutting himself off from his rank and file. Everything indicates that this is rather what the psychologists call "wish fulfillment" on the part of Hillman's foes than an exact statement of the truth. It is in line with the charge of the extremists that Hillman is losing his radical punch and turning his back on the revolutionaries of yesterday. You will find the answer to this charge in a speech that he made just after his visit to Russia where he and Lenin talked for hours about almost everything except the theory of revolution. Said Hillman:

"There is no patent medicine, right, left or center or any other kind. It takes men and women to build an organization, and not abstract theories. It takes warm hearts to maintain ideals, and not phraseology. . . . Conditions will arise, dictated by life, and not by the theories of a few dreamers, and it is much more important to have a proper policy than a great deal of noise."

A Statesman Can Be a Prophet

FRANCIS J. McCONNELL

ONE of the American Episcopal bishops who attended the Lambeth Conference last summer in London brought back a story for the truth of which he vouches with all the weight of his apostolic succession. The assembled clergymen, many of them in serried ranks of gaiters, bishops of the Church of England, the American Episcopal Church, of the Anglican Church in British dominions, were having a group photograph taken. The zero hour had come. Faces were being composed with fitting ecclesiastical gravity. The photographer, standing in front of them, just ready to snap the shutter of his camera, issued a last warning, *"Remember, any movement will spoil the group!"*

The photographer was not conscious of having made a generalization on church history, but he came very near summing up a common idea of the spiritual leadership of bishops. It is a conception they themselves have supported with ample evidence. Bishops as a class have not been distinguished for "movement." The hierarchy, time out of mind, has reiterated, "Remember, any movement will spoil the group. Hold steady." And as a group they have held steady with magnificent control. The picture has been unspoiled by any distressing degree of violent movement, either intellectual or spiritual. They have been for the most part a static group like the frieze on the front elevation of a cathedral, unruffled by dynamic upheavals. The typical bishop has been more

FRANCIS J. MCCONNELL

like the curator of a historical museum, than a Peter the Hermit.

"Our Fathers have been churchmen,
Nineteen hundred years or so,
And to every new proposal,
They have always answered, No."

Such at least is the common conception of bishops. We meet with it not only in the England of Oliver Cromwell, but in the New York of Jimmie Walker.

That is one reason many find it hard to fit Francis J. McConnell into a group of bishops for the essence of the man is movement. Not physical movement. In conference or on the platform or in the pulpit he is about as animated as the Sphinx. There is a rumor to the effect that about a dozen years ago he made a gesture in the pulpit. But as no confirmation of that can be secured, and as he has not done it since, it must be set down as legend. It is doubtful whether during the last decade or two he has taken any more violent physical exercise than that required to scramble into an upper berth in a Pullman car. But in all the years of his public life his mind has been in emphatic and incessant movement, pushing out into fresh fields of thought and action.

Canon Streeter in the concluding chapters of his book, "The Primitive Church" suggests that the First Christians achieved what they did achieve because the spirit which inspired them was "favorable to experiment." If that be true, Bishop McConnell would have been quite at home in the first century church. The temper of his mind is "favorable to experiment." That temper has carried him into scores of experiments and into the thick of many a fight for some fresh advance toward a social order which recognizes the primacy of human values and human welfare. It is that temper of his mind which has made him perhaps the leading social prophet of American Christianity.

Bishop McConnell has been a sort of enigma to many both within and without the church. He does not fit neatly into any pre-arranged pigeonhole. He is an odd size. And that is baffling. He combines qualities rarely found together, qualities which one does not expect to find together. Indeed, in one striking combination of qualities, that of uniting the administrative talents of an executive bishop with untrammeled and passionate prophecy on social questions, only one other man comes readily to mind—the late Bishop Charles D. Williams of Michigan. That does not mean that there are no socially-minded bishops in the United States. There are many. One of the most hopeful trends in present ecclesiastical life is that their number is increasing. Two bishops elected within the last two years are striking instances of this trend of putting prophetically-minded preachers into the office of bishop: Bishop William J. Scarlett of Missouri, and Bishop Charles K. Gilbert of New York. But in many instances the class just referred to are more accurately described as bishops with a social outlook rather than prophets who happen to be bishops.

The outstanding significance of McConnell in the life of the United States today is expressed in the title of this article—"A Statesman Can Be a Prophet." To those oppressed by the heavy weight of a conventional ecclesiasticism, to those who have seen so often the tragedy of some promising personality congealed and stiffened by the demands of the office of bishop, McConnell is a portent of hope. It is probably no exaggeration to say that the largest service he has rendered to thousands of ministers in the country is to furnish the spectacle of a man standing in the very center of the ecclesiastical machinery, neither overwhelmed nor suffocated by it, but putting it all to the service of an undeflected purpose— the purpose of carrying into the complex welter of modern life the spiritual and ethical implications of the Christian gospel.

It is significant that this forthright prophet has not done his work on a soapbox. There is a place for the soapbox. In the old complacent days of the foreign missionary movement a generation ago, it used to be said that missionaries were carrying "soap and civilization to the Orient." We have begun to be in doubt about the civilization; we are even weakening on the redemptive qualities of soap. And while it appears that the soapbox is more important than the soap, nevertheless, it has its limitations as an instrument of social transformation. It is fragile and it is very moveable. McConnell has undoubtedly accomplished far more as a responsible executive than he would have as a wandering firebrand. Within the framework of the ecclesiastical scheme, persuasively but relentlessly, he has carried into the minds of people the desire for a new social order which has the abundant life for all as its goal.

How did he "get that way?" What is it that has given him a unique position, this administrator whose chief distinction is as a prophet? We turn to *Who's Who* for an answer, and *Who's Who* answers in Biblical language, "It is not in me." We find a succession of different posts which he filled, an impressive chronicle of a rise to influential position; yet outwardly it is like many another "success" story. It would make an excellent feature for the *American Magazine* under some such title as "From Country Preacher to Bishop in Sixteen Years," thus establishing a new American speed record in ladder-climbing. The Trinway, Ohio, papers—if there are any papers in Trinway—would be entitled to reprint excerpts from the story with the usual formula, "Local Boy Makes Good in Big City." Nevertheless from the recital of the mere outward facts of the McConnell career we gain no more idea of the content of the story, the shaping of a great personality and social force, than we would get an idea of the meaning of Hamlet by reciting the location of the various scenes from the platform at *Elsinore* down to the location of the last act.

Let it not be thought, however, that this rise to the highest place within the gift of his own church is meaningless. It is vastly to the credit of the Methodist Church and organized Christianity in general that there has been this response to thoughtful, courageous, prophetic leadership as reflected in a man like Bishop McConnell, a man who has deliberately renounced all the devices of the popular orator and the ingratiating "beam" of the "glad-hander." Before looking at an outline of his life, let us take a further glimpse at several unusual combinations of qualities which he exhibits.

First of all, despite the fact that he is a competent philosopher, McConnell has a keen appraisal of all the forces that are making a din on the street corner—the jumble that is modern industrialism. Indeed, his understanding of and interest in economic and social questions do not go hand in hand with the usual conception of a mathematician and a philosopher. Fundamentally, however, it is as a philosopher that he has made a genuine contribution to his time. His first book, produced during a crowded pastorate in Brooklyn, bore the title *The Diviner Imminence*. Other books showing the mind of the man are *Is God Limited?* and *Public Opinion and Theology*. He frequently carries around in his pocket, as a means of recreation, an analytical geometry. This is one way he has kept his mind sharpened—like stropping a razor. One would expect a man of such interests and accomplishments to act as if he had a study on Mount Everest, far from the madding crowd's ignoble strife. A philosopher who fits into such a picture is Hegel—he who wandered into the little town of Jena on the day of Napoleon's colossal battle, and asked what all the disturbance was about! Frequently the philosophic thinker comes into the hurly-burly of industrial life like the gentle soul in George M. Cohan's drama *The Tavern* asking, "What's all the shootin' for?" McConnell knows what the shooting is about.

Recently the papers carried the announcement that Bishop so-and-so would speak on Holy Innocents Day. That sounds quite appropriate, for most bishops are "Holy Innocents." Some would raise a question about the holiness at times, but there would be no question about the innocents. Bishop McConnell would not qualify as a Holy Innocent.

This concern over economic and social questions is not exhausted in oratory, for there is no oratory. McConnell's leadership among groups outside the church and frequently antagonistic to religion rests, for one thing, on their knowledge that he can and does fight.

A shrewd observer said of another bishop sometime ago that whenever you urged him, "Now is the time we will have to take off our coats and fight" you always reached the end of the chapter. His ideas were excellent, his spirit was fine, but he never got out of the rhetorical and academic realm. He never in his life got his hands dirty or his shirt soiled by a rough-and-tumble fight. The McConnell coat strips off easily; in fact it is off a good deal of the time. This does not mean that he is a victim of the juvenile bad boy complex, with a fondness for breaking windows in order to hear the noise and watch the consternation of the higher respectabilities. Wherever a struggle is called for such as his participation in the campaign for old age security, in the Steel Strike

Report of 1919, and in the work of the American Civil Liberties Union, he has been in the midst of it. In his own church he has been responsible for a great deal of the advanced legislation as well as the declarations on social questions that have been written into the official pronouncements. In the last twenty years, with Harry F. Ward, he has made the Methodist Federation for Social Service a genuine force for projecting questions into the minds of the church and has given it an influence far out of proportion to its small membership and meager resources.

Another rare combination of qualities in Bishop McConnell is that of the expert ecclesiastical executive whose main interest in life is not the shell of religion but its soul. And, make no mistake about it, McConnell is an amazingly accomplished bishop in all the details of his job. If he were not, easy allowances could be made for him. People would say, "How can you expect a prophet to be an administrator? Let him alone, poor dear, he is a flaming soul. Of course, steering a ship through a rocky channel isn't his forte." But nobody has ever made that apology. There is no more efficient officer in his own church or in any legislative body in the United States. Behold him presiding over an annual conference, a task which must often be the dreariest occupation to which a man can be chained; you will see him on the platform looking like Macbeth contemplating the dagger, or an Indian *yogi* lost in meditation upon the absolute; or he is writing a letter on a matter thousands of miles away. The business gets into a nasty snarl. Then quietly you hear the voice of the bishop: "If the chair may be allowed to say a word, I would suggest that you got into this jam by the fact that the first amendment to the motion was out of order owing to its illegality, according to section 294, paragraph 5 of the Discipline. To loosen the knot you can push this end through that loop, give it a sharp move to the right and pull, and all will be straight."

Yet with this competence, which far surpasses that of many bishops who are noted for little else but complete devotion to ecclesiastical machinery, he has never allowed his interest to be absorbed in the means to the extent of forgetting the end. The best illustration of this faculty for refusing to dissipate his energy in fussy merry-go-rounds is expressed in a recent address he made to a group of ministers: "We have to guard ourselves against the idea that when we are busy we are necessarily busy with something worth while. Some men can come home tired out from what they have been doing all day long and none of it amounts to very much. . . . A good rule to follow is this: Anything you can get anybody else to do, let him do it. That is the mark of a true executive—turning over to anybody, who can do it as well as you, work that otherwise you would have to handle."

One of the shrewdest observations I have ever seen on this was made by Walter Bagehot of England who said that in the business world it is always a bad sign when the head of the house is too busy for it means ordinarily that he is getting lost in details. That certainly is true of ministers. "When ministers get too much to do and miss the main matters, then the minister begins to suffer and the church begins to suffer."

As a public speaker Bishop McConnell has shown complete disdain of the ordinary arts and devices of the consciously impressive orator; yet he has been heard with eagerness for a generation. Not for him the thunders of Niagara; not for him the music of the spheres! He has made himself understood in the vernacular of New York, Pittsburgh, and Denver. Let it be confessed there have been times when, to those who were looking for that harmonious bombardment of the organs of hearing usually associated with bishops, McConnell has been a frost—a complete frost. He has "busted up" camp meetings by speaking in the tone and language of truth and soberness. One of the standing jokes in his denomination is the tale of an audience which was "stampeded by McConnell's emotional appeal." To a large audience he talks in the same conversational tone that he uses to a small conference group. Those brought up on the tradition of the stereotyped "bishop's sermon" find him a puzzle. The McConnell type of oratory bears about the same relation to the old-fashioned, three-decked, full-rigged elocution that David's method of warfare did to Goliath's. One often thinks that Goliath would have made a great bishop. He had the figure, the resonance, the authority. David had none of these. But his five stones out of the brook were well selected. McConnell, like David, wields a wicked sling shot. The technique is simple but the words do what David's pebbles did to Goliath—they land in the head and make a decided dent.

By the undiscerning McConnell's lack of effusiveness has often been set down as coldness. Certainly the Bishop was never designed as the "greeter" at a hotel. But this seeming undemonstrativeness is in accord with his dominating concern for human welfare. His interest, having no outlet in mere emotionalism, is channelled into action. One Methodist bishop, giving expression to this false test which measures sensitiveness and sympathy by outward signs that cost nothing, declared not long ago that the episcopacy was too much of a strain on him. He could not, he said, appoint a man to a difficult place and then go on to the next order of business. He would toss about all the night afterward. "I am not a McConnell," he explained. A few months later Bishop McConnell, referring to this in a public address, remarked that he could go on to the next order of the day because he had done his tossing the night before and not the night afterward!

Many of his traits are hereditary endowments. His father,

the Reverend I. H. McConnell, was a minister, one of the vigorous preachers of his time, who served churches in Ohio and Indiana and, in the later years of his life, in Massachusetts. His mother, who died only three or four years ago, was a woman of amazing force and skill and spirit. It would be understating the truth to say that she combined the wisdom of the serpent with the gentleness of the dove, for we have never met a serpent endowed with the ability to rear a family of five children in the manner in which Mrs. McConnell did after the death of her husband.

Francis McConnell was born on a farm in Ohio and had reached the age of seventeen when his father died. He was at that time a student at Andover Academy, having already worked in the textile mills of Lawrence, Massachusetts. His mother took the family back to the farm in Trinway, Ohio, and set her heart and mind and will on securing an education for the children. Francis worked on the farm and acquired the physical robustness which has made possible his later energy. His competence may be judged from the fact that neighboring farmers offered to pay him twenty-five dollars a month for his services. But his mother insisted that this rapid road to wealth be put aside and that he go to school. In 1893 he was graduated from Ohio Wesleyan University, where he won several oratorical contests, and, as tradition has it, showed considerable genius for campus politics, and a flair for bringing results to pass while all the time maintaining the appearance of an innocent bystander—an accomplishment he has developed to a fine point in the years since.

After commencement he enrolled in the Boston School of Theology where unquestionably the greatest formative influence in his education was Professor Borden P. Bowne. It was the latter's recognition and enthusiastic appreciation of McConnell's rare capacity for philosophic thinking which gained him his first reputation. On graduating from the Theological Seminary, young McConnell accepted a Massachusetts pastorate and in 1903 was called to the New York Avenue Methodist Church of Brooklyn.

One of the first things which drew the attention of the church at large to the mental acumen of the young preacher was the incident known as the Mitchell case. Hinkley G. Mitchell, of Boston University School of Theology, Professor of Old Testament, failed to be confirmed for reelection to his position by the Bishops of the Methodist Episcopal Church, who at that time had the power of rejecting a professor. The case was one of the battles for a modern and liberal interpretation of Scripture, and it made history in the Protestant churches in general. When, later, charges of heresy were brought against Professor Mitchell, the vigilant defenders of the faith who were out for Mitchell's scalp struck a snag in their victim's counsel, young McConnell. As Clarence Darrow once said after a debate with Bishop McConnell on the question of a mechanistic universe, "It was like monkeying with a buzz-saw." The Mitchell Case was historic in establishing freedom of thought in the church.

That it is today practically impossible in the Methodist Church to convict a minister of heresy is in no small degree due to McConnell and his stand in the Mitchell case.

After a pastorate of six years in the Brooklyn church, McConnell was elected, in 1909, President of DePauw University, at Greencastle, Indiana. That office was a test, not only of his executive competence but of his courage. A college presidency is the most effective snare into which a prophet can step. The office has so many liabilities. A president is prone to develop throat trouble which prevents his giving expression to anything more dangerous than "Honesty is the best policy" or "The American Home must be maintained."

There are so many perfectly sound reasons for stepping on
the soft pedal that the utterances of college presidents are, as
a rule, quite pianissimo. What man of sense could not per-
suade himself that "It is no use to be quixotic"; "The time is
not ripe for entering this disputed field"; "There is a time
for everything"; "Don't bite the hand that is feeding you"?
These wise mottoes can be found all the way down the slippery
path that leads to new buildings and lost souls. During the
four years at DePauw, McConnell was not only a theological
progressive in a region filled with listening ears that were keen
to note divergence from sacred shibboleths, but he was outspoken on social questions when an interest in them was novel.
In all ways he threw himself into the work of making a
liberal college and refused the rôle of a financial go-getter.

Four years later in 1912 he was elected a Bishop of the
Methodist Episcopal Church. Those who are familar with
many such elections can sing with hearty faith Cowper's
hymn, "God moves in a mysterious way His wonders to
perform." But McConnell's election was a mystery of another
sort. It was a hopeful mystery that in a realm in which there
has been such an entanglement of wires of all sorts he came
into the office through faith of the ablest men of the church
and because of his combination of intellectual, prophetic, and
executive capacities. For eight years he was located in Denver
where he faced the issues of a rampant industrialism and
developed his peculiar method of episcopal leadership, which
can well be called peculiar in that it consists not in programs
but in holding up the goals for a dynamic church, in the
inspiration of ministers, and, above all, in backing them up
when they get into hot water.

An instance of McConnell's lifelong discovery of men was
his support of Dr. D. D. Forsyth who rendered memorable
services as Secretary to the Board of Home Missions. It is

no secret that it was McConnell's backing which gave Forsyth the position and resulted in bringing to the work of home missions, which to so large an extent had been the routine operation of a sort of ecclesiastic bureaucracy, a new social outlook and a readiness to experiment.

In 1920 Bishop McConnell was transferred to Pittsburgh. For this man to be projected into a great steel center dominated by a big-business psychology, in a time of growing tension, there were elements of irony. The outstanding feature of those years was McConnell's chairmanship of the Inter-Church Movement Committee which produced the report on the steel strike of 1919. About that achievement there are three striking things characteristic of the man. In the first place, he could easily have sidestepped the job. It was ticklish business at best. He could have said, as hundreds of men have said on similar occasions, "I would like nothing better personally than to do this but I cannot think of myself alone. There are the responsibilities of my position" and so on for a thousand glowing words, at the end of which the speaker really begins to pity himself for not being allowed to go into the fight. McConnell had never learned the crab sidestep. In the second place, he was largely responsible for the procedure adopted that the report should not be the cursory investigation of busy ministers and others on the committee, but should be the scientifically produced, documented investigation of competent experts. Consequently when the report appeared, the rains descended and the flood came, but it stood because it was founded upon a rock. The partisans of the steel company at the time attempted to apply the familiar smokescreen: "Here is what a bunch of harebrained preachers do when they get lost in unfamiliar fields," but it soon fell of its own weight. However, it was not enough merely to bring in the report. The committee went the further step of standing for it and fighting for it. In all this we see the dominating spirit of Bishop McConnell—his test of any institution by the extent to which it recognizes and serves human values. And that spirit has continued to make itself felt in New York where since 1928 he has served as resident bishop of the Methodist Episcopal Church.

In the field of social leadership McConnell possesses a quality that is most irritating to standpatters. He never rants. What can you do with a man who never gets caught off his base in relation to facts and never loses his sense of humor? Up to one hundred years ago it was permitted by the law of Massachusetts for a man to punish his wife "with reasonable instruments." It is interesting to speculate what a "reasonable instrument" might be, whether it would include a strap or rod or stop just this side. At any rate, whenever McConnell debates it is with a really reasonable instrument—with an open mind well stocked with relevant facts.

McConnell's prestige has come in part from indisputable intellectual strength. H. G. Wells said of English bishops, not long ago, that they were "socially much in evidence but intellectually in hiding." President Charles W. Eliot is remembered by a well-turned phrase in which he spoke of certain preachers conducting their mental operations with "a maximum of intellectual frugality." But neither frugality nor hiding have marked McConnell. As both Clarence Darrow and Harry Elmer Barnes found when they engaged in debate with him, his was a mind against which the stock arguments of the village atheist were about as deadly and impressive as peas blown through a boy's shooter against a stone wall.

Through all these approaches to current problems, Francis J. McConnell is a realist in that he is never interested in paper utopias. On the other hand, he has never been stopped from the most thorough-going ethical criticism of the economic and

social order by the bugaboo of not being "constructive." Of
all words in the English language, that word "constructive"
has given scarecrow service as well as any other. It has frightened off thousands of people from holding to the social implications of their own faith. McConnell is as interested in
constructive measures as anyone, but as he himself has pointed
out in characteristic passages, often before social construction
is possible there must be some radical destruction to make
way for the new.

The pioneers, he once declared, as a necessary step to con-
structing a new order in a virgin wilderness, engaged in some
thorough-going criticism with an axe.

When a boy the bishop first came into local prominence as a
long distance runner. On one occasion out in Ohio a man
who believed in him completely won a five dollar bet by trust-
ing the boy's ability to catch a calf. Young McConnell caught
the calf not by any brilliant or blood-stirring 100-yard dash;
he caught it by jogging along after the animal with a steady
stride until the calf finally sat down and said, "This thing has
gone far enough." Granting that it took all afternoon to catch
the calf, there was nothing in the bet about time; the only
point that was specified he covered—he caught the calf by
jogging on to the end of the day. It is a comforting thing to
think the child is father to the man. He will be found jogging on at sunset. And he will get his animal.

SCOTT NEARING

A Puritan Revolutionist

SCOTT NEARING

THE crop of native rebels produced in America has in these later years been extraordinarily meager for a land born in revolution and nurtured in the pioneer tradition. Our outstanding revolutionary figures have for the most part been foreign-born or once removed from it. They have led and spoken for the disillusioned who had sought a land of freedom.

The opportunity to get on in a country where classes are fluid, has put a premium on revolutionary thought and action. But there have always been native sons to rise in each generation to voice the old revolt against privilege and power. Scott Nearing is not merely one of them. He is doubtless the best known of them, both at home and abroad. His books and articles on American capitalism are accepted in radical circles throughout the world as the factual interpretation of our economic life, side by side with Upton Sinclair's propaganda novels exposing the American ruling class.

Like Sinclair, Nearing stands as a figure above parties and movements, though both men have worn party labels. Nearing as a revolutionary economist is no spokesman for a movement. He has never worked in harness. He has no mind for politics. He never led a strike, never walked a picket-line, never served a term in prison. He has met the enemy chiefly in debate and by the printed word. Yet his reputation is that usually attached to men who suffer martyrdom for the cause of labor. His position and his large following have been won not in the practical struggles of labor but by a force of character and purpose evident in his writing and his speaking, and advertised by the attacks upon him. That character arouses in his hearers and readers a sense of selfless loyalty to his cause —the destruction of capitalism, the triumph of the workers' revolution. With it is mixed a quality, rare in revolutionary leaders but always inspiring, a hard Puritan sense of duty and self-denial.

For some reason which I am not enough of a psychologist to analyze, we all seem to set apart and admire men with what we call "moral" qualities—the denial of the indulgences which the rest of us take. I do not know what virtue rests in austerity of life, but when it is obviously combined with selfless devotion to the welfare of mankind we accept it as service to us. The saints who wore hair shirts doubtless got a kick out of doing penance for men's sins (and their own) yet they were admired for their self-sacrifice if not for their achievements. Tolstoy carried this Puritan self-denial to amazing lengths. So does Nearing. But it is the discipline by which he drives himself.

Like most of us he is full of contradictions, but in him they are sharper, more apparent. Scott Nearing is at once a Puritan and a revolutionist. He is essentially a religious man, with a mystic's cosmic sense of destiny and a believer in a god. Yet he is a Communist—a Communist with the spirit of an individual anarchist. A lone man, he voices the multitude's hopes. A leader, he is too individualistic to work with organizations, yet he predicates his every hope on organized effort. A highly emotional spirit, yet he aspires to scientific objectivity. A pacifist at heart, he regretfully accepts violent revolution as the effective means to deliverance from capitalism. Nearing is apparently so little introspective as to be unaware of these and other contradictions which give an appearance of inconsistency

to a basically unified life. His mental and emotional com-
partments simply don't mix.

And now at 48 he adds to the confusion by concluding that
he is getting too old to contribute longer to directing the policy
of organized struggle. In a recent letter of resignation, quitting all the organizations with which he has been identified,
he said:

"Long ago I sensed the danger of old men in power.
Forward-looking movements need young blood. This is
particularly true of the revolutionary movement. I have
always planned to get out of the way before I began to
hold up the procession. Tentatively I fixed on 25 years as
the maximum of time that a man could usefully spend in
the direction of public policy. I have finished my quarter
century. I am resigning all my directorships and committee positions. Henceforth I shall not accept such offices.
The determination of policy belongs in the hands of
younger men and women."

From what origins and by what route has this apparently
hard, simple Puritan come to these complex contradictions,
unified though they are by an underlying purpose?

Scott Nearing came from a ruling-class home, as he would
call it, in a Pennsylvania company town. His grandfather,
who managed the coal mines, was known as Czar Nearing, a
paternal and benevolent despot. Scott's father ran grandfather's company store. The oldest of six children, Scott was
raised under the dominant influence not of his parents but of
a grandfather whose word was law, who tolerated no unions,
who controlled schools, churches, homes, jobs. The boy
worked in his father's store. He tried manual labor of all
sorts after school and in school vacations. He read hungrily.

He early learned hard work and the struggles of common men. There were strikes but, opposed by the Czar, they meant little to young Scott.

Off to Philadelphia for high school, he became at once interested in debating, which has remained his life-long field of battle. The first political movement to grip him was the fight against the trusts, then in full swing. In those years of growing independence the enemy must have had to him some unconscious identification with Czar Nearing. Grandpa was agnostic, if not atheist. Scott became religious. He joined the Baptist Temple, then under the leadership of an energetic man who combined with his church a school and a hospital. The boy went to Christian Endeavor and Sunday school with fervor. In 1905 when he was at the University of Pennsylvania, still a devout church-goer, the Baptist preacher, a political reform leader, was bought off by a contribution to his hospital. Scott got out of the church in disgust and never went back— nor to any other. He was through with organized religion although he hung on to a nominal Christianity until the World War. The treason of Christians to Jesus finished that.

In the University of Pennsylvania young Nearing continued his debating, specializing on anti-trust issues and preparing, as he fully expected, to be a lawyer. One year of the course, however, convinced him it was not to his taste and he went over to economics in the Wharton School, teaching and studying at the same time. Here he came under the influence of Simon N. Patten, the most daring intellect he had ever met, a man to whom nothing was sacred, who demolished shams and pretence, who penetrated to the core of things, and who without being a revolutionist had a revolutionary mind.

From studying, debating, and teaching, Nearing on his graduation turned to the practical job of fighting child labor. As secretary of the Pennsylvania Child Labor Committee, he put in three years on the job—one year at it exclusively, the others in combination with teaching, both at Temple University and at the Wharton School.

From then on for nine years he led an academic life at the Wharton School, teaching also on the side at the Philadelphia School for Social Work, at Swarthmore and, during the summer, at Chautauqua. Always he was the propagandist, the fighter against trusts and big business. Always he was for the underdog and against the upper. Serious, determined, he had no conscious revolutionary philosophy or connections.

He stirred his students by his earnestness, his dramatic and forceful simplicity. He was popular, and he was loved and hated like all men of pronounced convictions and uncompromising statement. He says he presented the facts and let his students make up their own minds—but I am skeptical of Scott's ever having been dispassionate.

With a little group of teachers at the Wharton School he was active in Philadelphia political reform movements, then dominated by the crusading Philadelphia *North American* under Van Valkenberg. Scott Nearing, unlike most of his associates, disliked and opposed both Roosevelt and Wilson. In the three-sided campaign of 1912, he voted for Debs, though he did not join the Socialist Party until the War. For ten years he spent his summers at the single tax colony at Arden, Delaware, but he never proclaimed himself a single-taxer. His was revolt against the existing system of unearned wealth, without any formulated political or economic program to abolish it.

His activities, of course, aroused business interests. Joseph R. Grundy, then as now boss of Pennsylvania industry, and chief defender of child labor, challenged the Wharton School in 1912 on the issue of Nearing's activities, threatening to get the legislature to cut its appropriation if he did not quit. Nearing's answer was characteristic. He went out on a speaking tour in the state for two weeks, sending to the press and to graduates copies of his attacks on big business, child labor and industrial slavery. Grundy raged but achieved nothing. Indeed within two years Nearing, supported by a strong group in the faculty and by the two crusading Philadelphia newspapers, was made an assistant professor in 1914 after serving eight years as an instructor. He then had eleven men under him in the department, and for one year directed most of its administrative work.

But his victory was short-lived. In June, 1915, he was suddenly dismissed without warning after the school had closed, so that there could be no protest by students or faculty. Grundy had finally sworn that if Nearing remained the state appropriations would be held up. George Wharton Pepper, member of the Board of Trustees, did Grundy's bidding and had Nearing fired.

At once Scott Nearing became a national figure. His case, among the first dismissals for reform activity against big business, aroused protest in the press, in academic circles, and among men and women in public life everywhere. A vigorous campaign for his re-instatement was organized. It continued without let-up until November. Professors Lightner, Witmer, and F. E. Shelly, totally disagreeing with Nearing's views and activities, led the fight for academic freedom. Witmer later wrote a book on the case. The fight was lost; Grundy and Pepper triumphed. Simon N. Patten, too, distinguished by years of service and about to retire, was likewise dismissed a year later, a sacrifice to big business. The insurgent group was broken and they all gradually left the school. Nearing says his best education was the five-year fight his group put up against the trustees.

He stayed around Philadelphia some months finishing a

book or two. He had published first in 1911 his *Social Adjustments* and in 1915 three books: *Wages and the Cost of Living, Income,* and *Anthracite Coal.* He accepted an appointment as Dean of the College of Arts of the municipal University of Toledo, an appointment secured by virtue of the fact that the board was composed of six trades unionists and five business men. He held that job just a little over a year, when his pacifist stand in the War forced him out. He had toured the country for the Union Against Militarism before the United States entered the War, speaking to huge audiences with a team including James Maurer, John Haynes Holmes, Rabbi Stephen Wise, and Max Eastman. His home in Toledo was searched by federal agents, the first domiciliary raid in the War. He was too hot a potato for a municipal university to hold.

That was Nearing's last teaching job in a "respectable" institution of learning. His friends tried to get him appointments elsewhere, without success. And yet he was regarded as a teacher of the first rank—but not for students from safe and sane homes.

Nearing plunged into the anti-war campaign, first, as a speaker for the People's Council, then as its chairman, elected at the memorable convention in Chicago which was broken up by state troops whom the governor sent in to overcome the treason of Mayor Thompson in permitting it to meet. He joined the Socialist Party and became a member of the faculty of the Rand School in New York. He also took an active part in the Fellowship of Reconciliation, radical religious fraternity of pacifists.

With amazing efficiency for a man who detested office routine, he directed the work of the People's Council. He spoke and wrote ceaselessly against the War. For writing a booklet *The Great Madness,* published by the American Socialist Society, he was indicted under the espionage act. Brought to trial in 1919 after the War was over he was acquitted by a jury to which he lectured on the War as to a class in college. The Society, which could not lecture, was convicted and fined for publishing the book on which Nearing was acquitted!

The war over, Nearing continued his writing, lecturing and debating, settling with his wife and two little boys in New York. He stuck to the Socialist Party through the Communist splits until 1922 when he left it because of its stand against Soviet Russian tactics. He even ran for office once on the Socialist ticket for Congress on a New York east side district in 1920. Knowing that he could not be elected, he used the campaign as an opportunity for educational work. Remaining pacifist, though disagreeing with what he deemed the bankruptcy in action of his middle-class pacifist friends, he still continued active in the Fellowship of Reconciliation, serving on its executive committee up to 1925, though always as a left-wing opposition. He then quit it because he felt that its supporters were too largely coupon-clipping Protestants to whom pacifism had become mere dogma. And his own pacifism had been weakened by his growing belief that despite his personal disinclination to use violence, only violent means would insure ultimate victory in the struggle of workers to overthrow capitalism.

Nearing's ardent sympathy with the Russian revolution had been intensified by a visit to Soviet Russia in 1925, a trip in which he made a study of the educational system, publishing the first book in English on it. His revolutionary outlook had led him to apply for admission to the Communist Party, but his admission was held up for over a year because the leaders felt that his previous pacifism and strong individualistic convictions unfitted him to subscribe wholeheartedly to Party principles or to work in Party harness. He was finally admitted in 1926 and remained a member three years, longer than most of his friends expected. He resigned because of the refusal of the Party authorities in Moscow to approve a manuscript on imperialism which he had submitted to a Party publishing house. To him it was more important to publish his work than submit to a party decision with which he disagreed.

While in the Communist Party Nearing took no active part in its internal affairs. He lectured at the Workers' School and spoke for the Party in political campaigns. Privately he disagreed with the Party management and he refused to accede to suggestions as to his work in the Party. His ideas of popular education, his view of the reactionary mind of American workers as well as of their leaders, both differed sharply from the Party's more dramatic and optimistic outlook. His exit from a party to which he was never temperamentally adapted was a foregone conclusion.

Nearing's devotion to the Russian revolution and its colossal adventure has inspired most of his thinking and activity in recent years. He visited Russia again on the tenth anniversary of the revolution; he organized a series of studies of Soviet achievements, published by the Vanguard Press and financed by the "Garland Fund," of which Nearing has been a trustee since its establishment in 1922. He wrote one book in a series on *The Economic Organization of the Soviet Union,* jointly with Jack Hardy.

His production of books since 1920 has been phenomenal: *The American Empire,* 1920; *The British General Strike* in the same year, after a visit to England; pamphlets on workers' movements in France and Germany; *The Next Step,* a sketch of future society which might well have been called the "Last Step," syndicalist rather than Communist in thesis; *Where Is Civilization Going?* an excursion into faith; *Dollar Diplomacy,* with Joseph Freeman, a survey of American foreign investments; *Whither China,* 1928, after a trip there; *Black America,* 1929, a vivid picture of the industrial life of the American Negro, and *The Twilight of Empire,* 1930, which caused his resignation from the Communist Party, and *War,* 1931.

Scott's future labors in research and writing, for which his resignation from all organized activity prepared the way, are apparently to be even more prodigious. He has sketched a lengthy series of books interpreting the future growth of a world society. It is to be a synthesis of all his thinking and study on economics and social reorganization.

Despite these many volumes Nearing's income from his books is negligible. They represent on the whole an investment of the surplus he saves from his lectures and debates above his meager living expenses.

He does a hard season's work, October to May yearly, on the road lecturing and debating. He arranges his own dates. He meets working-class and middle-class audiences in forums and societies. His frequent debates attract great audiences, for he is one of the most forceful and skillful men on the platform, winning frequently by hammering out hard, black-and-white simplifications of his case. Nearly devoid of humor, anecdote or ridicule, he is more than a match for most of his opponents by the force of his utterance and unfailing adherence to his thesis. His speeches and debates, simple as they appear, are prepared with scrupulous care and delivered with a dogmatic assurance—usually irritating to those who disagree with him and by them often labelled fanatical.

Such is the picture of the external man in action and the road he has traveled to his present position as our leading radical economist. Behind his activity lies a curious combination of driving motives, moods, and habits of life which must be understood so as to see the mainsprings of his life and power.

Scott Nearing is essentially a religious man. He lives by faith—faith not only in the future freedom of mankind but in a cosmic order over and above directed human effort. Indeed, his social philosophy flows from his religion. He believes, rather naïvely it seems to a non-mystic, in a world behind the appearance of reality. The real world is yet unknown. He is eager to explore. He has approached it via spiritualism. He follows Sir Oliver Lodge's excursions into the other world. He accepts the evidence of communication with the dead. In the real world there is no death; we merely go on. He sees a god as the form of a planned universe. The human race is working out its destiny in a prescribed pattern, not a destiny of arrival at some final social state but a destiny of continuing greater growth and fulfillment, to be tested always by the opportunities it gives to release the creative power of individuals. To this end the environment must change that man may evolve. Social revolution alone can change it.

For a Communist all this is a large order! The orthodox Communist is first a materialist; he accepts the natural world as the only reality. He asks scientifically what, how, why? Nearing is philosophically an idealist; he begins with the cosmos, the unseen world, and accepts the material world only as an aspect of the greater. His is essentially the unscientific, mystical approach. He is a man of feeling, not a scientist. His thinking is increasingly cosmic, synthetic. Yet this religious approach to life can hardly be detected in his debates, his speaking, and writing. It is only the overtone, the large outlines that reveal the mystical aspect of his nature.

His books, objective as they are, revealing little of his personal views, are nevertheless charged with emotion. This emotional power is responsible for his extravagant statements in speech, often so sweeping as to be amusing. He will qualify them at once on being challenged without apparently even sensing the contradiction. His fundamental honesty is convincing even when he takes two opposed positions on the same subject in a half hour, as his friends have often heard him do.

Education is his passion. It flows from his evangelical qualities. His world of struggle is the field of propaganda. He sees the world more or less as a debating society. Hence his tendency to persuasion, to argument and away from identification with the practical activities of labor or radical parties.

Nearing never plays to the galleries nor talks for publicity. For a man so well known, he gets remarkably little newspaper attention. He scorns it anyhow, refusing even to talk to the capitalist press. His natural approach to his public is from teacher to student.

His personal life, unlike that of many radicals, squares in its main outlines with his ideas. He has disciplined himself to it. Duty is the first law of this Puritan—a law to keep him on his set path and to resist the lure of hidden and feared sensualities. He has no little vices. He does not smoke, drink, swear. He does not even indulge in social frivolities. He lives simply because it satisfies him more to share the way of life lived by those whose bondage he so deeply feels. And I suppose that a little self-mortification compensates for a strong man's sense of potential sin.

But the call of duty will sanctify pleasure for him. A friend asked him on a canoe trip for the sheer pleasure of it. No, said Scott, he had to work in the garden. He had an article to write. But when the friend reminded him that they had a joint job on a report and suggested a canoe as a place free of interruption, he consented at once.

"Did you have a good time in Russia?" asked another friend. "I did not go there for a good time," replied Scott. Of course, he had enjoyed it hugely.

Nearing's Puritan self-denial in the joy of doing his duty

leads him to shun all middle-class extravagances. He usually dresses like a farmer—cap, unpressed old clothes, colored shirt, heavy boots. He scorns taxis, even when street cars are inconvenient. He long resisted getting even a second-hand Ford car for his family and, after he got it, took pride in the fact that it was old and rusty.

He is a vegetarian in principle but he will make adjustments in practice. A fellow-vegetarian who had also toured Russia, asked him what he ate when the bill of fare often consisted only of bread and soup with a hunk of meat in it. "I ate the soup and left the meat," said Scott.

He lives as simply as a farmer or worker. He is endlessly, almost painfully energetic, rising often at dawn and working till late into the night. For years he has run a garden. He revels in manual labor around the place—anybody's place. When visiting he is often embarrassing by his insistence upon washing the dishes. When he indulges in sport—baseball, tennis or swimming, he plays as hard as he works. I once said to his son, apropos of a family argument, "Johnny, you can get your father's consent if you will wait till you catch him stretched on the grass with his hands behind his head looking at the clouds float by." Johnny opened his eyes wide. "Then I will never get it," he said.

In his home life Scott is still the Puritan. The old grandfather is in him there. And the older son, strikingly like his father, shows the same revolt that marked father against grandfather. The boy still in his teens, has struggled to free himself from the domination of the father he admires and loves, by changing his name.

It would be hard to call Nearing a happy man, save as duty-loving Puritans are happy. Among the strong lines of a face weather-beaten and tanned by much outdoor living are lines of conflict, even suffering. He is not the happy warrior. He is the rockbound selfless revolutionist, driven by duty and a sense of union with mystic powers.

Though he thinks he is retired from active struggle after twenty-five years of it, he cannot help continuing his essential drive. He will continue to hurl his philippics against the kings of capital. He will continue research in the libraries, teaching from the platform, writing and debating until a real old age —not 48—tames his fierce energies. For thousands in the radical movement, whatever their politics, he will continue to be an inspiration as a teacher, not through his propaganda so much as through rare qualities of rigid honesty, a lovable selflessness, and the essential integrity of the contradictory virtues that go to make up his character.

Ambassador to the Court of St. Francis

VIDA D. SCUDDER

IDEAS rather than people," Miss Scudder often tells her young disciples, "seem to me important." One wishes to respect her preference, but it is not easy to compose a biographical sketch of the ideas and omit the provocative personality. For Miss Scudder, it must be admitted, is a paradoxical person. Daily she resolves that difficult problem, existence as a Socialist in a capitalistic state, by the same grace that allows her character to unite aloofness and ardor, caprice and austerity, mysticism and shrewd common sense. A puzzle to those who know her by hearsay, she appears to those who acknowledge her guidance as something of a miracle. They are abashed before one who rebukes them like an Old Testament prophet and loves them like an early follower of Saint Francis.

Accepted as comrade in several groups of radical and religious thinkers, she regards herself, first of all as a writer, and next, as a teacher of English literature. The teaching, which held her for forty years in the Department of English Literature at Wellesley College, began casually enough. While youthfully uncertain about a choice of occupation she was persuaded by an old friend of the family, Professor George Herbert Palmer, to take a position at the college of which his wife had been president and which he always supported with his loyal interest. To the teaching of English literature, Miss Scudder says she gave during her professional life her concentrated attention; she has, moreover, loved the work. From the first she must have been an extraordinary teacher. She gave her classes heavy assignments and saw them accomplished; scrupulous to avoid making application of principles, she nevertheless often set her pupils to active work in social reform; most frequently of all, these young women who assembled before her several times a week grew more continually aware of the delicate shades of integrity, of courtesy, of wise and noble living. It is difficult to believe that anyone who has sat at her academic feet has not developed a desire to make life, socially and individually, more admirable. Now that she has retired from college teaching her home is frequented by alumnae who feel impelled, upon revisiting Wellesley, to run down to Miss Scudder's for advice about all sorts of problems and for congratulation on their triumphs.

The group which claims Miss Scudder as teacher is a large one, but other roads to her door have carried almost as many disciples. "I have never brought out any book," she has said, "that did not bring me friends." And it is a long shelf that holds her volumes. Many had their origin in the classroom, college lectures that demanded a larger public. *Social Ideals in English Letters* runs parallel to one of her most popular courses. *The Witness of Denial,* a study of the nineteenth century agnostics, is something of a companion volume to *The Life of the Spirit in the Modern English Poets.* The *Morte d'Arthur* of Sir Thomas Malory is more than an entrancing guide to mediaeval romance, and *The History of English Literature* sweeps the whole academic field. Selections and editions bear her name as well—Bede's *Ecclesiastical History* and *The Works of John Woolman* in the Everyman's Library, *English Poems* in the Lake English Classics, Macaulay's *Lord Clive,* Shelley's *Prometheus Unbound, The Poems of George MacDonald,* and *Selections from Ruskin.*

Apart from studies in English letters Miss Scudder's thought

VIDA D. SCUDDER

runs chiefly in two channels: the religious psychology of the past, and the necessity and means of achieving social justice in the present. It is her contribution to modern thought that she is able to make these streams mingle. A translation and edition of the letters of Saint Catherine of Siena, mystic and reformer, published in 1905, was followed two years later by an historical novel of the same time, *The Disciple of a Saint*. The period of the early Franciscans has been Miss Scudder's field of recent literary work. Four years ago she paused by the way to publish *Brother John, A Tale of the First Franciscans,* and has recently been rounding out her large history and interpretation of the first hundred years after the death of the saint, *The Franciscan Adventure*. To those who know Miss Scudder it is not surprising that these books on mediaeval sainthood have almost as much to do with modern social theory as have those whose titles indicate that she is dealing with contemporary problems: *Socialism and Character* and *The Social Teachings of the Christian Year*. Of them all, *Socialism and Character* is her favorite. In her own opinion this study of Catholic theology as the source of socialism contains her best thinking. She adds lightly, "Of course it was funny, and of course people didn't like it." And of course this statement must be taken with an ample pinch of salt. The book may not have run into many editions but it was of such importance to some who read it that it changed or confirmed irrevocably their course of life. One young man, who was about to start on a canoe trip through unexplored Russia, copied it out on onion-skin paper that he might have it at all times conveniently on his person.

The solution which Miss Scudder offers the sick soul and the sick world is one which curiously combines the old and the new, the traditional and the radical, the mystical and the practical. It is a paradox and, like all paradoxes when understood, an illumination. Briefly, she believes the panacea of

social and personal evil to be Christian socialism, or, since that
term has become obsolete, and "socialism" itself has undergone
several transformations, she would perhaps prefer "social justice revealed by Christian dogma." The phrase used for the
new school which she has a share in directing under the
auspices of the annual Episcopal conference at Wellesley is
"Christian Social Ethics."

A synthesis of a tendency towards social radicalism with a
demand for spiritual impulse is not over-common in either
radical party or church. The man of religious temperament
concerned with personal ethics finds it easy to dismiss social
problems with the conviction that if all men led blameless
lives the trouble originating in social conditions would disappear. The radical, impatient with the previous blindness of
the church to injustice and oppression, refuses to believe that
any help can come from a Christian institution. It is Miss
Scudder's belief that each needs the other. To her the way
out is less by proletarian revolution than by the quickened
sensitiveness of intelligent people. Although she has read
Marx and been enlightened by his analysis of the situation she
has never endorsed the idea that a class struggle was inevitable
or proletarian revolution the only means towards the establishment of a new order. She believes that the impulse of social sacrifice pervading the Christian Church must coöperate
with the righteous self-assertion of the working people in the
development of any socialist commonweal which shall be
stable. That is, she explains further, she has always believed
that a psychological transformation must accompany any
drastic change in social institutions while at the same time
no such transformation is authentic unless it produces such
change.

Happily today Miss Scudder does not find her point of view
quite so unusual or so isolated as it was when she first de-

veloped it. To some extent, perhaps, because of her own efforts there are now in good working order many small groups in harmony with her synthesis and to which she can give freely her energy. Chief among these is the Church League for Industrial Democracy, an organization in the Episcopal Church which is working for closer contact between Church and Labor, and for the quickening of social interest—the impulse of social sacrifice and social reconstruction among church people. Of this Miss Scudder is an officer, as she is of the League for Industrial Democracy and several other similar groups. But further questions about her place with those engaged in striving for reform will bring forth only a shake of the head. "I do not know how to give the impression," she says, "of my own entire obscurity in these organizations."

If Miss Scudder calls her place low it is because she wishes to make it seem so. Speaking of another matter she has said that to choose the lowest place in any group is a matter rather of good breeding than of virtue.

"It is the law of life," she said—and she did not add "that the meek shall inherit the earth." It is characteristic of paradoxical natures that their humility can be sustained by pride. Yet although based in some instances upon its contrary this humility may be true. So integral a part is it of Miss Scudder's attitude that during the War when she was asked to compose a prayer for the Episcopal Church she incorporated the words of Saint Paul, "in honor preferring each other" as a petition for the allied nations, and was a little regretful when they were struck out.

Incidentally, it is impossible, in such a sketch as this to ignore Miss Scudder's reaction to the Great War. Hers was an intellectual, almost an academic reaction. She accepted the War, as did some other Socialists, seeing the struggle as the inevitable result of the anti-social system of international anarchy under which the world was rushing toward Armageddon. In her mind there was no hatred, no intolerance, and no weakness. If this attitude was disappointing to her pacifist admirers, it was equally unsatisfactory to the War Department which found itself obliged to keep a careful watch over this lover of St. Francis.

Born of New England parentage, she very likely caught from her father a fiery idealism and a taste and equipment for mental and spiritual battle. At the peak of missionary fervor David Coit Scudder consecrated his life to the hazardous task of converting the heathen. Immediately upon his ordination he set sail with his young bride for Southern India. Here his daughter was born and here his life came to a quick and tragic close. Eager to return to his wife and baby after a journey made to distant villages in the rainy season against the advice of his native guide, he attempted to swim a turbulent river and was drowned. Mrs. Scudder immediately took her child to America to be brought up, as she had been, in Boston. There was the fashionable girls' school, the instruction in the arts, and always (then, at least) the company of lofty minds. Her two uncles in the world of books, Horace Scudder, editor of *The Atlantic Monthly,* and E. P. Dutton, the publisher, may early have encouraged in her literary talent that developed with the flowering of the mind. Often the mother and daughter were abroad.

In *A Listener in Babel* Miss Scudder tells of a child who with her mother visited lovely places and lived among unworldly people "who made a cult of the beautiful." "They moved about," she wrote, "these cultured, innocuous, expatriated men and women, in a phantom world of charming memories, perpetuated by charming art." She writes also that this little girl's painful shyness "coöperated with the nomadic conditions of their life to shut her off from intercourse with other chil-

dren but the sense of isolation encompassed her not unpleasant-
ly." The book is not an autobiography; it does not tell the be-
witching anecdotes attributed to the fair-haired child. It does
not tell of her visits to England where her prim playmates admired the way she avoided the nursery stairs to walk straight
down the front ones, and credited her with a courage of which
this was possibly no valid example. Nor does it tell of a summer in a château in Normandy and the lasting friendship with
a Frenchwoman of title who belonged to the legitimist faction.
Many pretty stories it leaves untold, but it expresses the sense
of unreality, the consciousness of moving about in a world
unrealized that alternately soothed and troubled the author's
spirit until her return to America for formal education.

The Girls' Latin School of Boston, of whose first class she
was a member, brought her sharply against the reality of the
class-room and sent her eager mind running in prescribed
paths. In 1880 she entered Smith College. Here for the first
time, gathered with a group of young women her own age, she
learned that "individuals can be as exciting as cathedrals."
Forgetful of time she sat up after the retiring-bell, discussing
with her best friends the meaning of life and the intricacies of
personality. She was one of an ardent little group. Looking
back upon those days Miss Scudder has been amused to recol-
lect how she reorganized a course in English literature, which
had rather tentatively been inserted by authority in the midst
of a classic curriculum, to serve as intensive study of the Lake
Poets.

The instructor, who willingly transferred her direction to
the keen students, may not have been the same one who introduced another course with the following remarks: "Young
ladies, we are gathered here for the study of poetry. The field
is large; we have little time; we must be eclectic. Let us
therefore select a topic which we may trace throughout the

realm of verse. Let us choose for our subject this year 'Wifely Fealty'." But this instructor belonged to the same school of sentimental approach, the school which the generation of her more scholarly pupils has entirely routed.

Still more amused Miss Scudder grows when she thinks of the sort of person she was then—in her own words, "an impossible intellectual snob who ignored all persons unfamiliar with the works of Alfred de Musset."

American colleges did little in the eighties to turn the eyes of young ladies toward the actualities of an increasingly industrial society. One teacher at Smith, to be sure, Professor J. B. Clark, made in his classes the social approach. But it proves how unprepared was the mind of the student that Miss Scudder, although she admired and honored the teacher, found the point of view at that time bewildering.

It was natural that this enthusiastic young graduate should crave to study in foreign countries, and at Oxford University she enrolled for Ruskin's last course of lectures. Already she knew well his criticisms of art and was in sympathy with his sensitive and moral judgments. But like the rest of the world she thought it a "pity that he had turned to crazy social theories." Listening at length to that "vital, wistful, appealing, arresting" personality she saw, beyond the pathetic ruin of his broken mind, an intelligence and an attitude that sent her to his social writings and a consideration of the appalling economic conditions of the age.

Reading *The Fabian Essays* shortly after her study with Ruskin converted Miss Scudder to socialism, a position from which she has never wavered although the content of the word has varied with the decades. It was no easy humanitarianism, no flood of weak pity, which moved her to take this stand so distasteful to the friends of her early environment. It was not the oppression of the people by an unjust economic situation which caused the rebellion of this fastidious member of the intelligentsia. It was the unreasonableness of the situation itself. Of the poor and unfortunate she knew but little. Of logic she knew a great deal. As an intelligent young woman, possessing a college degree, she felt it necessary to protest against such prevailing stupidity.

How to protest was a problem. To the group of Smith graduates, aflame like herself with social passion, there seemed available nothing more than personal means of protest. Encouraged by the work being done at London's Toynbee Hall, they proposed to create a similar settlement in America managed by the women of the colleges. Adult education, an opportunity for under-privileged people to share in the advantages of culture and training, was their hope. Temporary relief for those in need was merely incidental to the importunate desire for opening the eyes of those sitting blindfolded by their complacent culture. In the same year that Jane Addams opened Hull House, these young women, joined soon by representatives from other colleges, established in Rivington Street, New York, which before had offered as community centers only the dance-hall and the saloon, a gracious home where they played hostess and neighbor to all who longed for the amenities of living.

Looking back today, that first College Settlement seems like a dream of some Victorian poet. Yet the sentimentality, which to contemporary eyes seemed to envelop the movement at its beginning, is due not to the attitude of the first earnest workers, but rather to the books written about them in a period which put a premium on sentiment. The young workers were met less by unreal approval than by actual disapproval from their frequently exasperated parents. Unsupported by church or organization which their elders considered respectable, they were forced to depend upon their own courage and sense of duty for a justification.

The justification is, we may believe, complete. There is less need now for the settlement as a benevolent institution. But to Miss Scudder the settlement never was benevolent. To her it was a means of improving an economic system not by giving charity to one class but by "paying the debt owed by the privileged to the dispossessed." "My practical association with working people has not been on philanthropic lines," she has said; "I sought it for myself and others because I felt sure contact at first hand with industrial conditions and under-privileged people would not only quicken the social compunction of any intelligent and sensitive college woman, but would lead to conviction of the need for drastic social reconstruction. I wanted people set free from the prison of class."

Denison House in Boston, during the years she was teaching, was the center of her most intense social interest. For ten years she sustained in this college settlement for women a club in the Department of Italian Relations which provided lectures by Italian scholars and recitals by musicians, and fostered an interest in folk handicraft. Miss Scudder rejoices in the remembrance of its success as a "revelation of the rich contribution that other races can make to American life." Drawn to the group because of her studies of the saints she gained from it an insight into national character and a knowledge of the national tongue. The way in which her talks were received at first bewildered her. The audience, though courteous and sympathetic, seemed much amused. "I know I make mistakes," she finally exclaimed, "but please tell me why you laugh so much." "Signorina," a woman answered, "you do not speak Italian. You speak Latin." She had been speaking in the mediaeval idiom of Dante.

The class-room and the public platform are the places where

Miss Scudder's most striking natural talent is readily apparent. Here, in intimate communion with abstract ideas, which she regards as so much more important than people, her excitement is contagious. For Miss Scudder is an exceptional speaker. With no display of conventional oratory she yet casts a spell over her audience which puts them in her power before they realize what has happened. Had American women earlier had the opportunity of training themselves in statecraft she might today be in a position of national responsibility. Had she remained in England, after the tutelage of Ruskin, in association with the movements which created the Labor Party, who knows whether we should not now find her speeches in Parliamentary reports?

Temperamentally close to the intelligent English Socialist, of the same stock and knowing intimately the literature of the race, there appears to be, nevertheless, no affinity between her and the English people, between her and the English soil, except in so far as they are comprehended by her instinctive international sympathies. A national complacency, founded though it may be upon affection, is to her obnoxious. Even blatancy about liberty seems to her more hopeful than the smugness of established privilege. She professes democracy and chooses to be a citizen of a government called democratic.

The United States on principle, Franciscan Italy for love. So one accounts for her territorial preferences. It has been her good fortune to return often for refreshment to spiritual Umbria. The mist that seems to linger wistfully on the slopes, the steep little sterile hills that appear to exist solely for the upstanding purpose of praising God, the olive trees so intimate with Christian legend; these converse with her more directly, one believes, than the features of any other landscape. A follower of Saint Francis might accept the fancy that the country of the saint had taken his vows of chastity, poverty and obedience. Unearthly land, unsoiled by man, it is Miss Scudder's spiritual home.

Long she has been interpreting Italy and Italy's saints. She has lived in the Siena of Saint Catherine; with her she has gone on perilous pilgrimages of social reform; like her, one supposes she has known the experience of the mystic. To the modern world, a world that prides itself on a modernity of tangible earthliness, she has dared to offer the teachings of Saint Catherine and Saint Francis. To a world to which she would bring a more effective social justice, an opportunity for greater happiness to a greater number, she offers the cult of the unimportance of all personal happiness. And yet, the absurdity on the face of the paradox is often a measure of its common sense. What was once accepted as spiritual discipline often remains as practical guide. It is no new unproved theory that the gospel of unworldliness may save the world.

Here, as always, crops up again the eternal debate between the so-called realist and the mystic. It may perhaps be fairly argued that the intellectual, relying on logic and the force of ideas, may as easily become twisted in judgments as those whose lives are less intellectually deep but who continually rub elbows with stern human and material conditions. To a miner evicted from his home in a labor struggle, compelled to see his children hunger, denied the right to meet with others and express his sense of loyalty to his cause, Miss Scudder's cry for justice might seem trivial, remote, aristocratic in effect, and cold, no matter how warm to her, no matter how sincere and passionate. And there are not a few who stoutly still proclaim that from such a miner comes as sound a sense of primitive values as from scholar, saint, and seer. Among these, certainly at times, must be this scholar, saint and seer herself.

Like the ironic twist of a parable, Miss Scudder's life appears to be recompensed with all those things she most scrupulously has renounced. Personal happiness, on principle a negligible part of existence, seems to dog her footsteps. Refusing to avoid any troublesome issue, her mind, nevertheless, meets such issues halfway and resolves them often before they have become defined. She who is most serious about the condition of mankind, who profoundly searches unrevealed motives, who preaches a doctrine indefatigably austere, often indulges in a fascinating capriciousness. She loves to surprise, to play with her mind; occasionally, it must be admitted, to tease and shock. It is this quality, combined with her wit, that makes her conversation so enchanting.

Speaking once of her books by which she so earnestly makes known her creed, she said she supposed that they "had played their part in the pleasant symposium of conversation to which literature seems to be descending." Requested by a group of religious women to compile a Lenten reading list she inserted a pamphlet by Lenin. One remembers that a sense of the dramatic, amounting at times to the absurd, was the prerogative of the early Franciscans.

Play is the manifestation of those who are free. Joy is a condition of spiritual grace. *"Per crucem gaudium"*—through the cross, joy—Miss Scudder tells those of uncertain stamina. Her strength, her capacity for resilience, are drawn from a reservoir deeper than that of solitary conviction—the great body of garnered faith.

Great-Grandson of the Revolution

JOHN NEVIN SAYRE

ONE destined to carry the pacifist banner, especially through troubled waters, is fortunate to have behind him a host of ancestors who never took life lying down but as a great adventure. The hysterical patriot is at all times color-blind, particularly so in time of stress, when everything appears red to his distorted vision except the battlefields stained with human blood. The men of the Nevin and Sayre families were stout fighters for their faith. Though not all thought alike, all fought alike; when they rallied to their respective colors they stayed for the finish, and at the front. The Sayre coat of arms has for its crest a dragon head crushed by a strong hand. The voluminous genealogy shows them a prolific family that produced a strong hand in each succeeding generation with which to squeeze a dragon head. They intermarried with other eminent families, were prominent in church and state as well as in the arts, and generally speaking, led rather than brought up the rear of the procession. Ethelbert Nevin, the musical composer, belonged to the clan, and Blanche Nevin, poet and sculptor, has a statue in the national Capitol at Washington. They have left not only footprints on the sands of time, but name plates in divers places—Nevin on the coast of Wales and Sayre in the State of Pennsylvania.

The founder of the Sayre family, Thomas by name, left Leighton Buzzard in England for the new settlement at Lynn, Massachusetts, in the year 1638, and Sayres have kept on coming with unfailing regularity ever since, until the posterity of the original Thomas is spread far and wide over the country.

In the turbulent Revolutionary period the Reverend John Sayre, great-great-grandfather of the subject of this sketch, was rector of a church in Fairfield, Connecticut, a man who took his religion seriously. The Revolutionary committee circularized the townsmen demanding a subscription to what was then the equivalent of our Liberty Bonds, and exacting a pledge to deny "the kind offices of humanity and hospitality" to any who were unfriendly to the cause. The reverend gentleman replied at some length and without equivocation. He loved the colonial land, but his fundamental loyalty was to his divine Master. As a Christian he could neither aid in war nor turn from his door any stranger or traveller who sought his hospitality. War and politics, he said, "belong not to my profession, and I find sufficient employment for my head and for my heart in that honorable though arduous calling to which . . . I have vowed to devote my whole life." War and Christianity have always been at variance, and the patriots ordered the good man to move on. Finally with his family he trekked to Nova Scotia. But time brings its revenges; not long since Nevin Sayre was invited to preach at the second centennial of the church from which his great-great-grandfather had been ousted!

At the same time another Sayre was making himself offensive to patriots on the other side of the water. Though high sheriff of London, he was outspoken in his sympathies for the American colonists in their resistance to governmental tryanny. Accordingly, he was sentenced as a traitor and escorted to the Tower. Later, when released, he assisted the cause he believed to be a rightous one by deed as well as word, and did some good work for the American commissioners in Europe.

But that is not the whole story of John Nevin Sayre's Revolutionary ancestry. A great-great-grandfather on the Nevin side was Dominie Carmichael, Scotch by race and temperament, grand-nephew of the Duke of Argyle. Though he was a parson, it was not the Dominie's idea to keep out of a good fight by hiding behind his cloth. Moved by a letter from General Washington telling of the awful sufferings of the men at Valley Forge, he lost no time in firing his flock with his own spirit. The closets of his parishioners were ransacked and every garment that could be spared, every scrap of linen was gathered, till at last the women protested they had nothing left but their petticoats. "Shorten your petticoats," he thundered. If hair could have been used at Valley Forge, he would have preached to a flock of bobbed-haired women. The American army had left only the Dominie's horse for use in the community; and when that solitary animal was not employed in visiting the sick and burying the dead, it was loaded with the parish loot and the parson galloped off at midnight to Valley Forge, straight through the British lines, unconcerned that

"The British had put a price on his head,
Capture him living, capture him dead."

Finally word came that a British force was on its way to take him. With a cool head and Scotch thrift he gathered his family, his silver, and a precious store of salt, and slipped off to the forest, where the red men concealed and sheltered him.

Robert Heysham Sayre, great-grandson of the exiled Connecticut preacher, and father of Nevin Sayre, built the Lehigh Valley Railroad, of which he was chief engineer. The town of Sayre, Pennsylvania, takes its name from him. He was vice-president of the Lehigh Valley and of the Bethlehem Iron Company, which blossomed into the Steel Trust. His connection with these enterprises, and his investments during the period of our extraordinary industrial expansion, have placed his succeeding generation beyond the grasp of the gaunt hand of poverty.

The old gentleman, however, was no swivel-chair official; he worked side by side with his men and knew them. Wakened in the middle of the night by news of trouble somewhere down the line of the road he had built, he would leap from his bed, dash for an engine, and hustle to the scene in order personally to direct the work.

He was a typical gentleman of the time, able, cultivated, conservative, a trustee of the Episcopal Church of the Nativity, in Bethlehem, a staunch Republican from the time Lincoln ran for the presidency, a fervent patriot. Every year on the Fourth of July he invited the community to join him in commemorating the great national event in the manner prescribed by John Adams as appropriate to its celebration throughout the ages. When Dewey defeated the Spaniards in Manila Bay and sank six ships, Mr. Sayre ran up six small flags in addition to the usual large one.

His son, John Nevin, was born at Bethlehem in 1884, heir to all those things that make for a good and pleasant life. He was sent first to the Moravian School, later to Lawrenceville Preparatory School, and finally to Princeton. Scotland had contributed money generously toward establishing a college at Princeton, and great-great-grandfather Dominie Carmichael had been one of its early graduates.

As a student, Nevin Sayre was neither a long-faced Christian nor a "pale-faced" pacifist—not any pacifist at all—but a genial, athletic youth, who entered heartily into the diversions of young men of his class and means. He was a good dancer, and served on the college dance committee; he was the champion club swinger of the University, and an enthusiastic horseman. During his college days and later in the Wild West and in Mexico he was as hard a rider as the old Revolutionary Dominie.

After graduation, he put in a year at Williams College, where he became leader of the Young Men's Christian Association. For a time education seemed likely to be his chosen field of labor. Always of a deeply religious temperament, he finally decided to enter the ministry, a calling in which so many of his forbears had been distinguished. He entered Union Theological Seminary in New York, and went on from there to the Episcopal Theological Seminary at Cambridge, Massachusetts. He was ordained to the Episcopal ministry in 1911. During the following year he taught Old Testament History at Princeton.

His interests have never been parochial and, yielding to the urge for a more active life and wider fields of usefulness, he entered the mission field in China, under Bishop Roots. The climate, however, proved a serious menace to his health, and it seemed wise to give up the work and return home. Crossing through Siberia and Russia proper, he finally reached Germany where he broke the journey by a year of study at the University of Marburg.

He made a flying trip to America to officiate at the White House wedding of his brother, Francis Bowes Sayre, to Jessie Wilson, daughter of the President. It was a happy reunion for him, for his brother's best man was Sir Wilfred Grenfell with whom Nevin Sayre had spent two summers in Labrador, assisting in Grenfell's work, an important feature of which was the battle against tuberculosis. Chugging up and down the coast in the doctor's motor boat, he spent his holidays preaching what he called "Don't-spit sermons."

After the wedding he hastened back to complete his course at Marburg. It was there that he first became acquainted with Norman Angell's anti-war literature which deeply interested

JOHN NEVIN SAYRE

him and set in motion a train of thought that was to carry
him far. His studies at the University ended, he set off to explore Palestine. The day he reached Damascus he got news
of trouble brewing between Mexico and the United States.
Norman Angell had focussed his mind on the economic absurdity of war. If, however, his country became entangled, he
debated with his conscience whether, as a young man un-
encumbered by immediate family ties, it was not his duty to
shoulder arms in its service. He hurried home, fortunately
to find the war scare over, and took up the more peaceful and
pleasant occupation of teaching again at Princeton.

Then came the great catastrophe which overwhelmed the
world in 1914. War had gradually become less and less respectable to people of thoughtful minds. Empty minds, glad
of any relief from the boredom of existence, simple minds,
stirred by brass buttons and brass bands, jingo minds, that go
off at the touch of the trigger, all respond to the romantic appeal of the skilful war propagandist, and these in 1914 descended on the world like locusts. Talcott Williams came down
to Princeton to lecture and rivalled the kaiser in providing a
religious cloak for the War. Jesus, it appeared, was no pacifist,
though in his early ministry he seemed inclined that way. He
was a realist, and as he grew older and wiser, he advised his
disciples to exchange their cloaks for swords.

Since the Marburg days when Norman Angell had convinced him of the economic imbecility of war, Nevin Sayre
had given much thought to other angles of the subject, and
after hearing Williams's lecture he decided to come to grips
with it. He sat down one day determined not to rise till he
had taken a definite stand as a professing Christian toward
mass violence. He went through the New Testament dili-
gently and rose from his search a convinced and uncompromising pacifist. Although at the time he was unfamiliar with

the history of the old John Sayre of Revolutionary days, he came by the same reasoning to precisely the stand taken by his ancestor.

He left Princeton to become rector of a church in Suffern, New York, and during his four years' pastorate there America entered the War. He continued to preach pacifism unflinchingly, and without alienating his flock, from which there were only half a dozen withdrawals. Many of the clergy in that strenuous time ceased to preach a Christianity which was unpopular, and joined in the hymn of hate. Nevin Sayre bore testimony to the faith that was in him without rancor, as becomes a good Christian. He expressed a willingness to resign if the congregation so desired. Though many of them disagreed with his pacifist creed, they respected his courage and sincerity, they too behaving as becomes good Christians. By the time men of his class were called to the colors, his resolve was made to waive exemption as a clergyman and refuse service as a conscientious objector to war. The armistice was declared before this conflict with government became necessary.

A handful of English Christians to whom war was utterly abhorrent and who deplored the poisonous hate engendered by vicious propaganda, banded together to form a Fellowship of Reconciliation. Nevin Sayre joined the American branch of that International Fellowship. For the first time in all his wanderings over the face of the earth he found, in the activities of the Fellowship, work which completely absorbed him and into which he could throw himself without reserve. He had first-hand knowledge of the plodding masses in Labrador, Asia, Europe, in his own country. His conscience was highly socialized, his loyalty to the teaching of Jesus profound. With Jane Addams, he believed that "the things that make men alike are stronger and more primitive than the things that separate them." The brotherhood of man could not be reconciled with the practice of war. The time had come, he felt, to talk of many things which needed change in this everchanging world. First and foremost on his list of things to be changed was the general belief in the inevitability of war.

Nevin Sayre was born with a silver spoon in his mouth, a circumstance which has always pricked his sensitive conscience, although many worthy persons and unpopular causes have been fed from it. He disapproves of the social order which started him in life with that useful article of table furniture in his mouth, while innumerable others started with their little noses to the grindstone of sordid poverty. That system which is unsocial and un-Christian comes second on his list of desirable changes.

As education seemed the most effective weapon with which to effect these changes, he resigned his pastorate to assist in founding the Brookwood School, and became a member of the teaching staff. Kellogg Pacts and naval reduction conferences, he believes, are of service in putting peace on the front page, but these agreements will continue to be mere scraps of paper while the history taught in the schools is little more than a glorification of war. A silk purse is not made of a sow's ear, nor genuine peace lovers by that sort of education.

A strange result of the war to end war was the intensification in America of the European system of compulsory military education. Schools and colleges throughout the land have been subsidized by the War Department, and many ingenious methods have been used to sell the idea to reluctant American students. Army and Navy groups, the American Legion, and patriotic societies gave it vigorous support. All friends of peace fought it just as vigorously, none more than Nevin Sayre.

In this fight the militarists have not scrupled to use unfair methods. Before an investigation dimmed the bright luster of his career, Fred Marvin furnished articles to *The Army and Navy Journal* which were apparently read, and acted upon by officers all over the country, although Marvin's statements were laughable. He also furnished a so-called black list of "plotters" for the information of patriots, dangerous persons who must be condemned unheard. The Nevins and Sayres have not been this blatant type of patriot; useful citizens who perform their bounden duty and reasonable service to society as a matter of course make less noise. Marvin succeeded in convincing nervous ladies that the anti-military movement was stimulated from Moscow by bribes of Russian gold, and having no other visible means of employing their time they set about saving their country from the machinations of traitors, oblivious of the fact that even President Coolidge and Senator Borah had opposed compulsory military training in American institutions of learning.

This black-list of Bolshevists was headed by Jane Addams, and Nevin Sayre had the honor to be included in the good company. All is fair in war, and it was the strategy of the country's defenders to suppress meetings which advertised the speakers on their list.

In Gibbons' *Fall of Rome* occurs a passage which should be better known. He tells that when the Romans waxed fat and flabby and fearful of a possible foe, they decided to raise a great standing army for their protection. This army soon became powerful and had its heel on the neck of Rome, exercising a tyranny over those who had planned it as a protection which no alien foe was sufficiently strong to accomplish. The experiences of Nevin Sayre as a pacifist speaker suggest that history may and often does repeat itself.

As an instance, a talk advertised to be given in the University of Oklahoma was called off. Norman, the University town, is a military post and Colonel Lewis "requested" the faculty to prohibit the meeting. As the college is one of those subsidized by the War Department the request was obeyed. But the students called the meeting on again by securing a church basement. Colonel Lewis hastened from a nearby town for the fray. In his heckling talk he made some irrelevant though fervent remarks on the subject of lawlessness. "Yes?" shouted an irreverent youth, "well what have you to say about bootlegging in the army?" The doughty colonel was determined to play only with marked cards, and continued his efforts to break up meetings of Mr. Sayre. Fair war, but poor sport. Daughters of the Revolution helped on the good work of the army.

By right of distinguished ancestry few Americans are as eligible as Nevin Sayre to membership in those societies of patriot descendents who regard the virtue of patriotism as a personal and private inheritance, and live on that unearned increment. Nevin Sayre is not a fundamentalist patriot who believes that the faith was once and for all delivered to the fathers in 1776, but an evolutionist who accepts new revelations that will carry American civilization on from glory to grace.

As a speaker, he is always in demand. He talks sound sense, even though he does mix up the genial, informal speech of a true democrat with a hangover of broad a's—horribly broad a's—which break through unconsciously as reminders of the silver spoon origin or his formal homiletics.

The zeal of the big army and navy group; the worthy citizens of both sexes who get their inspiration from the Fred Marvins and their ilk, have kept liberals and radicals on the jump. Yes, give them this well-earned credit! During the War a drastic suppression of liberty was inevitable; there can be no liberty in wartime. But cruel and unusual punishment, in war as in peace, is a violation of the Constitution. For a time Nevin was practically a commuter to Washington, working in the interests of war victims. Once a friend, Evan Thomas, brother of Norman, was suffering in Leavenworth Penitentiary as a result of a rebellion led on behalf of fellow prisoners. This conscientious objector had his arms chained for eight hours a day to a beam above his head—the Leavenworth style of prison reform. When Nevin laid the facts before his brother's father-in-law, President Wilson promptly put an end to this form of punishment, so far as Leavenworth was concerned.

Considering that Senator France's brother was arrested during the War in Passaic, New Jersey, for reading aloud the Declaration of Independence—a document with which the officers of the law were unfamiliar—and that other people were rushed off to jail for distributing copies of the Sermon on the Mount, it is not strange that an outspoken paper like *The World Tomorrow,* edited then by Norman Thomas, should catch the eagle eye of the press censorship. As a menace to the state, even since the War, it has been allotted several pages of space in that delightful magazine of humor, *The Congressional Record.* During the conflict it was all but driven out of business. Nevin fought to keep the paper going, along with Norman Thomas, and since the War he has on one occasion had to undergo a four-hours' grilling before a Congressional committee, in the course of which revelations were made by these investigators that would have brought envious flushes to the cheeks of the original authors of the *Arabian Nights.*

When the American Civil Liberties Union was begun to campaign for the rights of the oppressed guaranteed them by the Constitution, he was on the job as usual, and "in on it," taking an active part in all its efforts to see that justice is done to men and women everywhere, no matter what their honest views.

Upon Norman Thomas's retirement from the editorship of *The World Tomorrow* in 1921, Nevin Sayre, not without some reluctance, took over the job, brought in new blood to share his editorial labors, and started a task which he laid down some two years later because he found the routine of writing—though he writes with force and has a good swinging style—wearing and less to his taste than functioning through committees and groups on specific projects. Although he has steadfastly continued his work as Secretary of the Fellowship of Reconciliation, he has also found time to organize the Committee on Militarism in Education, for which he was cited in 1929 on the annual honor roll of *The Nation*.

Since he has found a full-time job in the crusade for economic justice and the abolition of war, Mr. Sayre has again become a world-trotter. In 1920-21 he was one of an international quartet—American, English, French and Dutch—who toured war-desolated Germany, spreading the gospel of reconstruction through love and justice. In 1928, with a group of Quakers, he engineered a good-will mission to Nicaragua. This mission made many contacts in southern republics and resulted in the establishment of a Fellowship secretariat in Central America. He has covered all of Europe in his numerous trips abroad.

A few years ago Nevin Sayre was married to Kathleen Whitaker, a member of the English Fellowship and a Quaker relief worker, as devoted to the cause as himself, and if justice were done, worthy of a biographical sketch quite on her own account. They have a pleasant home close to the Palisades on the Hudson. The young Sayres have not yet learned that their daddy is a fighter for peace on duty, and they disapprove of his frequent absences. His little daughter, Faith, took the matter to the Lord in prayer. "Please God," was her evening petition, "bring Daddy safe home, and please let him be keeped here in this house."

Glancing into the laughing brown eyes of this quiet, cultivated, bookish-looking man, it is difficult to find anything remotely resembling the pictures of radicals painted by inventive or fearsome standpatters. It is refreshing to note how often he laughs—he is one of those persons who seem to enjoy laughing and therefore can't help it. He has a good collection of jokes, which, in moments of relaxation, he uncorks, though it pains me to write that often these are very, very stale.

Bookish he may look; but he is essentially a motor type of person. He must be on the move. He does some of his best thinking, as many people do, when strolling aimlessly about in a small room, circling within a radius of five feet, while hunching his shoulders, putting his hands into his trousers pockets, and turning a corner of thought each time he escapes running into some piece of furniture. Fond of movement, impatient as all good radicals ought to be, he sometimes becomes almost as driving as your professional go-getter; he likes his own way rather well, and as a matter of fact when very young he once sought to obtain it by dashing a plate of food violently on the dining-room floor. But withal, he is warm and generous in spirit, and when he drives, it is always because he visions some goal the attainment of which is of vital social import. He is not the only radical leader who wishes in his heart that he were six men, so tremendous is the need, instead of one and a half.

Genuine pacifists like Nevin Sayre are still comparatively few, though their numbers are markedly on the increase. They fight in the open, their only weapons fair means, persuasion, and non-violent insistence. Surely those who believe in convincing their erring fellowmen by killing them have nothing to fear from such antagonists. No, they fear the force of an idea which may change this best of all possible worlds, for an idea has always been stronger than armies or navies. Hear the words of Thomas Paine, one of our great founding fathers, a man of mighty faith, who passionately hated war, and believed it would be eliminated from the future history of mankind: "An idea will go where armies cannot penetrate. It will march on the horizon of the world, *and it will conquer.*"

Bishop to the Universe

PAUL JONES

"SO THIS is the Bishop's palace!" The speaker was a Scots woman, full of years and of wisdom, and the gentle irony of the remark was inspired by the modest domicile in Orange, New Jersey, which had, for many years, been the episcopal residence of the Right Reverend Paul Jones, Bishop of the Protestant Episcopal Church. To find one of so high ecclesiastical rank housed in such complete simplicity, was for a British subject a new and startling experience. True—one does hear of such a mode of living among bishops who have gone forth as missionaries, but in the "States" as well as in Great Britain, the rank of chief Diocesan carries with it the assumption of high material, as well as high spiritual, standards of living.

Scant wonder then that the typically small suburban dwelling should call forth an exclamation. Scant wonder, on the other hand that *Bishop* Jones should choose just such a house for homing his family. For this bishop would find material ease incompatible with the habits of behavior which have developed as a result of auto-conditioning over a long period of years. For these behavior-habits have in turn so affected the mental processes of Paul Jones that the convictions set forth by him seven years ago in "The Philosophy of a Madman" have become the nucleus of a social philosophy to which he applies the pragmatic test in every detail of his personal as well as of his official life.

It has become customary in writing biography to use, in so far as material is available and deduction possible, the method of cause and effect. If such a plan is adopted in approaching, however briefly, the life of Paul Jones, material concerning antecedents and background is easily procurable and, in logical sequence, deduction just as easily determinable. But with this difference—that following the rules of logic the deductions thus made must disagree with the known facts. And just herein lies the superior value of biography of the living over that of the dead. Certainly behaviorist psychology receives a challenge in Paul Jones' life-story.

Sprung from Welsh and English forbears, whose progeny had settled in New England and New York, Paul Jones was born in Wilkes-Barre, Pennsylvania. At that time Wilkes-Barre numbered among its population more persons of large fortune than any other city in Pennsylvania—Philadelphia and Pittsburgh only excepted—and the source of this material prosperity was anthracite coal. For Wilkes-Barre was happily situated, not only because it occupied the centre of the anthracite coal-belt of northeastern Pennsylvania, but also because it had a water-front on the Susquehanna River which made easily possible the shipping of the mined product. Hence, since the opening of the first coal-beds in 1813, Wilkes-Barre had grown in population, wealth, and fame.

At the zenith of the coal era in the history of this industrial town, the family of the Rector of St. Stephen's Church there was augmented by the advent of a son. Yes, Paul Jones was of the house and lineage of Levi in the Protestant Episcopal Church. His father and his father's father had, each in turn, served the Church in the capacity of priest, the latter for 33 years as Rector of the Church of the Epiphany, New York; the former, for 40 years as Rector of St. Stephen's, Wilkes-Barre. At this juncture source-material and logic are consistent in accepting the sequential fact of the falling of the mantle of *Elisha* upon the shoulders of Paul. This boy, destined to stand for the rise and fall of many in Israel, was the sixth and youngest child of Henry Lawrence and Sara Coffin Jones. Thus his infancy and childhood were endowed by nature with those social factors which inhere in real family life. Paul had two brothers, two sisters, two parents. "Everything," he says, "in my family was perfectly *regular.*" Everything which birth, early environment and training gave him was, according to known tests, calculated to result in his case in the production of a citizen whose well-regulated reactions would lead him easily to accept the *status quo.*

His father, as has been indicated, was a clergyman, of the Broad-Church School of Episcopalianism,—one of the best examples of his period and his kind in his simple loyalties, his sweet contentment, his practical demonstration of religion. "The atmosphere in which I had grown up was a liberal one in its theology," says Paul Jones, "so that I had never been troubled by questions of the literal inspiration of the Bible or of rigid ecclesiasticism. For that very reason I was led to believe that the validity of the teaching of Jesus rested upon its essential truth rather than upon some outside or supernatural authority." His mother, of New England ancestry, one of the New Hampshire branch of the Coffin family, was high principled but, like her husband, quite conventional in her adherence to established social mores. This minister's family was a fine example of traditional virtues, and as such was deservedly regarded with admiration by the parishioners of St. Stephen's, Wilkes-Barre.

By the time Paul had reached the age of ten, Wilkes-Barre had widened its industrial scope to include, in addition to coal, the manufacture of wire, lace, and axles, and this industrial expansion had been a factor in increasing the population to 55,000. Wilkes-Barre was an industrial city! But this fact was of neither conscious nor sub-conscious moment to Paul. In the last decades of the nineteenth century, with rare exceptions, the clergy of the Episcopal Church did not, as now, minister to "industrialists." "Working-men" or "laborers," as they were then called, were usually attached, according to national inheritance, either to Roman Catholic or Protestant evangelical branches of Christendom.

It is but natural that the Jones children should have grown up "in association only with right-thinking people of the best type," and so it was that the boy, born and reared in an important industrial centre, was impervious to it as such, because he was surrounded by the protective influence of a refined home, a liberal but thoroughly orthodox Sunday-school and Church, and a traditional private-school, the Harry Hillman Academy. That the boy's reflexes *at that time* responded properly to environmental conditioning two facts attest: in Sunday-school he was rewarded for perfect attendance during a period of four years, and in the Academy he was for several years first in his class! Thus Paul Jones, well-grounded in the standards of respectability—accustomed to conform to the accepted social and national code—locally distinguished by academic achievement—assured of future success by reason of the behavior-habits established through the *best* environment—Paul Jones entered Yale!

The first years of college life were for Paul Jones insignificant beyond the fact that his keen intellect, his healthy pleasure in athletics and in social events made them in the main happy. Nevertheless even during these years the question of the future and a career began to give him pause. When, during the second half of his collegiate period, the question demanded an answer, Paul determined to "think through" (afterwards a favorite phrase and modus solvendi) the problem. This process, the first complete experiment of the kind brought him face to face with certain facts, facts which struck a blow at the supporting-beams of the super-structure of life-standards as he had been taught to see them. The facts are two—one academic, the other practical.

The former entailed a definition of "success," and here despite the environment of his childhood, he saw himself as a non-conformist. Success, as he viewed it, was entirely apart from the connotation of the terms which was commonly accepted. For him, it meant a life devoid of ambition of a subjective kind; devoid of acquisitiveness even when exerted toward the attainment of laudable qualities. Success for him was in a purposeful life lived objectively.

The second of the two facts was that a life-work which would be a definite expression at one and the same time of his own inclinations and of service to society might eventually involve him in the repudiation of more definitions than that of "success." How much of struggle there may have been in the serious process whereby Paul Jones thus relinquished his first hold on the principles which his youthful training had given him, we are not permitted to know. For it was typical of him then, as it is typical of him today, that such struggle is never allowed to waste in emotional reminiscence, but finds instead immediate application in the affairs of life.

So it was that Paul Jones, considering Forestry Service and the Ministry of the Church as two possible ways of living an objectively useful life, chose the latter and in the fall of 1902, following his receipt of the baccalaureate degree from Yale University, entered the Episcopal Theological School at Cambridge. How rudimentary was the first "thinking through" method is shown in the fact that aside from its effect on the vocational destiny of Paul Jones, it in no way influenced his concepts of right and wrong in other departments. Proof of this is his activity as a strike-breaker in the anthracite strike during the summer of 1902, the interim of his graduation from Yale and his matriculation in the Cambridge Divinity School.

Now that the first great problem, that of profession, was settled, Paul Jones devoted himself heart and soul to the preparation necessary for the life-work he had chosen. The habits of study which had developed during adolescence were not lost during the years at Yale, but were rather balanced by a fine interest in extra-curricular activities. Now, however, with the inspiration of a definite purpose study was pursued with zest, and among the most intelligent of the theological students then at Cambridge, he was a distinguished figure. During three years family and friends watched his progress and looked forward eagerly to a future of ecclesiastical distinction for this young man in whom habits of industry coupled with mental endowments of high order gave promise of the attainment of greatness. Nor were they to be disappointed of their hope, save that ecclesiastical distinction was to meet Paul Jones not in the moment of triumphal entry as Bishop into Jerusalem, but in the hour of the long march to his Calvary; and save that greatness was to be his by reason—not of intellectual attainment or pastoral achievement but of spiritual and mental integrity.

For the second time Paul Jones faced the problem of the future. At the completion of the usual three year theological course of the Episcopal Seminary he decided to add to this one year of graduate study, and it was during this period that "thinking through" his problem, he resolved to decline a pleasing offer from St. George's Church, New York, and even the opportunity to become assistant to and ultimately to succeed his father in the Church in Wilkes-Barre which had nurtured his youth. How momentous was this decision is easily discoverable in the series of results which it produced. Far from rudimentary in its effect, this time, the re-defining of values carried with it a cleavage from the established order not only in the matter of connoting the term "success," but in that of evaluating all social and moral concepts, not according to their general acceptance but according to their merits as a means of liberating the spiritual forces latent in humanity. It is a truism that the individual suffers *one* greatest grief, experiences *one* greatest love, holds *one* greatest struggle: after it, should he rise victorious, future contests of a similar sort are frequent but increasingly easy. In this victory at the very outset of his career of service, had Paul Jones already known his greatest struggle?

The fact that he was to receive the degree of Bachelor of Divinity from the Cambridge Theological School would under ordinary circumstances have been a cause for satisfaction. But, in the case of Paul Jones the circumstances were not ordinary. For across the horizon of his vision had appeared the figure of a man, and with that intrusion the horizon had receded— the vision broadened. Franklin Spencer Spalding, Missionary Bishop of Utah, had come East for several purposes, one of which was to find a young man who would see in his diocese opportunity not for promotion and prestige, but instead for service. To convey in words a true impression of the power and magnetism of this great personality is impossible. Bishop Spalding, outstanding Socialist, was as feared in the Church as he was respected. Like Paul Jones, Spalding was of fine lineage and the story of his conversion to socialism is an interesting one. Whatever his belief none could doubt his sincerity, and so strong, so magnificent even, was his expression of conviction that his greatest opponents both within and without the Church regarded him with respectful admiration. A long hard battle he fought for "his people." His letters to his mother, written over a long period, reiterate again and

PAUL JONES

again the depth of his disappointment in those who could have supported him and would not. Yet wherever he went, he left something behind him, for none could lightly hear his words, and the Church Socialist League, part of whose purpose was "to further social justice by prayer and study of socialism," owed much of its sustained impetus to the vigorous social Christianity of Bishop Spalding.

When therefore Paul Jones, eager for sight of the star which should guide him to the land of his desire, listened to Spalding's account of Utah and its crying need of men who could find among gray lives in lonely places adventure for God, he decided to follow. Such were the immediate circumstances which led Paul Jones to begin his ministerial career in the little town of Logan, Utah. In reference to this incident, a biographer of Bishop Spalding, speaking of his trip East says: "He stirred up interest, however, in the Cambridge School, and elsewhere, and one man destined to become one of his most intelligent and devoted assistants offered himself for service in Utah. The coming of that one man, like that of St. Andrew and St. Philip, makes financial results, however necessary, seem insignificant. This trip, judged by that alone was a triumphant success."

From 1906 to 1911 together with his friend, D. K. Johnston, and from 1911 to 1914 alone, Paul Jones lived in Logan. "There they" (Johnston and Jones) "lived on terms of genuine friendship with the Mormon people, drawing about them by means of club, gymnasium and classes other young men. On Sundays they preached Christian sympathy and were able to draw encouraging congregations of young Latter-Day Saints to listen to them. Their audience usually consisted of Mormons, the proportion at times being about thirty of those to one Church member."

Very early in their period of activity there, on October 13th,

1906, Bishop Spalding wrote of these two men: "Jones and Johnston are doing splendidly. They are very happy and the people like them. . . . I think they appreciate that it is to be slow, hard work, but they see the need and are full of enthusiasm, and they propose, too, to get other men from Cambridge. It is wonderful what an impression they have made on the town. It's the first time really well-educated gentlemen have been sent there. I'm hoping great things for Logan."

And the Bishop was not to be disappointed of *his* hope. *The Portal* which was edited by the two young men at Logan became an important factor in the growth of the work there, and its pages bore continuous evidence of the influence of the great Bishop upon Paul Jones. Christian socialism, a movement within the Church to apply the social Gospel of Jesus to all human relationships including those of race, industry and nations, became for Paul Jones during these years, a spiritual passion. More and more, as he himself whimsically expressed it, he "easily moved still further away from the sound conclusions on which the stability of our institutions rests."

In 1913 he visited California and while there married Mary Elizabeth Balch, of Coronado Beach, whom he had known for several years. Miss Balch had been fostered in a home where the term "success" had much of the connotation which her husband, years before, had given it. She has contributed to their union not only a rich companionship, but also a naturally progressive and liberal outlook which has enabled her to sympathize completely with the ideals and ideas of her husband.

Just a little more than a year after his marriage, in September, 1914, Paul Jones was made Archdeacon of Utah. The travel which the duties of this office require was, although unforeseen as such, a helpful preparation for the heavier responsibilities which were so soon to be his.

On what slight contingencies hangs the web of Destiny! In November of that year, in Salt Lake City, just as a certain man was crossing a street, a car shot suddenly around a corner, struck the man with full force and jammed, in response to steering effort, into the nearest lamp-post. The man was Franklin Spencer Spalding. Within a month after the tragedy, Paul Jones was elected Bishop of Utah and joined the Socialist Party!

By the time Paul Jones was consecrated Bishop of Utah, the Great War was already four months old. That the new Bishop was anti-war neither surprised nor disturbed anyone. Many persons who had no socialist leanings were equally so. Hence sermons, and addresses dealing with the possible inconsistency of the inclusion of war in the Christian program were received with slight if any opposition. But the new Bishop was too close a student of men and affairs to be caught by the idealistic slogans whose use was a part of the preparedness program of the United States. Accordingly during 1915 and 1916 he was active in opposing all measures which pointed to the future entrance of this country into the conflict. Finally in the fall of 1916 at the General Convention of the Episcopal Church in St. Louis, Paul Jones leading a forum on "Christianity and Force" openly declared himself by taking the full pacifist position. He had "thought the problem through," and like Luther of old he faced his peers with the unanswerable challenge: "Here I stand; I can do no other!"

Less than a year later, in the Spring of 1917, the United States entered the War. Although Bishop Jones merely continued to interpret the Christian attitude toward war in the terms which he had been using since 1914, he was now looked upon with suspicion. Among those who thus questioned him, not one seemed to see the consistency of the Bishop's position, the inconsistency of its reversal. His own words express the situation clearly: "I had committed myself to an interpretation of Christianity that had no place in it for war, and I did not see how a mere declaration by Congress could alter the principles involved. The inevitableness of it, as I look back, was the most striking thing about the whole experience."

Just one year after the entrance of the United States into the War, Paul Jones resigned the bishopric of Utah. The story of the series of events which resulted in this loss to the Episcopal Church is a familiar one, and its details are easily obtainable. The spark of antagonism kindled at a "time of excited public opinion" needed only a zephyr to fan it into flame. The zephyr breezed over it when Bishop Jones, en route for Coronado Beach, California, to bring back to Utah his little daughter who had been visiting her grandparents, attended and addressed a Conference of Christian pacifists in Los Angeles. The drama, showing how garbled reports of this conference in the Utah press led to an official protest from the Council of Advice of the Diocese of Utah; of how the wardens and vestry of St. Mark's Church, Salt Lake City, endorsed this protest; of how these two bodies demanded his resignation and filed copies of their resolutions with the House of Bishops; of how the House of Bishops, granting Paul Jones a brief leave of absence, appointed a commission to inquire into the matter; of how he was invited to meet the commission to state his case, *but was actually accorded no such opportunity*— this drama reached its climax when, in response to the decision of the commission Paul Jones having offered his resignation, the House of Bishops "in view of Bishop Jones' impaired usefulness in Utah" accepted it.

Even when summarized briefly, minus stage-settings and lighting-effects, minus the sordid "close-ups" of hatred and bitterness, minus the actors' portrayal of cowardice in high places, this story of shocking injustice is harrowing enough. Only one fact softens slightly this incredible act of the Episcopal Church; that many of her members, both clerical and lay, and among them some who could not take the full pacifist position, protested vigorously the action of the House of Bishops. But one voice was not lifted in protest. Paul Jones, true to the principles which had been so dearly bought, refrained from words, and while he retained his title, he lost his seat in the House of Bishops.

For two years he labored as missionary in the Diocese of Maine, working and preaching there, much as he had done in the old days at Logan.

Back in 1916, while he was endeavoring to prevent the future participation of the United States in the War, he had happened to read in *The Literary Digest* an account of the first conference in this country of the Fellowship of Reconciliation. Part of the statement of principles of this organization was contained in the article. He describes his reaction thus: "When I read it I said to myself, '*That* says it; that's what I have been looking for.' So I applied for membership . . . there wasn't anything else for me to do." In 1920, Paul Jones was called to succeed Norman Thomas as Secretary of the Fellowship. To it he gave ten years—ten years of constructive work—ten years of ripe and wise leadership—so that much of the steady and fine growth of the Fellowship was due to his careful guidance.

During the decade from 1920 to 1930, his personal life was enriched by the birth of a son, as well as by the blessings which accrue in family relations that contain no problem. During this decade, his life incalculably enriched the lives of many.

Paul Jones is physically large and well-proportioned. His

appearance gives a sense of balance. A strong face in which kindness and humor are blended, contains brown eyes which look directly, very directly and steadily at the object of their gaze, whether it be a person, place or thing. His hands are large, and they wield a pen or a saw with equal facility.

He has dignity about him, dignity rooted in an imperturbable serenity. Indeed, I have heard people say who know him well that they would give a lot to see Paul rise up in wrath or excitation. He is the sort of man who sits calmly and fills his veteran of a pipe while everybody else rushes to watch the thrill of fire-trucks shrieking their way to a two-alarm fire. Yes, a trifle maddening! I have heard those who know him only a little describe him as merely easy-going, irresponsible. But he is sensitive, warm, immediately responsive to unimportant people if not always equally so to big-wigs.

No man on earth is more approachable. His ideas on high-pressure efficiency methods are more Oriental than of the West. In ten years I have called him on the telephone hundreds of times. The only time I ever heard about his being "in conference" was late in 1929, and I felt much the shock of one hearing about a staid daughter's elopement. All kinds of people are drawn to him, all colors, creeds, conditions, citizens from every corner of society. He has spoken successfully before Rotarians and wobblies, he has almost literally expounded the gospel and pounded the—soapbox. More than many a bishop entrenched in splendor, he reaches subtly out, and far. He is veritably Bishop to the Universe.

Eleven years after the action taken by the House of Bishops, the diocese of Southern Ohio called upon Bishop Jones to assume the duties of Acting Bishop during the interim of the Diocesan's illness and the election of a coadjutor. To this call, Paul Jones responded and from the city of Cincinnati the Acting Bishop administered the Diocese, preaching and teaching, *without protest now,* his Christian social gospel in its entirety.

In the fall of 1930, following nearly a year in Southern Ohio, Paul Jones went to Yellow Springs to act as College Pastor. "Happy is the man who has found his work," and equally "happy" the work which has found its man! Antioch College, unique among educational institutions, now has Paul Jones, and Paul Jones has Antioch College. And pendant from the contingency of this union we see again the finely wrought web of destiny!

What is this Christian Social Gospel, the subject on the one hand of so much bitter controversy, on the other of such exalted incentive to sacrificial love? For Paul Jones, it is a social order wherein "Jesus' principles are applied to all human relationships." For Paul Jones, it is a social order which recognizes in Jesus' teachings three fundamental principles: first, "the supreme value of personality," second, "the necessity of putting the kingdom of right relationships before everything else," and third, "the use of the creative power of love as the great method of overcoming evil." No Christian could do other than agree with it—*in theory.* But for Paul Jones there is no theory apart from its application. "Had the bishops of the Church," he says, "thought to have had my spiritual I. Q. taken when I was elected to succeed Bishop Spalding, the difficulty for the church would have been avoided." His spiritual I. Q. would have shown conclusively that he recognized no national, industrial or racial problem to whose solution a method other than that of the creative power of love should be applied. Paul Jones is still an ardent and an active member of the Socialist Party. His socialism has grown with that of the movement, and somewhere the spirit of Franklin Spencer Spalding must smile, appeased! For Paul Jones is always cognizant of the mighty influence of that episcopal pioneer of socialism upon his own philosophy.

In the story of his conversion to the socialist point of view, Spalding once said, "I was forced to realize that thousands who had as good a right to the fulness of life as I had, did not have a ghost of a chance. . . . I was forced to realize that the power to make and save money carries with it the destruction of the impulse to give it away." And the illuminating experience of that rugged leader was duplicated in the case of his disciple. In the socialist aspiration to a new society wherein co-operation shall supersede competition, Paul Jones finds the cure for many of the social ills which are not recognized as such by those who accept, without question, the present social code.

In the story of Paul Jones is found a challenge to the theses of that school of psychology which holds that the reflexes of the young child may be consciously, and are unconsciously, so conditioned by the environment of his early life that his adult behavior-habits are easily predictable. Here is the testimony of Paul Jones: "The natural right of the best people to have the best things, wealth as an evidence of individual probity, punishment as the only proper treatment for crime, the foreigner to be kept in his proper place as a drudge and to be treated kindly but firmly, the army and navy as the loyal defenders of the nation, the worship of the Church as the proper expression of all decent and respectable people— *all these conceptions were mine by ordinary training and association.*" Ergo—Paul Jones must in adult life develop into a thoroughly *safe* citizen; one who may be counted upon to attain respect through conformity to all the conventions of society in a capitalist civilization. Yet observe again the testimony of this same Paul Jones: "From questioning war as a method for aiding the cause of democracy or achieving peace . . . I have been led to examine other fields, where we have been careless of the method because of our devotion to the goal. Thus the whole subject of our treatment of offenders seems to need re-examination; for the average person seldom seems to ask whether, when we have punished such an offender, anything has been done to cure him or make society safer. Or in another field, that of race relations, even if it should be granted that the fears that some people have of other races are justified, I am led to believe that the methods of discrimination and suppression which such people justify are, after all, merely going to intensify the problem." Alas poor reflexes! They did not make Paul Jones safe for democracy!

An impression of Paul Jones as he appeared to some of the members of the office staff of the F. O. R. is couched in these words, written out as an informal tribute:

Paul Jones is privileged to use the official "Right Reverend."
But he never exercises this privilege. By the members
Of the F. O. R. he is addressed as "Paul."
I have observed that when
One wishes to *know anything,—*
One goes to—Paul!
Paul is large; he sees things in a large way—
But his broad vision, his generous mind,
Have not prevented him from remembering
Details. His memory is prodigious.
Added to that, he has the gift of clarity.
Not only can Paul see, himself;
He can tell others about it, in such a way that—
They too, see!
Always busy, never hurried;
Always sympathetic, never without judgment;

He neither praises nor censures,
But faces the Truth with a *smile!*
Best of all, he has a rare
Sense of humor,—a spiritual qualification,—
Which is a part of the courage
That emanates from him!

Having nothing yet possessing all things; being poor yet making many rich, he toils with hands, head and heart for his brother-man. And the daily life of Paul Jones attests that to him "all men within the four seas are brothers."

B. CHARNEY VLADECK

Barricades and Business Management

B. CHARNEY VLADECK

FROM the top of the building of *The Jewish Daily Forward,* one of the tallest in the neighborhood, you look down over the tenement roofs of all the lower East Side, with the new Empire State Building and the Chrysler tower aflash in the sunlight for background. To the south are the skyscrapers of lower Manhattan, to the east, the river and the spires of Brooklyn.

Under the tower of this most famous of Jewish daily papers sits a man whose keen eyes have long since taken in every significant detail of the swarming city life below him and yet who knows that New York's East Side where he has spent so many busy years is still largely alien to the rest of America and that the Socialist Party in which he plays so prominent a rôle has not yet struck firmly down into the grass roots of the country. This man in the office of the general manager of *The Forward* is B. Charney Vladeck, one-time professional revolutionist, who spent most of his young manhood in Russian and Polish jails, former alderman of New York City, now manager of one of the most successful foreign language papers in the United States, lecturer, teacher, writer and all the time a Socialist.

Stroll with him through the East Side that he knows so well and it seems as though every third person must stop to shake Vladeck's hand, comment on something he has written or said, or, as often as not, ask him to aid in some money-

raising campaigns. For there are few liberal, labor, or socialist causes in America that have not at one time or another
called on Vladeck for help when they have found themselves
in financial straits—as most causes of that nature often find
themselves. Go to a socialist dinner and when you have eaten
your revolutionary way through the traditional tepid soup,
broiled chicken, and brick ice-cream, if you find Baruch Charney Vladeck rising to preside over the speech-making, be prepared to give and give all but your carfare home, when the
collectors come around. For the man can simply charm
money out of the closest pressed wallets. He can give gaiety
and gusto even to that terrible ordeal known to all attendants
upon radical gatherings as "the money-speech." "Sometimes
I think," he remarked almost wistfully once, "that the comrades think more of me as a 'schnorrer' (beggar) than a
speaker."

But here we are not concerned so much with the financial
abilities of the man, which would have given him a high place
among those skyscrapers in the money markets near him, as
with the genuine brilliance of his intellect and the fire that
glows in those eyes behind the spectacles. For Vladeck is a
curious compound, typical perhaps of the newer school of
Socialists, of skepticism and self-sacrifice, of caution and true
courage, never forgetting the ordeals of his revolutionary days
and yet distrustful deep down of the dogmatic Marxist and
the amateur American revolutionist.

He has the professional's scorn for the amateur, whether
that amateur is performing in the parlors of Greenwich Village or in "mass demonstrations" in Detroit. You see he
became a professional revolutionist at the age of fifteen and
he still bears on his body scars from the whips of the Czar's
Cossacks. So he smiles rather grimly when he hears himself
denounced as a "betrayer of the labor movement" by some

fledgling American Communist, and again he shrugs his shoulders when he is told by the old Marxists in his own Party that he and the paper which he manages are becoming dangerously "liberalized."

To be sure, there are many responsible critics of genuine integrity within the ranks of the Socialist Party today who feel that *The Forward* is not always true to its Socialist faith, that it compromises too readily in order to keep on the right side of the ledger, that its editorials lack their old-time fervor, and that many of the salaries paid its officers are way beyond any Socialistic levels. To be sure, also, it is not fair to place the blame for what seems to be a steady rightward movement of this influential paper upon Vladeck alone.

He has been up and down and all about this country for many years now, and he has come to the belief that the Russian formula and even the more advanced European socialist formulæ will make small headway with a people who as he says, "are children economically and politically." He sees ahead the most intensive sort of educational work, with the infiltration into the Socialist Party of more and more of those who have an American rather than a European background. He hails the recruiting of such men as Harry Ward, Reinhold Niebuhr, Sherwood Eddy, Heywood Broun and others because he feels that they can bring socialism out of its East Side milieu into America proper. And this attitude has cost him the friendship of many of those who thought years back that he would be the fiery leader of the "militant" wing of the Party.

In a recent review of Norman Thomas's book, *America's Way Out,* Vladeck wrote:

"The weakness of the socialist movement in America has always been a challenge to the accepted notions of

Marxism. Here is a country in the highest stage of industrialization—a stage set by history for a great social upheaval. Economically it has developed in full accordance with scientific socialism, but socially and politically it is as backward as China. For some reason the actors have failed to appear for the enactment of the social drama, the lines and rôles for which have been written for quite some time. Karl Kautsky tried to explain away this contradiction several decades ago. Most of his reasons are no longer valid, and yet the socialist movement in the United States is as weak or perhaps even weaker today than it has been in the past. We have always thought that there was something fundamentally wrong with the country. After reading *America's Way Out,* one begins to ask whether there isn't something wrong with the Socialist Party. Thomas is not very specific on this particular question. His answer is rather halting and indirect, but one cannot help but feel that Thomas is saying to all of us: 'Now look here, you have been at this work for decades and you have failed. The American people neither assimilated your thoughts nor approved of your battle-cries. Perhaps the fault isn't with the cause but rather with its presentation. So let me explain socialism to the American people in a new way.' "

Small wonder that Vladeck's frank recognition of the weakness of his Party's propaganda causes consternation among the old timers. "What can they know of socialism who only Karl Marx know?" he asks in effect and stands up at Party meetings to urge a fresh orientation of socialist propaganda. To "explain socialism to the American people in a new way"— that is the man-sized job which Vladeck has cut out for himself, and to it he devotes the bulk of his burning energies.

There is fire a'plenty in the man when he is campaigning in New York. He knows his city and the way of its rules. He knows what so many Socialists do not know, the complexities of capitalism and its psychology. Vladeck has given heed to the advice of G. K. Chesterton that it is more important to know the philosophy of your enemy than the number of troops at his disposal. When he was elected alderman on the Socialist ticket, after a red-hot campaign in a Brooklyn district, he took his job very seriously and decided that he must know all about the powers of the Board of Aldermen under the City Charter. He went straightway to the Municipal Reference Library and there asked for a copy of the Charter and the available literature pertaining thereto. The librarian looked at him with astonishment. "Mr. Vladeck," said he, "in all the years I have been here, no Alderman has ever before asked for a copy of the Charter." This was in 1918 and for the next four years in which he sat in the Aldermanic Chamber, first with six other Socialist colleagues and then with three, his conscientious study of the Charter and its provisions made many miserable moments for his old-line opponents. Likewise, when he speaks to his crowded weekly forum on current events, he makes no generalized denunciations, but shrewdly selects those facts and figures which have the most teeth in them.

"Never debate with that man Vladeck," was the advice given by a Tammany chieftain to a younger speaker. "When he shoots off his face, he's likely to hit you in the weakest spot you got."

But it is not only in the rough and tumble of a New York political campaign that Vladeck's ability as a speaker stands out. There was a group of liberals in a mid-west city which more out of curiosity than anything else decided to invite an East Side Jewish Socialist to address them. Vladeck came and spoke and conquered. It was a luncheon meeting but it was long after five o'clock in the afternoon before the chairman was finally able to shoo the members out of the hall, so anxious were they to hear more from this keen-witted man whose accent was so heavy, but whose bearing was so easy and good-humored.

Vladeck's technique of speaking is the envy of many a professional orator. His success lies in his ability to capture the interest of his audience from the start, and this in turn comes from his quick appraisal of the crowd before him. Many a youngster has joined the Socialist Party after hearing Vladeck speak, captivated by the shining sincerity and forthrightness of the man; again, he has given renewed hope to veterans drooping under the strain of the struggle.

If it is an East Side audience to which he speaks, he begins by some simple story dealing, let us say, with the relations between the rich and the poor and packing at the end an unexpected punch which brings to its knees all pretension and pomp. He knows that the Jews love to watch the thrusting of tackle under the seats of the mighty. He knows that they love a good story and its teller, and he can create the mood that will carry his listeners along with him through an involved economic argument on which he throws the light of humor and reasonableness so that when he is through economics seems anything but a "dismal science."

Never does he leave the argument to the mere marshalling of facts and statistics, whether he is talking to economists gathered at conferences of the League for Industrial Democracy or workers in a Brooklyn labor hall. Always toward the end of his speech he reveals the larger purposes behind the immediate program which he has developed. Always there is a glimpse of what Santayana has called "the inward landscape." Then Vladeck is at his brilliant best. Then you can see men and women stirred beyond all consideration of hours and wages and the bread and butter things, dreaming themselves, with the eloquence of the speaker, into a spacious, freedom-breathing world.

In debate he is devastating. In his last campaign he proposed an intelligence test for Congressional candidates and submitted to his opponents a series of questions on economic subjects from which they very wisely fled.

During a discussion of radical tactics held at a conference some years ago, a Communist spokesman, after making his usual attack upon the Socialists, said that what this country needed was a group of paid revolutionists who should devote all their time to the making of a new American Revolution.

Vladeck, when it came his turn to speak, uncoiled himself and said: "The gentleman forgets that there is, after all, some difference between Russia and the United States. Over there we revolutionists had a mighty mass of class-conscious workers and peasants among whom we could make our propaganda. Here where the workers and peasants are alike imbued with a bourgeois philosophy, there is nothing left for your professional revolutionists to practice upon except the Socialist Party."

And the professional Communists lose no opportunity to practice upon B. Charney Vladeck. Rarely does an issue of their paper, *The Daily Worker,* appear without some scathing reference to *The Forward* and its business manager. The mere mention of the name Vladeck is a trigger that sets off fireworks of hatred from the Communist leaders. The early history of the man had led them to expect that he would be heart and soul with them in their catastrophic gesturings, and here he is talking such "middle-class methods as education and political action."

Vladeck's boss, Abraham Cahan, editor of *The Forward,*

once wrote a novel, and a grand good book it was, called *The Rise of David Levinsky*. In it he traced the rise of a young Jewish immigrant to material success in New York. A novel could be written with Vladeck as its central character and with not only material success, for Vladeck has achieved that, but with spiritual success as well, at its conclusion. In spite of the fact that just now many of the causes and movements with which he is connected seem to be in the doldrums, Vladeck gives you the sense of a man who knows where he is going and how to get there. He gives confidence to his followers. You come away from a speech of his convinced of the logic of its premises and that here is a man with feet firmly planted on the American soil for all his foreign upbringing, a man who may, after all, have the social compass that will show the right way out.

The first chapters of our Vladeck novel would take us to the tiny village of Dookorah, near Minsk in Northwest Russia where Charney was born on a bitter cold January day in 1886. His father died when he was but two years old, leaving his mother to care for the family of six children. She was a store-keeper and it was a small store and a large family, but she was resolved to give her children the best of religious educations. "So we lived on baked potatoes and cereals and the Hebrew prophets and the Talmud," says Vladeck. Those were the days when revolution was in the air. It drifted through the windows of the Minsk Academy and laid its red hand on the heart of the fifteen-year-old boy. It was then that he made the first of his life-long series of speeches against tyranny and began attending underground meetings in obscure, working-class side-streets.

By the time he was eighteen, the police had become sufficiently interested in his activities to march him off to jail, where he spent the next eight months as a political prisoner.

He came out a veteran revolutionist, resolved to devote his entire time and all his young energies to the cause. For a year he spoke for the Social Democrats in industrial cities and small towns until the police again caught up with him. In Vilna in May, 1905, he was once more arrested and jailed, this time for six months. When he was not in jail he was hounded by the Secret Police and the Cossacks and was several times severely beaten. On the whole, as he looks back on it, Vladeck thinks he received better treatment inside jail than outside. For the politicals were a proud lot, segregated from the other prisoners and treated courteously by the officials. Once Vladeck led a hunger strike of six days' duration because one of his fellow politicals was not asked to sit down by the keeper of the jail when he was brought to that worthy's office. This so enraged Vladeck and the others that they would take no food or water until the keeper had apologized. But it also had its lasting effect upon Vladeck's rather frail constitution, for he still suffers from stomach trouble caused, the physicians say, by that long fast.

How did they live, these professional revolutionists, who went about among the people stirring up trouble? Well, for one thing, they had friends among the peasants and workers almost everywhere who would give them food and lodging and a bit of money to take them to the next town. They shared and shared alike, but today few of them can tell you how it was they managed to survive. They traveled under aliases, constantly feeling the sinister shadows of the Czar's police over their shoulders. They spoke to little groups leaning desperately on their words in dingy holes-in-the-wall. They read and wrote grandiloquent manifestoes against czardom and capitalism. At times in their despairing moments it must have seemed to them as though no yeast so small could leaven the great lump on which they worked. But out of them was made the revolution that swept capitalism off one-sixth of the earth.

Of course there were purple patches. There were two thrilling days for Vladeck, fighting on the barricades in the streets of Lodz in Poland. And there was that history-making conference in a little church in the Poplar district of London, where after a month's discussion Lenin and his Bolshevists won the dispute over tactics with Plekhanov and his Menshevists. There Vladeck came into daily contact with all his revolutionary heroes—Lenin, for whom, by the way, he voted at that time, Trotzky, Mortov, Axelrod, and other outstanding Social Democrats.

After the crushing of the 1905 revolution, the chances for any sort of effective agitational work became less and less. Vladeck's brother in America wrote to him urging him to come overseas and in 1908, aided by a man who is now a member of the Soviet's Gosplan, Vladeck took boat and settled in Philadelphia. For awhile he lectured for the Jewish Socialist movement here. He came to know and love Gene Debs and the other leaders of the American movement. "The picture of Gene Debs was on the walls of our working people," says Vladeck, "alongside those of Sir Moses Montefiore, the Rabbi of Lubawich, 'Goan of Vilna' and others of their heroes. For them Debs was the liberator, the first who had come from the ranks of the American workers, holding out his hand and saying, 'I am your brother.' They had respect and admiration for radicals of their own race. But they worshipped Debs." Vladeck kept in constant touch with Debs when the latter was in jail, and to this day he has not forgotten the significance or the promise of Debs' peculiarly American type of Socialism.

He became manager of the Philadelphia edition of *The Forward* and studied at the University of Pennsylvania. He came on to New York to take the city-editorship of *The Forward* and in the campaign of the autumn of 1917, two years after he obtained his citizenship papers, he was elected alderman. They had to "gerrymander" his district finally to defeat him for he won by large majorities over his old-line opponents running on fusion tickets.

When Vladeck today is not doing about every job that there is on a newspaper from the editorial to the advertising office and back, when he isn't heading what must seem to him endless drives for funds for the Socialist Party, for tools for the "declassed" Jews in Russia, for this cause and that ranging all the way from Pioneer Youth to the League for Industrial Democracy, when he isn't making speeches in the Middle West or the Lower East Side, he is out with his family consisting of three children and his wife watching the ways of the people who make up this fantastic America. He loves to read, and no Vladeck vacation can begin without the packing of from ten to fifteen books; but he has a distrust of mere "book-larnin'."

"Nothing that is going to live can be built up on books," he says. "I keep away from people whose only idea of a social movement is something written down in a book of rules. The theoreticians who never go out-doors have been the curse of the radical movement in America. Life comes from a study of life. If radicalism is ever to succeed in this country, the radicals must know from their day-to-day contacts what the people are thinking and feeling and hoping. I know some radical speakers who always make the same speeches no matter what the occasion or the audience. The movement has become a formalized religion for them—something that you devote one day a week to—but not a way of life itself."

Whether or not his earlier radicalism has been modified by his contacts with the realities of the American business and political world, it can truthfully be said of Charney Vladeck that he is never guilty of making "set" speeches or uttering the hackneyed phrases of so many left-wingers. He loathes a *cliché* as much as he despises demagogy. With all his romantic beginnings, realities alone interest him. He wants to get ahead himself but he wants the rank and file to come along with him. At forty-six B. Charney Vladeck may not be the colorful, flaming personality that leveled a rifle over the barricades at Lodz, but he is someone very much to be reckoned with in any roll-call of American radicals.

GRACE ABBOTT

Champion of Women and Children

GRACE ABBOTT

NONE of the labels attached to Grace Abbott tells you much about her. As chief of the United States Children's Bureau, she is a Government official. But her breezy Nebraska manner freshens the stagnant Washington atmosphere and blows mental dust out of corners in a way somewhat terrifying to timid bureaucrats.

She is a social worker. Not, however, the slightly unhuman sort of person conjured up in most people's minds by that phrase. She can do good to people without their disliking her. She can even get after them for nefarious doings and still keep on good terms with them. A friend of hers, Ernestine Evans, tells how, when Miss Abbott was working on behalf of immigrants in Chicago, she fought pirate cabmen who fleeced incoming aliens. In spite of her successful campaign against them, the cabbies liked this downright young person so much they used to offer her free rides whenever she appeared!

Then, of course, she's a spinster. That label, frequently used by portly gentlemen who deplore her attempt to save children from exploitation, is just as meaningless. Grace Abbott doesn't fit that noun in appearance or temperament. She has a fine, lofty face, with brown eyes that are candid and warm; a wide forehead, from which dark hair is drawn back smoothly; a look of facing with clear, swift directness whatever life has to bring, and a manner that is unselfconscious, frank, eager. She grew up with several brothers, was somewhat of a tom-boy, and has always been a woman to whom men talk as easily as women do. Her own family life is richly happy. She has a charming home in Washington where she lives with her school-girl niece, Charlotte, whom she has mothered for half a dozen years. Boys and girls and children spill all over the place, for Grace Abbott likes children, in the piece as well as the mass, and they like her. She will pause in a moment of her campaign against infant mortality to send baby turtles to a youngster sick in the hospital, or an ingenious new toy to the small child of one of her Children's Bureau staff.

That Nebraska breeziness of hers comes from a childhood spent in the prairie town of Grand Island. She was born of a family of New England abolitionists whose adventuring spirit took them pioneering to Nebraska. She grew up while the Populist movement was seething all over the Middle West, and the rights of the under-dog engaged the public spirit. The family were progressive, but not radical. Susan B. Anthony was an exciting visitor at the home as were other pioneers of the liberal cause. Yet the family stayed within the Republican fold, and her father served a term as Lieutenant Governor of the State.

Grace herself was a clever, healthy-minded child who lived the wholesome life of an average small-town youngster. Back of her, through all the struggles of childhood and the problems of young womanhood, were the warm security of a home and the affection of a devoted family. Later she was to lead in the movement to save hundreds of thousands of fatherless children from the cold efficiency of institutional life—preserve for them, too, the sanctuary of home.

After Grace had finished with the A's and B's of the little red schoolhouse, she went through Grand Island College, did graduate work in the University of Nebraska, and then more or less drifted into teaching. It didn't satisfy her. There must be more exciting, more demanding, types of work. Her pioneer spirit drove her on.

Her next move was to Chicago. After receiving her Master's Degree in Political Science from the University of Chicago, she came into touch with that vital focus of idealism, Hull House. Here, in the midst of Chicago's foreign-born population, she became deeply stirred by the immigrant's problems—his bewildered attempt to adjust himself to American conditions. While still in her twenties she was made Director of the Immigrants' Protective League. As its Director and later as Executive Secretary of the State Immigration Commissions of Massachusetts and Illinois, she was the friend of these helpless newcomers.

It was in this work that her interest in children first began to manifest itself. The American-born child of foreign parents has an especially hard row to hoe, and his problems interested Miss Abbott. His chance to get schooling—his freedom from being put to work at too early an age—these have to be saved for him by American institutions, for old-country parents often don't understand.

So it was not a far cry to the next job young Grace Abbott tackled—director of the child labor division in the United States Children's Bureau. The task of this division was to enforce the first Federal child labor law, passed by Congress in 1917. This law established certain protective standards for all children—chiefly, that no child under fourteen should do factory work—and the Children's Bureau was to coöperate with state labor departments in carrying out these provisions.

Since the days of the prohibition amendment it seems hard to believe that such Federal-State coöperation can be amicably and efficiently carried on. But some of the strongest advocates of this law were the state officials themselves, who found the Children's Bureau officers, under Miss Abbott, their best allies and helpers.

After a short time, however, the child labor law was declared unconstitutional and Miss Abbott turned to other activities, including that of adviser on the War Labor Policies Board, and later, Secretary of the Children's Commission of the First International Labor Conference. Her work impressed both official Washington and the social welfare and women's group whose sponsorship had created and nurtured the Children's Bureau. Naturally, then, when its beloved and first Chief, Julia Lathrop, resigned in 1921, Grace Abbott was chosen to take her place.

Since then she has given herself so unstintedly to the Children's Bureau that its story is hers, its achievements in large share hers, its friends and enemies are hers. The outstanding fact about Grace Abbott today is that she has identified herself so completely with the welfare of the 43,000,000 children who are the Bureau's constituents that she interprets most issues in politics and economics from the point of view of the child.

An illustration of this single-mindedness is found in an interview in the fall of 1930, during which she was asked to talk about herself as a possible candidate for Secretary of Labor. "What I really want to talk about is the disease of unemployment and what can be done to keep it from inflicting too great an injury on children," she exclaimed. Then she described the studies made by the Bureau and what they revealed about the toll taken of children during a period when fathers are out of work. As always, she had an immediate practical suggestion to make. "I suggest an extension of mothers' aid laws, making the *unemployment* of fathers as well as their death or sickness a cause for which aid to mothers could be given."

Notice that she speaks of unemployment as a "disease."

Grace Abbott's point of view is that of the social economist—she is no sentimental lady bountiful. She sees many symptoms of an ailing economic order, and if she cannot cure she can and must shield the child from their cruel effects.

Poverty, for example, she recognizes as an economic disease which has its most devastating effects on children. The Children's Bureau first pointed out—and proved by a study of 23,-000 babies born in eight American cities—that poverty can actually *kill* babies. In Baltimore, for example, it was found that in well-to-do homes only one out of every 27 babies dies during the first year, while in poor homes one out of every seven failed to survive.

These facts were sufficiently startling to the smug complacency which holds a baby's death, like his birth, "an act of God." But the Children's Bureau did not rest with stating the case of the 200,000 babies sacrificed annually. The bureau reports hammered home the disgrace of our high infant and maternal death rates until Congress passed, in 1921, the Federal Maternity and Infancy Act, granting Federal aid in promoting the health of mothers and babies. When Grace Abbott became Chief of the Bureau that year, she at once began the work of carrying it into effect.

This act permitted the National Government to give the sort of aid to the states in promoting the welfare of mothers and babies that it had long since given in the building of good roads and the raising of better pigs. A million dollars was appropriated for a limited period, to be matched by state appropriations and expended in this work. The Children's Bureau had pointed out that the health of mothers as well as of babies must be included in the program, by statistics showing our disgracefully high maternal death rate (higher than that of most other civilized nations) and by studies revealing how large a proportion of women bore their babies without medical and nursing care of any kind. Perhaps such incidents as this helped to shock Congress into action. . . .

Out in the sheep country of a Western state, young ranchmen diffidently approached the nurse from the Bureau and asked:

"Tell us, ma'am, where we can get something to read about mothers. We know about the sheep—that's our business, but sometimes there is no one to do for the women and we've got to help. We want to know how."

The Maternity and Infancy funds were stretched to their utmost to reach as many of these neglected mothers and babies as possible. During seven years a magnificent beginning was made: 124,000 child health conferences were held, attended by a million and a half children; three-quarters of a million expectant mothers were reached through prenatal conferences, classes, literature, etc., and three million home visits were made by nurses.

This indicates the sort of attack Grace Abbott makes on the disease of poverty as it affects child health. Poverty also affects older children in many ways, notably by depriving them of their chance for school and play, driving them during tender years into industry. The Children's Bureau investigations of child labor brought this problem before the nation. Patient, first-hand study of more than 50,000 inarticulate Marys and Johns, Antonios, Michaels, Rosas, and Hannahs, told the stories of stunted lives and starved personalities. And these were typical of hundreds of thousands of child workers.

Again Grace Abbott began stirring people to do things about it. And from an aroused public sentiment grew the demand for an amendment to the Constitution which would make it possible to give boy and girl workers at least as much protection as had the former national child labor laws.

This movement ended in defeat—of which more later—but

its defeat left Miss Abbott's philosophy unchanged. When well fed gentlemen wailed in the lobbies of Congress: "Think of the poor homes which need the money these children bring in," like an avenging sword came Grace Abbott's challenge: "If you continue to use the labor of children as the treatment of the social disease of poverty you will have both poverty and child labor to the end of time."

Infant mortality and child labor are only two parts of the broad program of the Children's Bureau. It also includes all phases of child dependency, neglect, delinquency. To cite but one of the fundamental social movements sponsored by the Bureau in behalf of the dependent child, take the so-called "mother's pension" laws. These laws today keep over 220,000 children with their mothers, who might otherwise be in orphanges.

In all the phases of the Bureau work, Grace Abbott's academic training has been extremely valuable. The basic function of the Bureau is that of a "fact-finding" agency. Her scholarly habit of mind had made its 200 child welfare studies in 45 states models of social research. They are standard in their field, referred to by experts at home and all over the world.

She has other qualities, too, that have made her direction of the Bureau successful. Her administrative ability was proved in her frictionless enforcement of the child labor law before she became Chief of the Bureau. Later, the same talent was shown in the magnificent work done under the Maternity and Infancy Act, in which 45 state bureaus of child health were linked with the Children's Bureau in harmonious coöperation.

But she is more than a good researcher, a skilful executive. She has the ability to get direct to the Joneses, Browns, and McCoys—the everyday parents who need her help. She has sponsored the series of popular yet authoritative booklets on

child care that have reached the astounding circulation of 11,-
000,000, and have been translated into healthier babies in every
hamlet of the land. She has sent the Bureau's message out
through motion pictures, posters, exhibits, radio, and the press.

Her sound practical sense has also led her to perform an
extremely valuable service to the Bureau in maintaining close
contact with the social service and women's organizations
whose support has frequently saved it from being a political
football. The confidence of these groups was manifested, for
example, in her appointment—the fifth woman in 50 years—as
President of the National Conference of Social Work in 1923.
The power of such backing and its necessity, Washington being what it is, is illustrated by this incident.

During one of the Harding pencil-saving economy waves,
the Children's Bureau appropriation was cut in committee.
"It's safe to do that," said a wise politician. "We wouldn't dare
cut the Bureau of Labor statistics and hope to get it raised
again on the floor of the House, but cutting the Children's
Bureau will make the women mad. They will walk up to
Congress and get it back."

This warm support sustained Miss Abbott in the two bitter
attacks she has met during recent years. The first of these was
the fight against the child labor amendment. Manufacturing
interests sponsored a feverish "anti" campaign intended to
throw the country into a panic. They told the farmer's wife
that the amendment would prohibit her daughter from washing the dishes. Told the farmer his son would not be allowed
to milk the cows. Told Catholics that the Government would,
if the amendment were passed, reach out for control of the
schools. They cried "states' rights"—bolshevism—communism, whatnot—anything but the truth: that child labor control might endanger profits.

Not only the Children's Bureau, but Grace Abbott herself,

became the object of this anti-amendment campaign. It was impossible to find grounds for personal slurs. Miss Abbott's life is an open book. So these opponents resorted to the "meddlesome old maid" line of talk.

A witness at a Congressional hearing would say: "I hear that there are very few mothers connected with the direction of the Children's Bureau," and the implication was plain. No unmarried woman could possibly know as much about child welfare as the simplest, least tutored mother.

The "red" argument also did valiant duty. A publication would discover that Miss Abbott once attended a meeting which was also attended by Rosika Schwimmer and that Madam Schwimmer had been called a German agent by the Lusk committee. Such facts were enough to prove that the Children's Bureau and its Republican Chief were either German, Russian, socialist, bolshevist, or all four.

Great ingenuity was displayed in twisting statistics and misinterpreting facts. For example, it was discovered by the opponents of the amendment that there were in existence no statistics on juvenile delinquency comparable to those on child labor. True, the Children's Bureau was making studies in this field and working with court authorities in an effort to collect uniform statistics. However, the fact that less was known about delinquent children than about child workers was twisted into this classic remark at a Congressional hearing: "The Children's Bureau would rather see children go to jail or to hell than to work."

It was a tribute to the sound direction of the Bureau's work by Miss Abbott that no flaws could be picked in its many child labor reports or in the statements of its Chief. Grace Abbott herself has a prodigious capacity for keeping a mass of statistics at her fingertips. Before Congressional committees she is an effective witness. Her knowledge of her subject is evident to even the worst of the hecklers and her answers are so forthright, so free from weazel words, that she commands her opponents' respect.

Therefore when the Children's Bureau Chief could—at the request of Congress—meet opposition face to face, she won. Congress passed the child labor amendment. But in an appeal to the country she and the friends of children lost. The amendment has not so far been ratified by a sufficient number of states to make it part of the law of the land.

This struggle was taxing and disheartening. More than most women, Grace Abbott has a saving sense of humor. She is not especially thin-skinned. But neither is she as impersonal as the average man in political life. The attacks hurt, but never for a moment did she consider giving up the fight for children.

The second attack came, ironically enough, during the White House Conference on Child Welfare called by President Hoover in November, 1930. Ironically, because the very creation of the Bureau was in large measure the result of the first White House Conference, called by President Roosevelt in 1909, and the Bureau itself sponsored the second White House Conference, called in 1919 by President Wilson.

Hardly had the 1930 Conference convened when one of its committees recommended curtailing the activities of the Bureau, particularly with relation to its magnificent maternity and child health program. The Children's Bureau is dedicated to the theory that all phases of child welfare constitute an interrelated whole—that child health cannot be divorced from social and economic factors, that the doctor, the social worker, the economist must join forces.

The White House Conference committee, however, apparently represented a more narrowly medical point of view. Representatives of the American Medical Association have actively opposed the work of the Bureau under the Maternity and Infancy Act as meddling interference by the Government in a matter which is none of its concern. Many of the leading physicians of the country warmly endorse the Bureau, but the organized opposition swayed the Conference committee.

It was obvious that their report was expected to go through almost as a matter of routine. But the news leaked out, the press seized upon it, the delegates were aroused.

"After all,'" says a leading child welfare worker in reporting the Conference, "the federal Children's Bureau is the outstanding child-welfare agency in this country, if not in the world. Its two chiefs—Julia Lathrop and Grace Abbott—are among the foremost civic leaders of our time. The Bureau has affected the whole field of child welfare in ways that are far-reaching, constructive, and enduring. It has won sympathetic interest and support from the mass of the people, as well as the professional classes. It has not, however, been given the increasing financial support which it needs and merits. What the Conference did was to invite a great host of the Bureau's supporters to Washington and then ask them to agree to a plan which later on might be cited in Congress as a reason for reducing its sphere of usefulness. Naturally, such a plan could not be accepted."

After spirited debate, the anti-Children's Bureau report was tabled. This was a victory which, it is hoped, will be felt in pending legislation. The Maternity and Infancy Act, which lapsed in 1929, is again before Congress.

And now for the future. What can Grace Abbott look forward to? A man who had carried on successfully a work of such outstanding importance and appeal as hers might hope for political advancement. A woman has little chance for the "glory jobs." Grace Abbott herself apparently does not even hanker after them.

344 ADVENTUROUS AMERICANS

She was asked at a recent Congressional hearing which of two bills she preferred. One made the Chief of the Children's Bureau Chairman of the Federal Board of Maternal and Infant Hygiene; the other named the Surgeon General.

"I have no objection to the Surgeon General's being chairman," she replied. "I think he would like to be, and it makes little difference to me."

She was undoubtedly sincere in saying this. She lost no sleep when the movement to promote her as candidate for Secretary of Labor died the natural death political observers expected. It was an amazingly widespread movement which received the backing not only of women's organizations but of labor movement, of economists and business men. But it gained no encouragement from her. Even if she had felt it might be successful, she would probably not have lifted a finger to push the snowball along. Perhaps her lack of personal ambition is a fault. If so, its compensation is that it gives her an impregnable strength in the center of the political swirl of Washington.

She accepts responsible posts without hesitation, however, if she feels that by doing so she can advance the cause of children. She has represented the United States on the Commission for the Protection and Welfare of Children and Young People of the League of Nations. She is a member of the executive committee of the American Child Health Association and is connected with other similar organizations.

"Sometimes," she says, "when I get home at night in Washington, I feel as though I had been in a great traffic jam. The jam is moving toward the Hill where Congress sits in judgment on all the administrative agencies of the Government, and in that traffic jam there are all kinds of vehicles moving up toward the Capitol. There are all the kinds of conveyances, for example, that the Army can put into the street—tanks, gun carriages, trucks, the dancing horses of officers, and others which I have not even the vocabulary to describe. But they all finally reach the Hill and they make a plea that is a very old plea—one which I find in spite of the reputation for courage that they bear, men respond to rather promptly. The Army says to them, 'Give, lest you perish;' and fear as a motive is still producing results on a scale which leave the rest of us feeling very envious of the kind of eloquence the Army and Navy command. But there are other kinds of vehicles in this traffic jam. There are the hay-ricks and the binders and the ploughs and all the other things that the Department of Agriculture manages to put into the streets. When the drivers get to the Hill they have an argument Congressmen understand. They say to them, 'Dollars invested on this side of the ledger will bring dollars on the other side.'

"Then, there are still other vehicles. The handsome limousines in which the Department of Commerce rides, the barouches in which the Department of State rides with such dignity, the noisy patrol which the Department of Justice uses. I stand on the sidewalk with a great deal of timidity watching it become more congested and more difficult, and then because the responsibilty is mine and I must, I take firm hold on the handles of a baby carriage and I wheel it into the traffic. There are some people who think it does not belong there at all, there are some who wonder how I got there with it and what I think I am going to be able to do, and there are some who think the baby carriage is the symbol of bolshevism instead of the home and the future of America."

Though it's a perilous course this baby carriage pursues, the woman who guides it has courage, skill—and impatience. Is impatience, like discontent, sometimes divine? In this case, if ever. "They call me impatient," she says, "perhaps I am.

"I've said again and again, the only time we can save the babies who are going to die this year is *this* year. If we wait till next year they will be dead. The future rests in the hands of the children of today. What we do for them *now* is going to determine not only the future of the United States but the future of the world."

lations at the discretion